The Condominium Manual

The Condominium Manual

A Comprehensive Guide to the Strata Property Act

A Resource for Owners and
Real Estate and Legal Professionals in BC

Mike Mangan, B.A., LL.B.

with a contribution by
Anne-Marie G. Hammond, B.A., LL.B., M.A.

BRITISH COLUMBIA
REAL ESTATE
ASSOCIATION

Published by the British Columbia Real Estate Association • Vancouver

First Paperback Edition Published in December 2001.
Second Paperback Edition Published in May 2004.

Discounts on bulk quantities of this publication are available to corporations, professional associations and other organizations. For details and discount information, contact the Education Department at the British Columbia Real Estate Association.

Telephone: 604-683-7702; Fax: 604-683-8601.
www.bcrea.bc.ca; e-mail: condo@bcrea.bc.ca

Printed in Canada by Budget Printing.
This paper is acid-free and 100 per cent totally chlorine-free.

Photographs by Patrick L. Bouillet.

Cover Design by Gordon Finlay

Canadian Cataloguing in Publication Data

Mangan, Michael M.

The Condominium Manual: A Comprehensive Guide to the *Strata Property Act* / Michael M. Mangan; with a contribution by Anne-Marie Hammond.

Includes bibliographical references and index.

ISBN 0-921492-04-9 (paperback)
SECOND EDITION

Reader Input and Educational Seminars

If you have thoughts or suggestions that you believe would be helpful for future editions of this book, or if you are interested in having the author give a seminar or presentation to your group or association, please contact the British Columbia Real Estate Association.

Dedication

To Bea

TABLE OF CONTENTS

Part I

BACKGROUND

Part II

WHO'S WHO IN A STRATA DEVELOPMENT

Part III

OPERATIONS

Part IV

BYLAWS AND RULES

Part V
REPAIRS

Part VI

COURT ACTIONS AND ARBITRATION

Part VII

PHASING

APPENDICES

LIST OF TABLES

Acknowledgements

Although this book bears my name, I could never have written it without the help of many others.

In particular, to the outstanding staff at the British Columbia Real Estate Association, and especially June Piry, Director of Education; Bonnie Clogg, Publications Assistant; and Norma Miller, Director of Communications, my deep gratitude.

Thanks also to Adrienne Murray, Deputy Superintendent of Real Estate, and her staff, particularly Samantha Gale, Manager, Real Estate and Anne Napier, Condominium Officer. Adrienne Murray's relentless encouragement and friendly advice played a significant part in this book.

Thanks, as well, to Anne-Marie G. Hammond, a brilliant insurance expert and arbitrator, for providing the chapter on Insurance.

During my presentations to real estate boards around the province, thousands of real estate licensees contributed countless strata questions whose answers have found their way into this book. Finally, all of my strata clients, in one way or another, played an important part in emphasizing to me the subjects that matter most to strata corporations and owners.

To all of you, thank you.

Mike Mangan
December 2001

Acknowledgement to the Second Edition

When I learned that the publisher had sold approximately 4,000 copies of the first edition, I was surprised. When I discovered that the first edition had sold out and the publisher was taking names of persons who wanted early notice of the next edition, I was astonished. Clearly, there is a strong demand for plain language information about the way the *Strata Property Act* works.

In the nearly two years since the first edition, there have been many important court decisions concerning the *Strata Property Act*. In the second edition, I have incorporated these cases where appropriate and added roughly 60 pages of new material. The case law in the second edition is current to September 2003.

My continuing gratitude to the British Columbia Real Estate Association staff, and especially June Piry, Director of Education; Val Nelson, Program Assistant; Kim Spencer, Director of Member Services and Norma Miller, Director of Communications.

Thanks to the hundreds of strata property managers, real estate licensees, strata council members, and condominium owners who have adopted *The Condominium Manual* as their primary strata reference. The support of the Condominium Home Owners' Association and its Executive Director, Tony Gioventu, and of the Strata Property Agents of BC, including past president Rick Dickson, have been invaluable.

Thanks also to the strata lawyers, a group of Vancouver lawyers who regularly carry out strata work and meet informally to discuss emerging condominium problems.

Thank you as well to the Real Estate Council of British Columbia and its excellent staff, particularly Robert Fawcett, Executive Officer and the University of British Columbia, Sauder School of Business, Real Estate Division, especially David Moore, Director.

To all of you, my thanks.

Mike Mangan
May 2004

About the Author

 Mike Mangan is a Vancouver lawyer who, among other things, advises strata corporations and condominium owners in his law practice. Mr. Mangan is an Adjunct Professor of Law in the Faculty of Law at the University of British Columbia, where he teaches real estate law. He also teaches in the Real Estate Division of the Sauder School of Business at UBC. Mr. Mangan was called to the British Columbia bar in 1981.

Since 1994, Mr. Mangan has been the principal author of the British Columbia Real Estate Association's annual *Legal Update*, a comprehensive review of court cases, Real Estate Council decisions, and new legislation affecting real estate licensees. In addition, he has developed several seminars for real estate licensees, including two on *Strata Law for REALTORS*. By a conservative estimate, Mr. Mangan has taught over 18,000 REALTORS since 1992. He is also the current revisions author for real estate agency matters in the *BC Real Estate Practice Manual* published by the Continuing Legal Education Society of British Columbia. He is a contributing author to *Falconbridge on Mortgages*, Fifth edition, published by Canada Law Book Inc. In addition, he is the principal author of *What If. . .?*, a text for real estate licensees published by UBC and distributed, in part, by the Real Estate Council of British Columbia.

Mr. Mangan is also the editor of *Directors' Liability in Canada*, a national text published by STP Specialty Technical Publishers, Inc. In addition, he is the principal author of *The Annotated British Columbia Society Act*, published by Canada Law Book Inc.

Contributor

Anne-Marie G. Hammond contributed the *Insurance* chapter to this book. Ms. Hammond is a non-practicing lawyer with over 20 years' experience in the insurance industry. She was formerly the Director of Insurance for the Law Society of British Columbia and is now an independent risk and insurance consultant. In addition, Ms. Hammond serves as an arbitrator and mediator in insurance related disputes and advises strata corporations on insurance matters. She is a past president of the British Columbia Risk and Insurance Management Society and of the Law Society of British Columbia's Captive Insurance Company Ltd

TABLE OF CASES

STATUTORY INDEX

STATUTORY BYLAWS

Part I
BACKGROUND

Form follows function. Understanding the strata concept makes it easier to understand the legal structure of a strata development.

Chapter 1

INTRODUCTION

S trata development began in British Columbia in 1966 when the province enacted the first *Strata Titles Act*.[1] In 1974 a second *Strata Titles Act* was enacted.[2] In 1980 the government changed the name of the statute to the *Condominium Act*.[3] On July 1, 2000, the *Strata Property Act*, as amended, replaced the *Condominium Act*.[4]

The *Strata Property Act* retains nearly all of the legal principles expressed in previous condominium legislation. Although the Act is much easier to read and understand than previous legislation, it is longer and more complex than the *Condominium Act*. The *Strata Property Act* is the most important piece of legislation governing strata owners and those who transact with strata corporations.

This book is designed as a manual for strata owners and strata councils, and as a resource for strata property managers, real estate licensees and legal professionals. The manual begins by explaining the strata concept and the significance of a strata plan. Next, the book identifies the various parties in a strata development and describes their particular roles and responsibilities. This manual reviews the essential operations in a strata corporation including record keeping, meetings, voting and finances. After describing how bylaws work, this book explains the subject of repairs. The manual also examines legal proceedings and phased developments under the *Strata Property Act*.

---

[1] *Strata Titles Act*, S.B.C. 1966, c. 46.

[2] *Ibid.*, S.B.C. 1974, c. 89.

[3] *Condominium Act*, R.S.B.C. 1979, c. 61, later enacted in consolidated form as the *Condominium Act*, R.S.B.C. 1996, c. 64.

[4] *Strata Property Act*, S.B.C 1998, c. 43 amended by the *Strata Property Amendment Act*, 1999, S.B.C. 1999, c. 21. See also *Miscellaneous Statutes Amendment Act* (No. 2), 2000, S.B.C. 2000, c. 26, ss. 59-66; *Miscellaneous Statutes Amendment Act, 2002*, S.B.C. 2002, c. 22, ss. 11-22; *Trustee Investment Statutes Amendment Act, 2002*, S.B.C. 2002, c. 33, ss. 21-22; *Residential Tenancy Act*, S.B.C. 2002, c. 78, s. 116.

Throughout the book, we refer to the specific sections of the *Strata Property Act*, regulations or Standard Bylaws under discussion. When considering how the legislation might apply to a specific situation, readers should refer to the specific provisions in the Act, regulations or Standard Bylaws, as the case may be. From time to time, we include case studies of actual court decisions to illustrate some of the legal concepts. While some cases decided under the former *Condominium Act* continue to apply to matters under the *Strata Property Act*, other situations will require a court to consider the wording in the *Strata Property Act* before deciding how that Act should be interpreted.

The information in this book is not legal advice. This book is intended to provide general information of a practical nature. In particular, nothing in this book should be considered legal advice about a reader's own circumstances. Neither the author nor the British Columbia Real Estate Association assumes any legal responsibility for the information in this book. Readers must assess each situation on its own merits, bearing in mind that general information of the type in this book may not suit a particular situation. For advice about a specific problem, a reader should consult a lawyer.

Whenever we suggest consultation with a lawyer, we mean that the reader should consult a lawyer who is familiar with strata law. Although the Canadian legal profession does not recognize specialties, the fact is that most lawyers tend to restrict their work to particular legal areas. Our references to lawyers are not meant to exclude notaries, who carry out with excellence many real estate transactions in this province. We refer only to lawyers because we are usually speaking in the context of legal advice.

Chapter 2

THE CREATION OF
STRATA DEVELOPMENTS

Why Strata Developments?

Historically, the law allowed landowners to subdivide their land into two or more separate pieces. The owner of any piece of land also owned the buildings on it.

What if the owner of a building wanted to subdivide a building into several parts with separate owners? Although owners could subdivide *land*, the law did not easily permit them to subdivide their *buildings* into separately owned parts.[1]

The strata concept is the solution. A strata development is a special way of subdividing land *and* buildings for separate ownership with common features and shared expenses.

The *Strata Property Act* uses the term *owner developer* to describe the person who creates a strata development.[2] For simplicity, we will refer to the *owner developer* as the *developer.*

Anatomy of a Strata Development

A strata development consists of strata lots, common property and common assets. The part of the property that an individual separately owns is called the "strata lot." Informally, we often call this part the "strata unit" or a

---

[1]For information about the history of the strata concept, see D.J. Pavlich, *The Strata Titles Act* (Vancouver, Butterworths, 1978) at p. 4. See also P.J. Rohan, ed., *Condominium Law and Practice*, (New York: Mathew Bender, 1985) Vol. 1 at 2-1. For a comparison of the concept in different legal systems, see J. Leyser, "The Ownership of Flats-A Comparative Study" (1958) 7 Int. and Compr. L.Q. 31.

[2]*Strata Property Act*, s. 1(1) (definition of "owner developer").

"condominium." Every strata lot owner also owns a proportionate interest in the common property and common assets of the strata corporation.[1]

The owner cannot separate his or her interest in the strata lot, on the one hand, from the owner's proportionate interest in the common property and common assets, on the other hand, except as permitted by the Act.[2] Any document that deals with the strata lot also deals automatically with the owner's share in the common property and common assets of the strata corporation.[3] This means, for example, that a strata lot owner cannot sell his or her proportionate interest in the common property and common assets while keeping his or her interest in their strata lot.

For instance, in an apartment-style strata development, the owner purchases his or her apartment, being the strata lot. The owner also has a proportionate interest in the common property, which includes, in our example, the roof and the exterior walls of the building. He or she also owns a proportionate interest in the common assets, which may include, for example, a vacuum cleaner and any other cleaning equipment purchased by the strata corporation.

The Strata Concept

The owner of a strata property has less autonomy than someone who owns a conventional piece of real estate. An individual strata owner is always subject to the broader community interests of the strata development.

The *Strata Property Act* creates a democratic structure for the operation of a strata corporation. The strata development consists of strata lots together with common property and common assets. Every strata development has bylaws that reflect the strata community's values. The bylaws

---

[1] *Strata Property Act*, s. 66.
[2] *Ibid.*, s. 251(2).
[3] *Ibid.*, s. 251(3).

govern how owners and tenants may use their strata lots, the common property and common assets.

The owners of the strata lots make up the strata corporation. Every strata lot has a vote. Eligible voters in the strata corporation elect a strata council to carry out the day-to-day work of the strata corporation. Major decisions that affect strata owners or their strata lots must be made by the eligible voters in general meetings. Among other things, the eligible voters may, with sufficient community support, direct the activities of the strata council, requisition special general meetings or place items on a general meeting's agenda.

When using this book, it is useful to keep two rules in mind.

1. A Strata is a Strata

A strata is a strata is a strata. The *Strata Property Act* applies to every type of strata. The same legal principles that govern, for example, a 500-unit apartment-style complex, apply equally to a 100-unit industrial warehouse strata, and to a 20-unit bare land strata, and a two-unit duplex strata.

In some cases, the legislation adds special requirements for a particular type of strata, but the legal fundamentals remain the same for all.

2. The Strata Scheme is Self-Enforcing

The strata scheme is self-enforcing. There is no government body that regulates compliance with the strata legislation. There are no "strata police."

To enforce the *Strata Property Act*, every owner has the right to apply to the Supreme Court of British Columbia for an order requiring the strata corporation to comply with the legislation.[1] In addition, the Act

---

[1] *Strata Property Act*, s. 165.

permits owners and tenants to arbitrate certain disputes among themselves or with the strata corporation.[1]

The Strata Plan

To create a strata development, a developer must first subdivide the land, including any buildings, into designated parts for separate ownership together with common features. This is done by depositing a document called a "strata plan" at the Land Title Office.[2]

The plan must show which parts are strata lots for purchase by individual owners and which parts are common property. Although the requirements for depositing a strata plan are very technical, every plan must show, among other things, the following:

- a unique registration number (e.g., Strata Plan No. VR 150)

- the boundaries of the land

- the location of all buildings (except bare land strata developments[3])

- a drawing distinguishing the strata lots from one another by numbers or letters in consecutive order

- the area of each strata lot in square metres

- a schedule of unit entitlement

- a schedule of voting rights if there is at least one non-residential strata lot, and

- any bylaws that differ in any respect from the Standard Bylaws.[4]

---

[1] *Strata Property Act*, s. 177.

[2] *Ibid.*, ss. 2 and 239. For information about the two types of strata plan, see Chapter 4, *Strata Plan Types, Styles and Uses.*

[3] In a bare land strata plan the boundaries of the individual strata lots are defined by survey markers.

[4] *Strata Property Act*, ss. 2, 244 and 245 and *Strata Property Regulation*, ss. 14.3 and 14.4.

The strata plan is an essential document for every strata owner. Appendix A contains sample excerpts from strata plans that illustrate some of these features.

How to Obtain a Copy of a Registered Strata Plan

An owner can obtain a copy of the registered strata plan for his or her strata lot at the Land Title Office in the district where the strata development is located. The Land Title Branch publishes the locations and telephone particulars of the various Land Title Offices on the Internet at http://srmwww.gov.bc.ca/landtitle/. The local provincial Government Agent's office can also help an owner obtain information about his or her strata plan with an online search. For the nearest Government Agent, call Enquiry BC at 604-660-2421 or, from outside Greater Vancouver, dial 1-800-663-7867 (toll free). The Government Agent's website is www.governmentagents.gov.bc.ca/.

An owner can also use a lawyer or notary, or a private land registry search service (see "Title Service" in the telephone directory) to obtain copies of documents registered at land title offices. The cost of each search varies according to the nature of the information sought and the number of pages copied from the registry's records.

Strata Versus Co-op

A strata development is not the same as a cooperative housing project. The legal structure of a housing cooperative is different in some important respects. The *Cooperative Association Act* governs a housing cooperative created under our provincial legislation.[1] The *Canada Cooperatives Act* regulates a federally incorporated cooperative.[2]

In a housing cooperative, a corporation is created to purchase, or lease, and develop land for housing. The corporation is called an association. The corporation owns the land or buildings, or, in some cases, leases the property from a leasehold landlord. An individual becomes a member of the cooperative by purchasing a share in it. Typically, ownership of a share in the association carries the right to occupy a unit in the cooperative's housing complex.[3]

From a member's perspective, the most significant difference between a strata development and a housing cooperative is the nature of the member's interest in the project. In a strata development, an owner buys an interest in a strata lot. He or she owns real estate. In a housing cooperative, a member does not own an interest in land; rather, the member only owns a share in the association. The co-op member does not own real estate.

Strata Versus First Nations

With the exception of developments on Nisga'a Lands, the *Strata Property Act* does *not* apply to First Nations lands.[4] Some First Nations in British Columbia have developed real estate projects on Indian band lands. Outwardly, many of these developments may look like condominium projects, but they are not.

Aboriginal law is complex and rapidly changing. The following explanation is general in nature because the

---

[1] *Cooperative Associations Act*, S.B.C. 1999, c. 28.

[2] *Canada Cooperatives Act*, S.C. 1998, c. 1.

[3] There does not appear to be a great deal of information available to the public about cooperatives in British Columbia. For information about the structure of cooperatives, readers may find assistance in M. Mangan, ed., *Directors Liability in Canada*, loose-leaf (North Vancouver, STP Specialty Technical Publishers, 1994), Chapter 8.

[4] *Nisga'a Final Agreement Act*, S.B.C. 1999, c. 2, s. 6 (definition of "Nisga'a Lands"); and see, for example, *Strata Property Act*, ss. 70, 199, 237, and 242.

focus of this book does not permit a detailed examination of this area of the law.

Under Canada's constitution, "lands reserved for the Indians" are exclusively within the federal jurisdiction.[1] Accordingly, provincial and municipal laws do not apply if they deal directly with the use of Indian lands.[2] Since the *Strata Property Act* is provincial legislation governing the use of land, it does not apply to Indian lands.

Legal title to Indian reserve land is held by the federal government for the "use and benefit of a band."[3] Accordingly, Indian lands are excluded from our provincial land title system.[4] Instead, the federal Department of Indian and Northern Affairs Canada operates its own Indian Lands Registry.

In practice, non-Indians cannot acquire fee simple title directly from a First Nation. Rather, a non-Indian may only lease Indian land if various conditions are met.[5] A developer who creates a development on reserve land must first obtain a long-term lease (often called a "head lease" or sometimes a "ground lease") from the federal government. When the project is built, the developer sells a partial assignment of the developer's rights under the head lease to a purchaser. Note that a purchaser does not acquire fee simple title but rather the right to occupy the premises under a long-term lease.[6]

---

[1] *Constitution Act, 1867*, 30 & 31 Victoria, c. 3. (U.K.), s. 91(24).

[2] See, for example, *Derrickson v. Derrickson* (1986), 1 S.C.R. 285, (provincial *Family Relations Act*); *Surrey (Dist.) v. Peace Arch Enterprises Ltd.* (1970), 74 W.W.R. 380 (B.C.C.A.) (municipal zoning and health bylaws) and *Brantford (Township) v. Doctor*, [1996] 1 C.N.L.R. 49; (1995), 29 M.P.L.R. (2d) 300, [1995] O.J. No. 3061 (O.C.J. – Gen. Div.) (provincial building code applied where its provisions only incidentally related to Indian land).

[3] *Indian Act*, s. 12(1) (definition of "reserve").

[4] There is a rarely used mechanism to bring Indian lands into our provincial land title system, but it is complex and costly. For information, see W.J. Mackay *et al.*, ed., *Land Title Practice Manual*, loose-leaf (Vancouver, Continuing Legal Education Society of BC, 2001), Tab 24A.

[5] *Indian Act*, ss. 37-41 and 58.

[6] For several helpful articles on Indian land developments, see "*Indian Act Conveyancing*" (Vancouver, Continuing Legal Education Society of BC, April 14, 2000).

The legal specifics of real estate developments on Indian lands vary from project to project. Although nearly all developments are governed by head leases, the terms of those leases vary widely. Each head lease is typically a complex, lengthy legal document with features unique to the particular development. Among other things, a head lease may:

- include a rent review clause that exposes a purchaser to rental increases in the future,[1]

- incorporate agreements with local governments for services, whose costs are passed on to the purchaser,

- be subject to a band's zoning, assessment and taxation bylaws, or

- require the purchaser to belong to a homeowner's association, whose bylaws also affect the purchaser.

Before purchasing a leasehold interest in Indian lands, a purchaser should obtain legal advice from a lawyer experienced in such matters.

---

[1] See, for example, *Musqueam Indian Band v. Glass*, [2000] 2 S.C.R. 633; (2000), 192 D.L.R. (4th) 385; 82 B.C.L.R. (3d) 199.

Chapter 3

THE STRATA PROPERTY ACT

In June 1998, the province published the first report of former premier Dave Barrett, who chaired the *Commission of Inquiry into the Quality of Condominium Construction in British Columbia.*[1] In its report, the Barrett Commission recommended many changes to BC strata legislation.

In response to the first Barrett Commission report, the provincial government passed the *Strata Property Act* in July 1998,[2] which was not immediately proclaimed into force. In June 1999, the government fine-tuned the unproclaimed *Strata Property Act* with about fifty changes in an amending statute called the *Strata Property Amendment Act*, 1999.[3]

On July 1, 2000, the province proclaimed the *Strata Property Act*, and the *Strata Property Amendment Act*, 1999 into force.[4] The legislation repealed the *Condominium Act* and replaced it with the *Strata Property Act*, as amended. The government also issued comprehensive general regulations under its legislation. The regulations are found in the *Strata Property Regulation.*[5] Since July 1, 2000, the government has further amended the Act[6] and the *Strata Property Regulation.*[7]

---

[1]British Columbia, *Commission of Inquiry into the Quality of Condominium Construction in British Columbia* (Victoria, Queen's Printer, June, 1998).

[2]*Strata Property Act*, S.B.C 1998, c. 43.

[3]*Strata Property Amendment Act*, 1999, S.B.C. 1999, c. 21.

[4]B.C. Reg. 43/2000 proclaims the *Strata Property Act* [except s. 72 (2)(b)], as amended, in force effective July 1, 2000. Effective October 12, 2001, B.C. Reg. 241/2001 brought s. 72 (2)(b) of the *Strata Property Act* into force.

[5]B.C. Reg. 43/2000.

[6]*Miscellaneous Statutes Amendment Act (No. 2), 2000*, S.B.C. 2000, c. 26, ss. 59-66; *Miscellaneous Statutes Amendment Act, 2002*, S.B.C. 2002, c. 22, ss. 11-22; *Trustee Investment Statutes Amendment Act, 2002*, S.B.C. 2002, c. 33, ss. 21-22; *Residential Tenancy Act,* S.B.C. 2002, c. 78, s. 116.

[7]B.C. Regs. 237/2000, 265/2000, 289/2000, 241/2001 and 33/2003.

The *Strata Property Act* retains the same legal fundamentals found in previous legislation but adds many refinements.

Unless otherwise stated, all references in this book to sections of a statute refer to the *Strata Property Act*, as amended. The *Strata Property Regulation* will be referred to as the "regulations." When necessary, reference will be made to other statutes that play an important role in strata matters, such as the *Land Title Act*.[1]

The *Strata Property Act* also contains a *Schedule of Standard Bylaws*. When considering references in this book to the Standard Bylaws, readers should bear in mind that a strata corporation may amend its bylaws.[2] Accordingly, readers should check whether their strata corporations have amended any particular Standard Bylaw under consideration.

The Importance of the Regulations and Forms

Unlike the *Condominium Act*, which had very few regulations and forms, the *Strata Property Act* has extensive regulations and over 26 forms. It is not possible to use the Act without the regulations and forms. Anyone reading the *Strata Property Act* must have a copy of the regulations and forms at hand.

For example, section 132 of the *Strata Property Act* provides that the maximum amount of a fine established by a strata corporation cannot exceed the amount set out in the regulations. The reader must consult regulation 7.1 to know that the maximum fine is $200 for the breach of a bylaw, except for a rental restriction bylaw, in which case the maximum fine is $500.

---

[1] *Land Title Act,* R.S.B.C. 1996, c. 250.
[2] For information about amending bylaws, see Part IV, *Bylaws and Rules.*

Many sections of the Act refer to prescribed forms. For instance, prescribed forms now exist for an Information Certificate (Form B), a Mortgagee's Request for Notification (Form C), and to give Notice Beginning Arbitration (Form L). The forms are found in the regulations.

How to Obtain a Copy of the *Strata Property Act*

Readers can view or download the *Strata Property Act*, as amended, together with the regulations and forms at www.qp.gov.bc.ca/statreg/ or at www.fic.gov.bc.ca. The electronic versions of the statute and regulations may not always be up to date so it is important in each case to check an electronic document for the date of its last consolidation. Alternatively, readers may order a consolidated version of the *Strata Property Act* with the regulations and forms for the prevailing fee from Crown Publications Inc. at 250-386-4636 or www.crownpub.bc.ca.

Chapter 4

STRATA PLAN TYPES, STYLES, AND USES

Types

There are two types of strata plans: those that subdivide buildings and those that stratify land.

Building Strata Plans

Strata developments often involve buildings. Developers create these projects by constructing a new building or converting an old one (often called a conversion) into strata ownership.[1] In each case, the strata plan divides the building into two or more strata lots with common property. Unless the strata plan shows something else, the boundary of a strata lot in a building is midway between the surface of the structural portion of each wall, floor or ceiling that separates one strata lot from another strata lot, the common property or another parcel of land.[2]

Bare Land Strata Plans

Strata plans that subdivide land are called bare land strata plans. In addition to the *Strata Property Act*, the *Bare Land Strata Regulations* regulate the circumstances where land may be subdivided into strata lots and common property.[3]

---

[1] In the case of a conversion, the building must be previously occupied before the authorities may approve the building strata plan: *Burton et al. v. Harris et al.*, (2003), 37 M.P.L.R. (3rd) 200, [2003] B.C.J. No. 887, 2003 B.C.S.C. 523 (S.C.).

[2] *Strata Property Act*, s. 68.

[3] *Bare Land Strata Regulations*, B.C. Reg. 75/78 as amended.

The boundaries of a bare land strata lot exist in the horizontal plane by reference to survey markers, as shown in the strata plan,[1] in the same way a standard subdivided lot is identified. An important difference between a standard subdivision of land into lots and the subdivision of the land into bare land strata lots is the presence of common property in the bare land strata plan.

Buildings may be constructed on a bare land strata development after the strata plan is filed, or the land being divided may include buildings. Despite the presence of buildings, the development remains a bare land strata development. Because of the possible presence of buildings on a bare land strata plan, it can be difficult to know from looking at a development whether it is a building strata plan or a bare land strata plan. The only sure way to know is to look at the strata plan filed in the Land Title Office. Every bare land strata plan is identified as such on the first page of the plan.[2]

Some developers use the bare land strata concept very creatively. For instance, the author has heard of a marina development where the developer proposes to stratify the dock to create boat slips as bare land strata lots.

Styles

Strata developments can be built in a variety of styles and sizes. Some people believe that an apartment is a condominium and a townhouse is not. In fact, both styles, if stratified, are strata developments. Similarly, detached and semi-detached houses may form part of a strata development when shown on a strata plan as strata lots.

Strata developments can consist of as few as two strata lots or hundreds of strata lots.

---

[1] *Strata Property Act,* s. 68.
[2] *Strata Property Act*, s. 243; *Bare Land Strata Regulations*, s. 18.

Uses

Strata lots within buildings and bare land strata lots are developed for every purpose for which buildings or land can be used. Strata developments may be used exclusively for residential purposes, or they may be used exclusively for a commercial, industrial or recreational purpose. In some cases, a development may include both residential and commercial units. Such a development is commonly called a mixed-use development.

Land can be developed as a bare land strata plan for a variety of purposes. For example, suppose a developer owns a large piece of recreational land. The developer may subdivide the land into bare land strata lots and common property. The developer will likely provide various facilities in the common property, such as roads, tennis courts, barbeque sites and so on. The purchaser of each bare land strata lot may build a cottage on his or her lot. There may be requirements in the bylaws, or a building scheme, to ensure uniform standards of construction among the cottages. The owners of the bare land strata lots will share the use of the common property and the expense of maintaining it.

A manufactured home park is another good example of a bare land strata plan. Some manufactured home parks are bare land strata developments where strata lots serve as pads for manufactured homes. Ownership of a pad entitles the owner to put his or her manufactured home on it. Individuals own their respective pads and share in the ownership and maintenance of common areas, such as roads and recreational facilities in the park.

Air Space Strata Plans

At common law, a landowner has the right to control the air space above his or her land, subject to statutory restrictions for zoning, aviation and the like. A landowner may create one or more air space parcels above his or her land. The title to each air space parcel may then be dealt with separately from the other titles. Since an air space parcel is treated as land, it may be subdivided into strata lots with common property.[1]

The *Land Title Act* permits landowners to treat their air space as if it were land by depositing a survey of the air space above their land (called an "air space plan") at the Land Title Office.[2] If the landowner keeps the underlying land but permits someone else to occupy the air space parcel, he or she is sometimes called the "remainderman."

Developers have used the air space parcel concept to construct mixed-use strata projects.[3] This method is typically used where the same structure contains different uses. In effect, the developer creates separate air space parcels to contain single-use strata developments. By this means, the same complex may contain one or more separate strata plans, each having a different use. For example, one strata development may be residential while another is commercial. Though they share the same complex, each strata corporation controls a separate portion of the structure.

Virtually every air space development involves construction of a strata building over top of land or buildings owned by the developer as remainderman. It is very important to ensure there are appropriate arrangements to compel the remainderman to maintain the necessary physical support and related services to the air space parcel, even if the remainderman's property suffers damage.

---

[1] *Land Title Act*, ss. 3 and 141; *Strata Property Act*, s. 240.
[2] *Land Title Act*, R.S.B.C. 1996, c. 250, Part 9.
[3] See, for example, Christine S.K. Elliott and Eleanor M. Hart, *"Mixed-Use Condominium Developments & Parking in a Strata Development,"* Real Estate–1998 Update (Vancouver, Continuing Legal Education Society of BC, 1998).

In each air space strata development, there should be one or more written agreements between the strata corporation, as the occupier of the air space, and the remainderman, who is likely the developer. These agreements deal with obligations of support, access, provision of utilities, insurance and other important matters.[1]

The owner of an air space strata lot must be familiar with the relevant agreements between the strata corporation and the remainderman. Since these agreements are usually complex, an owner should obtain legal advice when reviewing such agreements.

---

[1]For information about the insurance considerations in such agreements, see Chapter 16, *Insurance.*

Chapter 5

FREEHOLD VERSUS LEASEHOLD

A developer who intends to develop a strata project will either purchase or lease the necessary land. The choice determines whether those who purchase the strata lots obtain a freehold or leasehold interest in their strata lots.

Freehold

If the land is purchased, the developer becomes the registered owner in fee simple. Fee simple means the owner exercises the greatest degree of control over the property that the law of private ownership permits.

When a developer subdivides land by depositing a strata plan, the Registrar of Land Titles records the developer as the fee simple owner of each of the newly created strata lots. The developer may then sell the fee simple title to a strata lot to a purchaser. We call these freehold strata developments because purchasers acquire fee simple title to their strata lots.

Leasehold

If the developer leases the land, he or she must do so for a term of fifty years or more from the federal, provincial or municipal government, a regional district or some other public authority.[1] According to the regulations, a public authority may also be a university, the Sechelt Indian Band, the Provincial Rental Housing Corporation or certain school boards.[2] We call the government or other public

---

[1] *Strata Property Act*, ss. 199 (definition of "leasehold landlord") and 201(c).
[2] *Strata Property Regulation*, s. 11.3.

body that owns the land, the "leasehold landlord." The developer leases the land under a document called a "ground lease" (sometimes called a "head lease") that sets out the terms and conditions upon which the developer has leased the property.

When a developer wishes to register a strata plan over land that is subject to a ground lease, we call it a "leasehold strata plan."[1] To ensure, among other things, that the leasehold landlord is aware of the developer's intentions, the Registrar of Land Titles will not accept the developer's leasehold strata plan unless it is signed by the leasehold landlord.[2]

When the developer, as the long-term tenant, deposits the strata plan, several things happen. First, the Registrar of Land Titles issues new fee simple titles in the name of the leasehold landlord for each of the strata lots created. Next, the deposit of the strata plan automatically converts the ground lease into individual strata lot leases of the leasehold landlord's interests in each strata lot.[3] The lease for each strata lot takes the form of a Model Strata Lot Lease attached to the ground lease.[4] This means that, in the case of each strata lot, the leasehold landlord is the owner and the developer is the tenant under a lease whose form is shown in the Model Strata Lot Lease.

Note that a Model Strata Lot Lease must be attached to the ground lease. Anyone checking the ground lease for a leasehold strata plan in the Land Title Office may view the attached Model Strata Lot Lease.

---

[1] *Strata Property Act*, s. 199 (definition of "leasehold strata plan").
[2] *Ibid.*, s. 201(e).
[3] *Ibid.*, s. 203.
[4] *Ibid.*, s. 203(1).

What the Purchaser of a Leasehold Strata Lot Acquires

When a developer "sells" an individual leasehold strata lot, the developer sells his or her interest as a tenant under the ground lease for that strata lot. When a buyer "purchases" a leasehold strata lot, he or she registers an interest as a "leasehold tenant." In effect, the strata buyer takes an assignment of the developer's interest as a tenant under the strata lot lease with the leasehold landlord. Unless the ground lease requires otherwise, the *Strata Property Act* dispenses with the requirement for the leasehold landlord to sign an assignment of each strata lot lease from the developer to its first purchaser.[1] When the first purchaser "sells" to the second purchaser, the first purchaser's interest is assigned as a tenant under the ground lease to the second purchaser, and so on with each subsequent "sale."

Since the buyer purchases an interest under a lease, he or she buys the right to occupy the strata lot for the balance of the term remaining under the lease. With each passing year, the term remaining diminishes.

The *Strata Property Act* permits the leasehold landlord to transfer fee simple title for each of the strata lots to the leasehold tenants.[2] However, the strata development can only convert from leasehold to freehold if the leasehold landlord transfers fee simple title to *all* of the strata lots.[3]

Terminology

By acquiring the developer's interest as a tenant in the strata lot, the buyer becomes a "leasehold tenant." Although the Act uses the term "leasehold tenant,"[4] most

---

[1] *Strata Property Act*, s. 204.
[2] *Ibid.*, s. 216(1).
[3] *Ibid.*, s. 216(2).
[4] *Ibid.*, ss. 1(1) (definitions of "convey" and "conveyance" and "owner" respectively) and 199 (definition of "leasehold tenant").

people informally refer to the buyer as the "leasehold owner" or, simply, the "owner." The definition of "owner" in the *Strata Property Act* includes a leasehold tenant of a strata lot in a leasehold strata plan.[1]

If the leasehold owner rents his or her strata lot to a tenant, the person who rents the unit is technically a subtenant.

What Happens at the End of the Strata Lot Lease?

As the end of the term of a strata lot lease approaches, the leasehold landlord has several options: renew the lease for a strata lot; buy out the leasehold tenant's interest in that strata lot; or sell all of the leasehold strata lots to their respective tenants and, in that fashion, convert the development to a freehold strata plan.

Renewal of a Strata Lot Lease

At least one year before the term of the lease expires, the landlord must advise each leasehold tenant in writing whether the landlord elects to renew the lease for the term specified in the notice.[2] If a leasehold landlord neglects to notify a leasehold tenant in writing about the landlord's decision, the *Strata Property Act* requires the landlord to renew the lease for a term of five years.[3] Granting renewals to fewer than two-thirds of the strata lots in the leasehold strata plan is not effective unless the leasehold landlord meets certain conditions.[4]

If a leasehold landlord chooses to renew the lease, or the lease is automatically renewed, the renewal must be on the same terms as the current strata lot lease, except

---

[1] *Strata Property Act*, s. 1(1) (definition of "owner").
[2] *Ibid.*, s. 210.
[3] *Ibid.*, s. 210(4).
[4] *Ibid.*, s. 212.

that the term and the rent may be changed.[1] In a renewal, the *Strata Property Act* requires that the rent for a strata lot reflect the current market rental value of the land included in the strata plan, excluding all buildings and improvements, in the proportion that the most recent assessed value of the strata lot bears to the total of the most recent assessed values of all the strata lots included in the leasehold strata plan.[2]

Buy Out of the Leasehold Tenant's Interest

If a landlord chooses not to renew the lease, the leasehold landlord must purchase the leasehold tenant's interest in the strata lot, as a tenant, according to the Act.[3]

If a leasehold landlord or a leasehold tenant wishes to determine the value of the tenant's interest in the strata lot, they must first check the Model Strata Lot Lease for a formula. If there is no formula in the Model Strata Lot Lease, they must look for a schedule filed with the leasehold strata plan in the Land Title Office. If no schedule is found, the Act requires them to use the fair market value of the leasehold tenant's interest, calculated according to the regulations, as if the strata lot lease did not expire.[4] To date, the province has not yet passed regulations to establish a formula for this calculation. If there is no formula in the Model Strata Lot Lease, or in a related schedule, or in the regulations, the leasehold landlord and the leasehold tenant respectively should obtain legal advice about the value of the tenant's interest.

Alternatively, a leasehold landlord may, with the unanimous consent of the members of the strata corporation, change the basis for calculating the final

---

[1]*Strata Property Act*, s. 211.
[2]*Ibid.*, s. 211(2).
[3]*Ibid.*, s. 210(5).
[4]*Ibid.*, s. 214(1), (2).

purchase price of each leasehold owner's interest by filing an amended schedule with the leasehold strata plan.[1]

Sale of Fee Simple Title to All Leasehold Strata Lots

At any time, a leasehold landlord may sell the fee simple title in a strata lot to its leasehold tenant, but only if the landlord similarly sells the fee simple title to each strata lot in the leasehold strata plan to its respective leasehold tenant.[2] After the leasehold landlord transfers the title to each of the strata lots, each strata lot lease ceases to exist and the strata plan continues as though it were never a leasehold strata plan.[3]

This procedure converts the owners from leasehold tenants to freehold strata owners. Instead of having only an interest under a long-term lease to sell, an owner may now sell fee simple title to his or her strata lot.

Restrictions on Lease, Assignment or Occupancy

A leasehold landlord may impose restrictions on the lease, assignment or occupancy of the strata lots included in a leasehold strata plan.[4] A restriction must be set out in a schedule of restrictions filed with the leasehold strata plan in the Land Title Office.[5] The restrictions are binding on the strata corporation and everyone who buys a leasehold interest in any of the strata lots.[6]

In some circumstances a leasehold landlord may, on his or her own, or upon the request of the strata corporation, change any of the restrictions. Before the strata corporation may ask the leasehold landlord to change a restriction, it must pass a resolution to change the restriction

---

[1] *Strata Property Act*, s. 214(3).
[2] *Ibid.*, s. 216.
[3] *Ibid.*, s. 216.
[4] *Ibid.*, s. 206(1).
[5] *Ibid.*, s. 206(2).
[6] *Ibid.*, s. 206(3).

by a 3/4 vote at an annual or special general meeting.[1] Except where the leasehold landlord is the government of British Columbia, restriction changes also require cabinet approval.[2]

If there is a change to an occupancy restriction in the schedule of restrictions, the amendment does not affect persons who were leasehold tenants immediately before the change. The amendment, however, affects persons who become leasehold tenants as a result of a sublease or assignment of the strata lot lease after the change occurs.[3]

Rent Review and Periodic Payment Clauses

Generally speaking, there are two types of ground leases: those which require regular rental payments throughout the lease; and those for which developers prepay all of the rent due under the lease. Before buying an interest in a leasehold strata lot, the purchaser should review the ground lease with a lawyer for the presence of any clause imposing a rent review or other similar liability as described below.

Where a ground lease requires annual rent payments throughout the term of the lease, every strata lot must pay its share of the annual rent under its Model Strata Lot Lease.[4] Typically, leasehold tenants are allowed to pay the annual rent in equal monthly installments throughout each year.

This type of ground lease *may contain a rent review clause,* which allows the landlord to periodically adjust the rent. Typically, a rent review clause allows the leasehold landlord to adjust the rent every 20 years or so to reflect the property's current market value. Rent reviews usually trigger substantial increases in the rent payable.

---

[1]*Strata Property Act*, s. 207(1).
[2]*Ibid.*, s. 207.
[3]*Ibid.*, s. 207(4).
[4]*Ibid.*, ss. 203, 205.

Begusic v. Clark, Wilson & Co.[1] illustrates the importance of checking the ground lease for a rent review clause. Although the case involves a housing cooperative, its ground lease governed the payment of rent in a manner similar to that found in leasehold strata developments.

Case Study

A cooperative association leased land in North Vancouver from the landlord for a term of 66 years under a ground lease. Members of the cooperative purchased shares in the association and took, in effect, an assignment of the ground lease as it applied to their respective units. Each cooperative member was responsible for her pro-rated share of the monthly rent payable under the ground lease. Many of the association's members were retired persons living on fixed incomes, who joined the cooperative for its secure, affordable housing.

The ground lease contained a clause requiring a rent review every 22 years. The clause required that the rent be adjusted to an amount equal to 7.5 per cent of the fair market value of the land. The ground lease scheduled the first rent review for 1990.

In 1983, the buyer purchased an interest in the housing cooperative. The buyer did not know about the rent review clause in the ground lease. Nor did the buyer expect a rent increase in the future. The buyer

---

[1]*Begusic v. Clark, Wilson & Co.* (1992), 69 B.C.L.R. (2d) 288, (*sub nom Reiger v. Croft & Finlay*), [1992] 5 W.W.R. 700 (B.C.S.C.) (decision on the liability of certain real estate licensees and lawyers). See also *Begusic v. Clark, Wilson & Co.* (1992), 69 B.C.L.R. (2nd) 273, 92 D.L.R. (4th) 273, [2002] 5 W.W.R. (B.C.S.C.) (decision on the liability of certain real estate licensees and lawyers); and *Flandro v. Mitha* (1992), 7 B.C.L.R. (2d) 280 (S.C.) (decision on the liability of certain accountants, lawyers, and the cooperative association).

thought her portion of the monthly rent would remain nearly constant for the 50 years or so remaining under the term of the ground lease.

In 1987, the association's members first took notice of the rent review clause. Calculations established that the 1990 review would raise the cooperative's annual rent from $21,225 to approximately $337,500. The buyer's pro-rated monthly share of the rent in respect of her unit would increase proportionately.

The buyer was one of many members of the cooperative who sued a variety of defendants, including the developer and various real estate licensees, lawyers and notaries.

Faced with the prospect of higher land value before the next rent review, the cooperative association decided to purchase the property from the landlord. It had to raise approximately $7.925 million in mortgage financing to complete the purchase and convert the property to a strata development.

The assessment of damages was complicated. The court assessed damages as at the approximate date when members of the association first learned about the pending rent increase. Generally speaking, the court assessed the global damages at $7.925 million less various amounts, including a 20 per cent discount for betterment. In mitigating their damages by purchasing the property, the cooperative's members converted their leasehold interests to freehold strata title, which gave them an advantage. The court took account of that advantage by subtracting 20 per cent for betterment.[1] The claimants were entitled to their respective pro-rated shares of the global award.

[1]*Begusic v. Clark, Wilson & Co.* (1991), 57 B.C.L.R. (2d) 273; 82 D.L.R. (4th) 667 (B.C.C.A.), with supplementary reasons (1992) 66 B.C.L.R. (2d) 253; 90 D.L.R. (4th) 319 (B.C.C.A.), leave to appeal to the S.C.C. dismissed without reasons February 20, 1992, [1991] S.C.C.A. No. 431 and [1991] S.C.C.A. 524.

Ground Leases with Prepaid Rent

If a developer prepays the rent under the ground lease, there will not usually be a rent review clause. However, a prepaid lease may contain a clause requiring periodic additional payments to the landlord based upon increases in the property's fair market value. This is similar to a rent review clause to the extent that it creates a potential financial liability for the buyer in the future.

Default Under the Strata Lot Lease

If a leasehold tenant defaults under the strata lot lease, the leasehold landlord is not entitled to re-enter and take possession of the strata lot. Instead, the leasehold landlord must apply to the Supreme Court of British Columbia for an order for sale of the leasehold tenant's interests in the strata lot.[1]

A title search usually reveals court proceedings against a leasehold tenant's interest in the strata lot. Generally speaking, the leasehold landlord registers a certificate of pending litigation (formerly called a "*lis pendens*" or sometimes an "*L.P.*") against title to the strata lot in the Land Title Office at the start of the landlord's default proceedings.

---

[1] *Strata Property Act*, s. 209(1).

Part II

WHO'S WHO IN A STRATA DEVELOPMENT?

Every strata development consists of various entities and individuals with specific roles, rights and duties. To apply the *Strata Property Act* to a particular problem, it is important to understand who's who in a strata development.

Chapter 6

STRATA CORPORATION

Creation

A developer creates a strata corporation by depositing the strata plan in the Land Title Office. Section 2 of the *Strata Property Act* says,

> **2. (1) From the time the strata plan is deposited in a land title office,**
>
> > **(a) a strata corporation is established, and**
> >
> > **(b) the owners of the strata lots in the strata plan are members of the strata corporation under the name "The Owners, Strata Plan No. ___" [the registration number of the strata plan].**

Subject to the *Strata Property Act* and the regulations, a strata corporation has the legal capacity of a natural person.[1] A corporation can enter contracts to buy or sell property or services, and a corporation can sue or be sued.

Although a strata corporation and a company are both corporations, the similarity effectively ends there. The following table summarizes some of the most important differences between a strata corporation and a company incorporated in British Columbia.

---

[1] *Strata Property Act*, s. 2(2).

Differences Between a Strata Corporation and an Incorporated Company

	Strata Corporation	Company
Liability	An individual member's liability is *not* limited to the same extent as in a company. If someone sues and obtains a judgment against a strata corporation, it serves as a judgment against every strata lot owner. Each owner is liable to pay his or her share of the judgment according to the schedule of unit entitlement, being the same formula that governs an owner's contribution to maintenance fees and the like.[1]	The members, in their capacity as shareholders, are not personally liable when someone obtains a judgment against their company. The judgment binds the company, not its members.
Incorporation	In a strata corporation, there is no certificate of incorporation. The strata corporation is created by depositing the strata plan.	The Registrar of companies issues a certificate of incorporation.
Shares	In a strata corporation, individual members do *not* purchase shares in the strata corporation. The *Strata Property Act* automatically makes every owner a member of the strata corporation.	The members acquire shares.
Company Act [2]	The *Company Act* does *not* apply, except as specifically provided.[3] For example, to cancel a strata plan and wind up a strata corporation, the *Strata Property Act* borrows the winding up procedure from the *Company Act*.[4]	The *Company Act* applies fully.

---

[1] *Strata Property Act*, s. 166.
[2] *Company Act*, R.S.B.C. 1996, c. 62.
[3] *Strata Property Act*, s. 291(1).
[4] *Ibid.*, s. 276.

Duties

The *Strata Property Act* requires every strata corporation to carry out fundamental duties, all of which are discussed in more detail later in this book. In general terms, the strata corporation's essential duties include the following:

Manage

A strata corporation must manage the common property and common assets of the strata corporation for the benefit of the owners.[1]

Repair and Maintain

A strata corporation must repair and maintain its common property and common assets.[2] Depending on the bylaws, the corporation may also have a duty to repair and maintain limited common property (LCP) or features in a strata lot.[3]

If the strata corporation receives an order from a regulatory authority to carry out work on common property or land that is a common asset, the corporation must carry out the work.[4] If the strata corporation receives a work order respecting a particular strata lot, the corporation must promptly notify the owner. If the owner fails to do the work, the strata corporation may do it and charge the owner for its cost.[5]

---

[1] *Strata Property Act*, s. 3.
[2] *Ibid.*, ss. 3 and 72.
[3] See, for example, the *Schedule of Standard Bylaws*, ss. 2 and 8. For information about repairs, see Part V, *Repairs.*
[4] *Strata Property Act*, s. 83.
[5] *Ibid.*, ss. 84 and 85.

Insure

A strata corporation must obtain and maintain property insurance on the common property, including any buildings shown on the strata plan, the common assets and any fixtures built or installed on a strata lot by the developer as part of the original construction of that strata lot.[1] In addition, the strata corporation must maintain insurance against liability for property damage and bodily injury.[2]

Every year the strata corporation must review the adequacy of its coverage and report about it to the owners at the annual general meeting (AGM).[3]

In *Lalji-Samji v. Strata Plan VR 2135*,[4] the court considered one of the consequences of a strata corporation's failure to insure its common property. The court held that a strata corporation could not claim against a strata owner whose carelessness apparently damaged the common property where the corporation had failed to insure the property under the former *Condominium Act*.

Case Study

A rug in the lobby of the complex was common property. The rug was ruined when bleach from a box belonging to one of the owners leaked on to it. Apparently, the strata corporation lacked insurance for damage to the rug.[5]

---

[1] *Strata Property Act*, s. 149(1). For information about insurance, see Chapter 16, *Insurance*.

[2] *Ibid.*, s. 150(1).

[3] *Ibid.*, s. 154.

[4] *Lalji-Samji v. Strata Plan VR 2135*, [1992] B.C.J. No. 176 (S.C.).

[5] In *Lalji-Samji*, the reasons do not explain why the strata corporation lacked insurance coverage. In a later case, the court referred to a commentary on the *Lalji-Samji* decision in which the author reported that the strata corporation in *Lalji-Samji* failed to file a proof of loss to claim coverage within the one-year period required by the corporation's insurance policy: see *Strata Corporation VR 2673 v. Comissiona*, [2000] B.C.J. No. 1681, 2000 B.C.S.C. 1240 at para. 8 per Levine, J.

The strata corporation sued the owner, who argued that the Condominium Act and the general principles of insurance law prohibited the corporation from claiming against him.

Section 54 of the Condominium Act (now section 155 of the Strata Property Act) required the corporation to insure the common property against fire and other perils which are usually the subject of insurance in similar properties. Section 54(3) also provided, in part,

> **54. (3) Notwithstanding the terms of the policy, ...**
>
> > **(b) the owners and tenants from time to time of every strata lot ...**
> >
> > **shall be deemed to be included as the named insured on a policy of insurance in force under (this section).**

The court dismissed the strata corporation's claim.

The court held that the strata corporation could not sue the owner. If the strata corporation had insured the rug as it was supposed to do, the corporation would have claimed against its insurance policy. After paying for the loss, the strata corporation's insurer could not recover it from the individual strata owner because the owner is one of the insured persons under the policy. Since the strata corporation failed to meet its statutory duty to insure the rug, it could not sue the owner for the damage in these circumstances.

Keep Records

The *Strata Property Act* requires every strata corporation to prepare and keep various records and to allow various persons access to those records.[1]

---

[1]For information about a strata corporation's records, including access, see Chapter 13, *Record Keeping.*

Chapter 7

STRATA COUNCIL

The law recognizes the need for an executive body to carry out the duties of the strata corporation and to oversee the corporation's affairs between general meetings of the eligible voters. This executive body is called the strata council. It is effectively a board of directors.

Duties

Section 26 of the *Strata Property Act* says,

> **26. Subject to this Act, the regulations and the bylaws, the council must exercise the powers and perform the duties of the strata corporation, including the enforcement of bylaws and rules.**[1]

The Act clearly makes the strata council responsible for carrying out the duties of the strata corporation. Thus, when the Act refers to a duty or a power of the strata corporation, it is generally the strata council that is responsible for performing the duty or exercising the power.

For example, the strata council ensures that the duty of obtaining the necessary insurance, which is a duty of the strata corporation, is fulfilled.

The Act states that the strata corporation has the capacity to enter into contracts in respect of its powers and duties under the Act, the regulations and the bylaws.[2] This means that through the strata council, the strata corporation can enter into a contract with a strata manager. If provided for

---

[1]See also *Strata Property Act*, s. 4.
[2]*Ibid.*, s. 38.

in the contract, the strata manager can perform the duties of the strata corporation that a strata council would otherwise have to perform. For instance, a strata manager could, by the terms of the contract, be required to obtain the insurance needed by the strata corporation.

When exercising authority under the bylaws, a strata council must act reasonably. That is, council must be able to demonstrate that its decision is in the best interests of the strata corporation as a whole and for reasons that rationally relate to the problem at hand. For instance, in *Baker v. Strata Plan NW 3304*[1] a strata corporation's bylaws required an owner to obtain strata council's permission before enclosing her balcony. From 1992 to 2000 the owner's balcony was enclosed. As it turned out, the building envelope leaked. After the owners contributed approximately $3 million in special assessments, in 2000 the building was repaired. To carry out the repairs, the contractors first removed the enclosed portion of the owner's balcony. In 2001, the owner applied to strata council for permission once again to enclose her balcony. The contractors who renovated the building envelope informed the council that any areas that are altered by others after the completion of renovation work would not be covered by the contractor's warranty. A municipal fire prevention officer had also recommended against completely enclosed balconies for fire safety reasons. The council refused the owner's request to enclose her balcony. The council cited its concerns to keep the building envelope warranty intact and fire safety. Council also took into account the new look of the building's exterior and the affect of an enclosed balcony on the building's aesthetics. The Council, however, did offer to compensate the owner for the loss of her original enclosure during the remediation work. When the owner sued the strata corporation, the court found that strata

---

[1]*Baker v. Strata Plan NW 3304*, [2002] B.C.J. No. 2518, 2002 B.C.S.C. 1559 (S.C.).

council relied on legitimate reasons that formed a rational basis for its decision. The council acted reasonably.

Number of Positions

The strata corporation's bylaws determine the number of seats on council.[1] The Standard Bylaws require a council to have at least three and not more than seven members.[2]

Eligibility

Each year at the annual general meeting, the eligible voters must elect from among themselves the members of the strata council.[3] The only individuals who can be council members are owners, some tenants, and any other class of person permitted by the strata corporation's bylaws.[4] For example, eligible voters may pass a bylaw permitting occupants who are spouses of owners to serve on council.

Owners

Every strata lot owner is eligible to sit on council.[5] If a strata lot is owned by more than one person, only one of them at a time may sit on council unless all the owners are on council.[6]

The *Strata Property Act* clarifies the status of corporate owners, who may choose an individual person to represent the corporate owner on council. Only one representative of the corporation at a time can sit on council.[7]

---

[1] *Strata Property Act*, s. 29(1).
[2] *Strata Property Act, Schedule of Standard Bylaws*, s. 9.
[3] *Strata Property Act*, s. 25.
[4] *Ibid.*, s. 28(1), (2).
[5] *Ibid.*, s. 28(1).
[6] *Ibid.*, s. 29(2).
[7] *Ibid.*, ss. 28(1) and 29(3).

Long-Term Residential Tenants

Tenants who rent residential strata lots for lengthy terms are eligible to serve on strata councils.[1] If the owner of a residential strata lot leases his or her unit to a tenant for a set term of three years or more, section 148 of the *Strata Property Act* automatically assigns the owner's powers and duties to the tenant.[2]

For example, if an owner rents his or her residential strata lot to a tenant for a term of five years, the owner's right to serve on council passes to the tenant. On the other hand, suppose the owner rents to a tenant on a month-to-month basis. After three years of renting month-to-month, does the tenant acquire the owner's right to serve on council? No. In a month-to-month tenancy, the term of the lease is only one month at a time. Typically, a tenant who remains in the unit elects each month to renew for another month.

There are some limitations on this automatic assignment. The tenant still requires the owner's consent to exercise any of the owner's powers or rights to:[3]

- acquire or dispose of land,

- cancel or amend the strata plan, or

- do anything that would affect the owner's interest in the strata lot, the common property or land that is a common asset.

A residential tenant must notify the strata corporation in writing of the assignment of the owner's powers before the tenant can exercise any of those powers.[4] The notice must state the name of the tenant and the time period

---

[1] *Strata Property Act*, s. 28(1).
[2] *Ibid.*, s. 148.
[3] *Ibid.*, s. 148(6).
[4] *Ibid.*, s. 148(3).

during which the lease is effective. The strata corporation must give a copy of the tenant's notice to the owner.[1]

The tenant can stand for election to council once notice has been given.

Family Tenants

If an owner rents his or her strata lot to a family member, the *Strata Property Act* automatically assigns the owner's powers and duties to his or her family tenant.[2] The regulations define "family" or "family member" to mean a spouse of the owner, a parent or child of the owner, or a parent or child of the owner's spouse.[3] The term "spouse" includes an individual who has "lived and cohabited with the owner, for a period of at least two years at the relevant time, in a marriage-like relationship, including a marriage-like relationship between persons of the same gender."[4] Neither the Act nor the regulations define the term "child." Presumably, the term "child" refers to the tenant's *relationship* to the owner, not the tenant's age. In the author's view, the term "child" in this definition includes an adult child.

This feature of the Act applies to rentals of residential and non-residential strata lots.

The same limitations that apply to an assignment of an owner's powers to a long-term residential tenant under section 148 of the Act, as noted above, also apply to a family tenant.[5]

A family tenant must notify the strata corporation in writing of the assignment of the owner's powers before the tenant can exercise any of those powers.[6] The notice must state the family tenant's name and the time period

---

[1] *Strata Property Act*, s. 148(4).
[2] *Ibid.*, ss. 142(3) and 148.
[3] *Strata Property Regulation*, s. 8.1(1).
[4] *Ibid.*, s. 8.1(2).
[5] *Strata Property Act*, ss. 142(3) and 148(4).
[6] *Ibid.*, ss. 142(3) and 148(3).

during which the lease is effective. The strata corporation must give a copy of the tenant's notice to the owner.[1]

Once a family tenant gives notice, he or she may stand for election to council.

Assigning Rights to Tenants

Apart from the automatic assignments of the owner's rights and duties to long-term residential tenants or family tenants described above, section 147 of the *Strata Property Act* permits any owner who leases his or her strata lot to assign some or all of the owner's powers to the tenant.[2] This feature of the Act applies to any type of strata lot, whether residential or non-residential.

The owner must notify the strata corporation, in writing, of the assignment of the owner's powers to the tenant before the assignment is effective. The notice must specify the name of the tenant, the powers that have been assigned and the time period during which the assignment is effective.[3]

Owners in Arrears

The strata corporation can pass a bylaw prohibiting a person from sitting on council if he or she is in arrears to the strata corporation to the extent that the corporation is entitled to file a lien against the person's strata lot.[4] A strata corporation must first comply with various requirements before it is entitled under the Act to file a lien. For information about liens, see Chapter 15, *Finances*.

The bylaw may also extend to the developer who owns one or more unsold strata lots but who owes money to the strata corporation for specified matters. However, it appears

---

[1]*Strata Property Act*, ss. 142(3) and 148(4).
[2]*Ibid.*, s. 147(1).
[3]*Ibid.*, s. 147(2).
[4]*Ibid.*, ss. 28(3) and 116(1).

the bylaw cannot disqualify the developer from council because of money owed for:[1]

- an interim budget shortfall or related penalty;
- a penalty for failure to call the first AGM; or
- reimbursement of the cost of obtaining copies of documents which the developer failed to deliver at the first AGM, as required by the *Strata Property Act.*

Standard of Care

Section 31 of the *Strata Property Act* sets out the standard by which council members must carry out their work:

> **31. In exercising the powers and performing the duties of the strata corporation, each council member must**
>
> **(a) act honestly and in good faith with a view to the best interests of the strata corporation, and**
>
> **(b) exercise the care, diligence and skill of a reasonably prudent person in comparable circumstances.**

This is the same standard of care expected from directors of provincially incorporated companies and non-profit societies.[2] Regardless of an individual council member's lack of experience, the court will hold the member to the standard expected from a reasonable person in comparable circumstances who is informed of all the facts. This is called an objective standard of care.

The statutory bylaws may exempt a strata council member from liability in certain circumstances. In the former *Condominium Act*, section 122(4) excused a council member from personal liability for acts done in good faith while

---

[1]*Strata Property Act*, ss. 28(3) and 116(1).
[2]*Ibid.*, s. 31. See also *Company Act*, R.S.B.C. 1996, c. 62, s. 118 and *Society Act*, R.S.B.C. 1996, c. 433, s. 25 respectively whose wording is nearly identical to section 31 of the *Strata Property Act.*

carrying out his or her duties as a council member. Under the *Strata Property Act*, section 22 of the Standard Bylaws relieves a council member from personal liability where the member acts honestly and in good faith while performing council duties. In the event of a lawsuit, the onus is on the council member to prove that he or she acted in good faith and, in the case of the Standard Bylaws, honestly.

The strata corporation may purchase insurance to protect council members against liability for errors and omissions in the performance of their duties on council.[1] This type of coverage is typically called Directors' and Officers' Liability Insurance. For more information about Directors' and Officers' Liability Insurance, see Chapter 16, *Insurance*.

Payment for Service

The *Strata Property Act* permits a strata corporation to pay strata council members for their service as council members if payment is approved in advance in the budget, the bylaws, or by a resolution passed by a 3/4 majority at a general meeting.[2]

A strata corporation that wishes to pay its strata council members for their services should consult the corporation's accountant before finalizing the method of payment. If the Canada Revenue Agency regards the payment as employment income, the strata corporation will be liable, among other things, to remit source-deducted income tax from payments to council members.[3] If the strata corporation fails to collect and remit any income tax due, the council members may be personally liable for the amounts due plus interest and

---

[1] *Strata Property Act*, s. 151.
[2] *Ibid.*, s. 34.
[3] *Income Tax Act*, S.C. 1970-71-72, c. 63, s. 153 as amended. For information about the approach taken by the Canada Revenue Agency, see *Employee or Self-Employed* (Ottawa, Canada Revenue Agency, undated) and *Information Circular 89-2R, Directors' Liability - Section 227.1 of the Income Tax Act and Section 323 of the Excise Tax Act.*

penalties. Merely calling strata council members "independent contractors" will not avoid liability under section 227.1 of the federal *Income Tax Act*[1] if the method used to pay council members falls within the Canada Revenue Agency's definition of employment income.

Conflict of Interest

Since strata council members must act in the strata corporation's best interests, they must avoid situations where their private interests might conflict with the corporation's interests.

Section 32 of the *Strata Property Act* requires council members to disclose their private interests in the following circumstances:

> **32. A council member who has a direct or indirect interest in a contract or transaction with the strata corporation must**
>
> **a) disclose fully and promptly to the council the nature and extent of the interest,**
>
> **b) abstain from voting on the contract or transaction, and**
>
> **c) leave the council meeting**
>
> > **i) while the contract or transaction is discussed, unless asked by council to be present to provide information, and**
> >
> > **ii) while the council votes on the contract or transaction.**

If a council member fails to disclose his or her interest to council as required, he or she may still avoid liability by disclosure to the members of the strata corporation in a general meeting. If the council member fully discloses his or her interest to the members, the eligible voters may ratify the contract or transaction with a 3/4 majority at a

---

[1] *Income Tax Act*, s. 227.1.

general meeting.[1] The council member in question is not an eligible voter for the purpose of the vote at the general meeting.[2]

If the council member fails to comply with these provisions of the Act, the strata corporation or any owner may apply to the court for relief. If a court finds that the contract or transaction was unreasonable or unfair to the strata corporation at the time it was entered into, the court can set it aside and require the council member to pay all of his or her profit from the arrangement to the strata corporation.[3] In addition, if the court finds that the council member did not act honestly or in good faith, the court may order the member to compensate the strata corporation or any other person for a loss arising from the arrangement or from setting it aside.[4]

Complaints

If someone complains that a strata council member has violated a bylaw or rule, then, with one exception, the council member in question must not participate in any decision about the allegation.[5] If all the owners are on council, however, the council member may participate in the deliberations.[6]

Meetings

For information about strata council meetings, see Chapter 12, *Meetings*.

---

[1] *Strata Property Act*, s. 33(1).
[2] *Ibid.*, s. 33(2).
[3] *Ibid.*, s. 33(3)(a), (c).
[4] *Ibid.*, s. 33(3)(b).
[5] *Ibid.*, s. 136(1).
[6] *Ibid.*, s. 136(2).

Chapter 8

MEMBERS

The owners of the strata lots are the members of the strata corporation. Although the powers and duties of the strata corporation are, for the most part, performed by the strata council, or by the corporation's agents or employees, the members have an essential role in the operation of the strata corporation.

Definition of an "Owner"

The *Strata Property Act* defines the term *owner* to mean a person who is the registered owner of the fee simple interest in a strata lot in a Land Title Office or, in the case of a leasehold strata plan, a person who is registered as the leasehold tenant of the strata lot.[1] In the case of a person who purchases a strata lot under an agreement for sale, the owner is the registered holder of the last registered agreement for sale. In the case of a life estate, an owner is the tenant for life.[2] In this work, the word *owner* is always used according to its meaning in the Act, unless otherwise stated.

Unless a person is an owner within the meaning of the *Strata Property Act*, she cannot exercise the rights of an owner under the statute. For instance, the definition of an *owner* under the Act may restrict the rights of a person who has a significant financial interest in a strata lot, but who does not meet the criteria of an owner. Suppose, for instance, that a husband and wife together purchase a freehold strata lot, but only the wife registers her interest on title in a Land Title Office. The common law regards

---

[1]For information about a leasehold strata plan, see Chapter 5, *Freehold Versus Leasehold*.
[2]*Strata Property Act*, s. 1(1) (definition of "owner").

the wife as a legal owner and the husband as a beneficial owner. Under the Act, however, the wife is the only one who meets the definition of an owner because she is the one registered on title. It follows, for example, that the wife is an eligible voter, but the husband is not.[1]

Control

Members direct the strata corporation's activities through general meetings.

The strata corporation must hold an annual general meeting (AGM) of the members.[2] Additional general meetings called *special* general meetings may be held during the year.[3] Each strata lot owner will have a vote at the annual and special general meetings unless the owner is ineligible to vote.[4] For example, an owner may be ineligible to vote if the strata corporation has passed a bylaw that prevents the owner from voting if there are unpaid strata fees, or if the owner's vote has been assigned to a tenant under the *Strata Property Act*.

Ultimately the members, and *not* the strata council, control the strata corporation.

At each AGM, eligible voters must elect a strata council and approve the budget. Additionally, there are a number of other decisions that *must* be made by the members at their general meetings.

In some cases, the decision is made by a simple majority vote. In other cases, the decision must be made by a 3/4 or unanimous vote. In some situations, a strata corporation's bylaws may require some other voting

---

[1] With a proxy, however, the husband could exercise his wife's vote. For information about voting, including the use of a proxy to vote on behalf of an eligible voter, see Chapter 14, *Voting*.

[2] *Strata Property Act*, ss. 40 and 41. For information about general meetings, see Chapter 12, *Meetings*.

[3] The former *Condominium Act* used the term, "extraordinary general meeting" (often informally called an "E.G.M.") to refer to a general meeting that was not an annual general meeting.

[4] For information about voting at a general meeting, see Chapter 14, *Voting*.

threshold for particular matters. Appendix C contains a list of certain decisions that must be made by the eligible voters. The type of vote required for each decision may vary depending on the specifications in the Act, regulations, or in some cases the Standard Bylaws.

Restricting the Strata Council

The *Strata Property Act* permits eligible voters, by a majority vote, to direct or restrict the strata council in exercising its powers and performing its duties.[1] There are, however, some limitations of the members' powers to direct or restrict the strata council.[2]

Eligible voters may not direct or restrict the council if their instructions contravene the Act, the regulations or the bylaws. For example, if the eligible voters pass a majority vote at a general meeting directing the strata council to close the strata corporation's contingency reserve account, the members' instructions are not enforceable because the Act requires every strata corporation to have such a fund.[3] Similarly, the eligible voters cannot interfere with the strata council's discretion to decide if someone has contravened a bylaw or rule, whether a person should be fined or whether to deny an individual access to a recreational facility.

In some cases, although there may be no requirement to do so under the Act, a strata council may choose to require members to vote on certain matters at a general meeting to ensure that the decisions made reflect the wishes of the majority of the eligible voters. Where the Act does not specify a certain type of vote, the type of vote necessary to pass a resolution at a general meeting is a majority vote.[4]

---

[1] *Strata Property Act*, s. 27(1).
[2] *Ibid.*, s. 27(2).
[3] *Ibid.*, ss. 27(2) and 92(b).
[4] *Ibid.*, s. 50(1).

Additionally, if eligible voters comply with certain requirements, they may influence the affairs of the strata corporation by requisitioning a general meeting and requiring an item to be placed on the agenda of that meeting.[1]

---

[1] *Strata Property Act*, ss. 43 and 46(2).

Chapter 9

STRATA MANAGERS

A strata corporation has the legal capacity to enter into contracts.[1] Although the strata council is responsible for carrying out the duties and responsibilities of the strata corporation, many strata developments hire strata managers to provide day-to-day management services for the corporation.

Although the strata council may negotiate a strata management contract with the strata manager, the costs associated with the contract must first be approved by eligible voters in the annual budget or by a 3/4 vote at a general meeting.[2]

When a strata manager acts for a strata corporation, the manager represents the corporation, not individual owners or tenants. In *McGowan v. Strata Plan NW1018*[3] the court described how the relationship between a strata property manager and a strata corporation ought to function:

> *In my view, both Council and (the strata property manager) should be very careful to ensure the property management position is seen for what it is—in service to, not in control of—the Council, the Strata Corporation and the ownership. It is critical to that perception that the property manager be responsive to directions of Council and requests from the ownership. It is also important to have the functions of the job open to scrutiny.*

---

[1] *Strata Property Act*, s. 38.
[2] *Ibid.*, s. 97.
[3] *McGowan v. Strata Plan NW1018*, [2002] B.C.J. No. 959 at para. 70, 2002 B.C.S.C. 673 at para. 70 (S.C.).

Only the strata council has the authority to direct the strata manager, unless the management contract requires the manager to also take instructions from individual owners or tenants.[1]

The relationship between the strata manager and the strata corporation is governed by the contract between the two parties. The activities to be performed by the strata manager, as well as the remuneration for such activities, should be clearly set out in the contract.

The *Strata Property Act* does not govern disputes between the strata corporation and the strata manager concerning the management contract. The parties must settle such disputes between themselves or through a court process.

Cancelling Contracts

If the strata corporation enters a contract for strata management services *before* the first annual general meeting (AGM), the agreement ends:[2]

- four weeks after the second AGM, unless the eligible voters decide by majority vote to continue the contract, or

- on the termination date in the contract, or

- when the contract is properly cancelled under the Act,

whichever is earlier.

The Act also permits a strata corporation to cancel a strata management agreement before its expiry upon two months' notice to the strata manager if the cancellation is first approved by a 3/4 vote at a general meeting.[3] Conversely, the strata manager may also cancel the

---

[1] *Strata Property Act*, ss. 4 and 26.
[2] *Ibid.*, s. 24.
[3] *Ibid.*, s. 39(1)(a).

contract before its expiry by giving the strata corporation two months' notice.[1]

Return of Records

When a strata management contract ends, the manager must, within four weeks, return to the strata corporation any of the strata corporation's records that are required to be kept under the Act and which remain in the manager's possession or control.[2] If a strata manager fails to comply with this requirement, the manager must pay the strata corporation an amount as provided in the regulations.[3] The regulations require the manager to pay $1,000 to the strata corporation for failure to return the records within the four-week period.[4]

Holding Proxies

Strata managers who provide management services to the strata corporation must not serve as proxies on behalf of eligible voters at general meetings.

Strata managers may only hold proxies if permitted to do so by the regulations.[5] At present, the regulations do not contain any provision that permits a strata manager to hold a proxy.

[1] *Strata Property Act*, s. 39(1)(b).
[2] *Ibid.*, s. 37(1).
[3] *Ibid.*, s. 37(2).
[4] *Strata Property Regulation*, s. 4.3.
[5] *Strata Property Act*, s. 56(3).

Chapter 10

SECTIONS

A section is a form of mini-government within a strata corporation.

Creating Sections

The *Strata Property Act* states that a strata corporation can create sections to represent the different interests of residential and non-residential strata lot owners, or owners of non-residential strata lots if they use their strata lots for significantly different purposes or among the owners of different types of residential strata lots.[1]

The regulations define "types" of residential strata lots as:[2]

- apartment-style strata lots,

- townhouse-style strata lots, or

- detached houses.

This means, for instance, that a residential strata corporation may create separate sections respectively for apartment-style and townhouse-style strata lots in the strata plan.

Sections can be created by either the developer or the strata corporation.

[1] *Strata Property Act*, s. 191.
[2] *Strata Property Regulation*, s. 11.1.

Developer

The developer may create sections for the strata corporation when the strata plan is filed in the Land Title Office. To create sections, the developer must file bylaws that provide for the creation and administration of each section. Additionally, if the strata plan does not designate limited common property (LCP) for the use of the strata lots in a section, the developer can file a resolution of the strata corporation to designate certain common property as LCP for the use of all the strata lots in the section.[1]

Strata Corporation

The strata corporation may also create sections. To create sections, the strata corporation must amend the bylaws at a general meeting. The resolution to amend the bylaws to create and administer a section requires at least two separate votes. There must be a 3/4 vote by the eligible voters within the proposed section, as well as a 3/4 vote by the eligible voters of the strata corporation.[2] The strata corporation may also pass a resolution by 3/4 vote to designate certain common property as LCP for the use of all of the strata lots in a particular section.[3]

Powers and Duties

Although the strata corporation retains its powers and duties in matters of common interest to all owners, the *Strata Property Act* provides that each section is a corporation and has the same powers and duties as the strata corporation.[4]

---

[1] *Strata Property Act,* s. 192.
[2] *Ibid.,* s. 193.
[3] *Ibid.,* ss. 74 and 193.
[4] *Ibid.,* s. 194.

Each section can establish its own operating fund and contingency reserve fund (CRF) for common expenses of the section. Additionally, the section can prepare its own budget and require the owners in that section to pay strata fees, or special levies, approved by the section.

The section can enter into contracts in the name of the section, sue or arbitrate in the name of the section, and acquire or dispose of land and other property in the name of or on behalf of the section. However, the section may not enter into contracts, or sue or arbitrate in the name of the strata corporation.[1]

A section may amend bylaws in respect of a matter that relates solely to the section.[2] A section can also enforce its bylaws and rules.[3]

Administration

The *Strata Property Act* permits a section to govern its own affairs concerning matters that relate solely to the section.

Executive

The eligible voters in a section must elect a section executive. The executive effectively acts as the strata council for the section. The executive has the same powers and duties on behalf of the section as the strata council has on behalf of the strata corporation.[4] Members of a section's executive are also eligible to be elected to the strata council.[5]

---

[1] *Strata Property Act*, s. 194(3).
[2] *Ibid.*, s. 197(2).
[3] *Ibid.*, s. 194(2).
[4] *Ibid.*, s. 196(2).
[5] *Ibid.*, s. 196(3).

Expenses

Expenses of the strata corporation that relate solely to the strata lots in a section are shared by the owners of strata lots in that section. As a general rule, each strata lot's share of expenses is determined based on the strata lot's unit entitlement in proportion to the unit entitlements of the other strata lots in that section subject to certain exceptions.[1]

In addition, where a bylaw creates a residential section of apartments, townhouses, or detached homes respectively, the bylaw necessarily identifies the relevant style of strata lot as a type.[2] The existence of a type bylaw enables a strata corporation to allocate certain expenses solely to strata lots of the particular type. For information about allocating expenses according to type of strata lot, see Chapter 26, *Paying for Repairs*.

Bylaws

In some cases, the *Strata Property Act* permits a section to create bylaws respecting matters that relate solely to the section.[3] Similarly, the executive of a section may make rules governing the use, safety and condition of land owned by the section or LCP designated for the exclusive use of all the strata lots in the section.[4]

---

[1]*Strata Property Act*, s. 195. For information about how a section allocates expenses among the owners of strata lots in the section, see Chapter 26, *Paying for Repairs*.

[2]*Strata Property Act*, s. 191; *Strata Property Regulation*, s. 11.1. See also *Strata Plan LMS 1537 v. Alvarez*, [2003] B.C.J. No. 1610 at para. 55 (S.C.); *Strata Corp. LMS 509 v. Andresen*, [2001] B.C.J. No. 225, paras. 18-23 (S.C.).

[3]*Strata Property Act*, s. 197. See also *Strata Property Regulation*, ss. 11.2, 11.3 and 17.11(6).

[4]*Ibid.*, s. 197(4), (5).

Insurance

A section is limited to obtaining insurance only against perils that are not insured by the strata corporation, or for amounts that are in excess of amounts insured by the strata corporation.[1]

---

[1]*Strata Property Act*, s. 194(4).

Chapter 11
DEVELOPER

The *Strata Property Act* uses the term "owner developer" to refer to the person who develops the strata project. The Act defines the owner developer as the person who, as at the date he or she applies to deposit the strata plan at the Land Title Office, owns the underlying land, or who leases the land from a public authority for a term of at least fifty years.[1] In this book we call the "owner developer" the "developer."

The Act prevents a developer from avoiding his or her obligations through a bulk sale of strata lots to someone else. According to the Act, the developer can be any person who acquires all of the developer's interest in more than 50 per cent of the strata lots in the strata plan.[2] Otherwise a developer, for example, might sell all the strata lots in a bulk sale to an affiliated corporation, which could then market the units without regard to the developer's obligations under the Act, arguing instead that it is a buyer who is simply reselling the strata lots.

At the time the strata plan is filed and the strata corporation is created, the developer owns or, in the case of a leasehold strata, leases all the strata lots in the development and is responsible for the governance of the strata corporation.[3] Somewhere in the course of the strata lot sales, a transition occurs. Governance of the strata corporation shifts from the developer to the buyers, who hold their first annual general meeting (AGM) and elect the first strata council.

---

[1] *Strata Property Act*, ss. 1(1) (definition of "owner developer"), 199 (definition of "ground lease") and 201(b).

[2] *Ibid.*, s. 1(1) (definition of "owner developer").

[3] For information about leasehold strata developments, see Chapter 5, *Freehold Versus Leasehold*.

The *Strata Property Act* imposes various duties on the developer at different stages of the cycle, creating three stages:

1. before any strata lots are conveyed,
2. after the first strata lot is conveyed, and
3. the first AGM.

1. Before Strata Lots are Conveyed

In the first stage, the *Strata Property Act* establishes a standard of care for the developer. The Act also gives the developer broad discretion to pass resolutions, including those required to amend bylaws.

Developer as Strata Council

Until the new owners elect a strata council, the developer must manage the strata corporation. The *Strata Property Act* specifically provides that, in the interim, the developer must exercise the powers and perform the duties of the council.[1] Section 6 of the *Strata Property Act* sets out the standard of care by which the developer must manage the strata corporation:

> **6. (1) In exercising the powers and performing the duties of a council, the developer must**
>
> > **(a) act honestly and in good faith with a view to the best interests of the strata corporation, and**
> >
> > **(b) exercise the care, diligence and skill of a reasonably prudent person in comparable circumstances.**

---

[1] *Strata Property Act*, s. 5.

This means, among other things, that the developer must make reasonable efforts to pursue any remedies under warranties in existence respecting construction of the common property or common assets of the strata corporation.[1]

Resolutions

Before the first strata lot is conveyed to a purchaser, the developer may pass any resolution of the strata corporation, including amending the strata corporation's bylaws. During this period there are no restrictions on the types of resolutions a developer may make.[2]

Finances

The developer must pay the actual expenses of the strata corporation until the last day of the month in which the first strata lot is conveyed to a buyer.[3]

2. After the First Strata Lot is Conveyed

In the second stage, the *Strata Property Act* restricts some of the developer's powers and creates new obligations for the developer. This stage begins when a developer conveys the first strata lot to a purchaser.

Developer Continues as Strata Council

As before, the developer continues to serve as the strata council until the first AGM. The developer's powers, however, are restricted after the first conveyance of a strata lot to a purchaser.

---

[1]*Strata Property Act*, s. 6(2).
[2]*Ibid.*, s. 8.
[3]*Ibid.*, s. 7.

Restrictions

The *Strata Property Act* gives eligible voters the power to hold special meetings to pass resolutions by majority vote to direct or restrict the developer in the performance of his or her "council" duties.[1]

Veto

As long as the developer owns the majority of units that remain unsold, the developer can exercise a voting advantage at special general meetings. To prevent abuses pending the first AGM, the Act effectively gives each owner a veto on important matters.

As a general rule, important decisions within the strata corporation normally require the support of 3/4 of eligible voters present at a meeting. For example, a 3/4 vote is required to approve a significant change in the use or appearance of common property.[2] However, before the first AGM the Act provides that resolutions at any special general meeting that would normally require a 3/4 vote need *unanimous* approval.[3]

Amending Bylaws

To amend the Standard Bylaws before the first AGM, the developer must call a special general meeting and, in most cases, obtain unanimous approval to the proposed change.[4] There are some exceptions to this general rule, especially in cases where a non-residential section has been formed.[5]

---

[1] *Strata Property Act*, ss. 9 and 27.
[2] *Ibid.*, s. 71.
[3] *Ibid.*, s. 11.
[4] *Ibid.*, s. 127.
[5] *Ibid.*, ss. 127(3), (4) and 197.

Contracts With Developer

The former *Condominium Act* lacked any effective restriction on the extent to which developers could, on behalf of strata corporations, enter into contracts with persons affiliated with the developer. For example, developers could easily award property management contracts to themselves or companies controlled by them.

After the first conveyance, the *Strata Property Act* prohibits the strata corporation from entering contracts with the developer or persons who are not arm's-length from the developer, with one exception. If the strata corporation wishes to enter such a contract, it must first hold a special general meeting and pass a unanimous resolution in favour of the transaction.[1]

Interim Budget

The first conveyance marks the point at which financial responsibility for the common expenses shifts from the developer to the strata corporation.

Prior to the first strata lot being conveyed, the developer must prepare an interim budget for the twelve months beginning the month after that conveyance occurs.[2] The budget must include:[3]

- the estimated operating expenses of the strata corporation,

- a contribution to the contingency reserve fund (CRF) that must be at least five per cent of the estimated operating expenses,

- each strata lot's monthly share of the estimated operating expenses and contribution to the CRF, respectively.

---

[1]*Strata Property Act*, s. 10.
[2]*Ibid.*, s. 13(1).
[3]*Ibid.*, s. 13(2).

The developer *must* deliver a copy of the interim budget to each prospective purchaser.[1]

Beginning on the first day of the month following the month in which the first conveyance occurs, the owners must start contributing financially to the strata corporation according to the interim budget.[2] Each month, every owner must pay his or her share of the estimated operating expenses and make their proportionate contribution to the CRF.[3] Like any other owner, the developer must make monthly contributions for each of the strata lots belonging to the developer.

At this stage, the developer still serves as the strata council. After the first strata lot is conveyed, the developer must collect strata fees in respect of each lot for the strata corporation. The owners must continue to pay their strata fees based on the interim budget until the date the first annual budget takes effect.[4] As the strata council, the developer must ensure that the strata corporation pays its bills.[5]

The Act encourages developers to budget accurately. If there is a shortfall between the actual expenses for the interim period and those set out in the interim budget, the developer must pay the difference.[6] If the shortfall exceeds 10 per cent of the estimated operating expenses, the developer is also liable to pay a penalty.[7] If the shortfall is more than 10 per cent and less than 20 per cent, the developer must pay the shortfall, plus a penalty of two times the shortfall. If the shortfall is at least 20 per cent greater than the estimated operating expenses, the developer must pay the shortfall plus a penalty of three times the shortfall.[8]

---

[1] *Strata Property Act*, s. 13(1).
[2] *Ibid.*, s. 14(1).
[3] *Ibid.*, s. 14(2).
[4] *Ibid.*, s. 14(1).
[5] *Ibid.*, s. 14(1).
[6] *Ibid.*, s. 14(4).
[7] *Ibid.*, s. 14(5).
[8] *Strata Property Regulation*, s. 3.1.

The transition provisions in the regulations relieve a developer of paying a penalty over and above a shortfall if the developer filed a prospectus or disclosure statement under the *Real Estate Act,*[1] or otherwise met certain requirements, before July 1, 2000.[2]

On the other hand, if actual expenses are less than those budgeted, the strata corporation must refund the excess to the owners in proportion to their respective contributions.[3] If, however, none of the owners will individually receive a refund greater than $100, the strata corporation may put the excess into its CRF rather than returning those funds to the respective owners.[4]

Contingency Reserve Fund (CRF)

The former *Condominium Act* did not require developers to create a CRF. In most cases, strata corporations did not start saving money for contingencies until the passage of the first budget at the first annual general meeting. This often meant that strata corporations lacked *any* contingency reserve for at least several years after construction of the project.

The *Strata Property Act* requires the developer to make a lump sum payment to establish the CRF when the first strata lot is conveyed to a purchaser.[5] The timing of the first conveyance determines the amount the developer must pay. If it occurs within one year from deposit of the strata plan, the developer's minimum contribution is five per cent of the estimated operating expenses in the interim budget.[6] If the first conveyance occurs after one year from deposit of the strata plan, the Act requires the developer to contribute up to 25 per cent of the estimated operating

---

[1] *Real Estate Act*, R.S.B.C. 1996, c. 397.
[2] *Strata Property Regulation*, s. 17.3(1).
[3] *Strata Property Act*, s. 14(6).
[4] *Ibid.*, s. 14(7).
[5] *Ibid.*, s. 12.
[6] *Ibid.*, s. 12(2).

expenses in the interim budget, depending on various factors.[1] The transition provisions in the regulations, however, relieve a developer of the requirement to seed the CRF if the developer filed a prospectus or disclosure statement under the *Real Estate Act*, or otherwise met certain requirements, before July 1, 2000.[2]

During this stage, the Act prohibits the developer and the strata corporation from using funds in the CRF to pay the strata corporation's operating expenses.[3]

Insurance

Every strata corporation must carry insurance on its common property, common assets, fixtures and buildings.[4]

After the first conveyance of a strata lot, the *Strata Property Act* requires the developer to ensure that the strata corporation's insurance coverage extends at least four weeks beyond the date of the anticipated first AGM.[5]

3. First Annual General Meeting (AGM)

The strata owners take their destiny into their own hands at the first AGM. This is the last step in the governance transition from the developer to the elected strata council.

Calling the First AGM

The developer must call the first AGM within six weeks of the earlier of the date on which 50 per cent plus one of the strata lots have been conveyed to buyers, or nine months after the date of the first conveyance.[6]

---

[1]*Strata Property Act,* s. 12(3).
[2]*Strata Property Regulation,* s. 17.3(1).
[3]*Strata Property Act,* ss. 12(4) and 14(3).
[4]*Ibid.,* s. 149(1). For information about insuring these features, see Chapter 16, *Insurance.*
[5]*Ibid.,* s. 15.
[6]*Ibid.,* s. 16.

If the developer does not hold the first AGM within the appropriate time, the developer must pay a penalty to the strata corporation.[1] If the developer has delayed calling the first AGM for a period up to 30 days from the date required, the developer owes the strata corporation $1,000. The developer owes the strata corporation an additional $1,000 for every delay of seven days thereafter.

Additionally, if the developer fails to call the first AGM, any owner may call the meeting by giving appropriate notice as described below.[2] The penalties for the delay in the first AGM continue to apply until the meeting is held.

The penalty provisions do not apply if the strata plan was deposited at the Land Title Office before July 1, 2000 *and* the developer holds the first AGM within the time required by the former *Condominium Act*.[3] The statutory bylaws under Part 5 of the *Condominium Act* required the developer to hold the first AGM when 60 per cent of the strata lots were conveyed, or nine months after registration of the strata plan, whichever occurred first.[4]

Notice

The developer must give at least 20 days' written notice in advance of the first AGM.[5]

Section 45 of the *Strata Property Act* requires "at least 2 weeks' written notice" of a general meeting.[6] According to the *Interpretation Act*, the phrase "at least" requires that we calculate this two-week notice period by excluding the first and last days.[7] For example, if the developer wishes to send out notice on the first day of the month, that day

---

[1] *Strata Property Act,* s. 17(b).
[2] *Ibid.,* s. 17(a).
[3] *Strata Property Regulation*, s. 17.3(2).
[4] *Condominium Act*, s. 123(1).
[5] *Strata Property Act*, ss. 16, 45(1) and 61(3).
[6] *Ibid.,* s. 45(1).
[7] *Interpretation Act*, R.S.B.C. 1996, c. 238, s. 25(4).

must not count as part of the two-week period because the developer must exclude the first day. Instead, the developer looks to the next day, being the second day of the month, and then adds two weeks (being 14 days) from that date, which comes to the 15th day of the month. Since the last date is also excluded, the meeting can be held on the day after that, being the 16th day of the month. In other words, the developer must allow at least 16 days between giving notice and the date of the meeting.

However, if the developer uses a method of giving notice which includes mailing, faxing, giving it to an adult occupant other than the person who is required to receive notice, or putting it under a strata lot's door, or in a strata lot's mail box, the Act deems that notice has not been given for four days.[1] Since these methods are often used to give notice of a meeting, the developer must add the four days to the 16 days. This means that the developer should allow at least 20 days (e.g., 16 + 4 = 20) between giving notice and the date of the meeting.

If the developer defaults, and an owner calls the first AGM, the same general notice requirements must be met, including delivery of the notice to the developer.

The notice must include a description of the matters that will be voted on at the meeting, including the proposed wording of any resolution requiring a 3/4 or unanimous vote.[2] The notice of the first AGM must also include the first annual budget together with a financial statement.[3]

The requirements for delivering a notice are described in Chapter 12, *Meetings*.

---

[1]*Strata Property Act*, s. 61(3).
[2]*Ibid.*, s. 45(3). For information about general meetings, see Chapter 12, *Meetings*.
[3]*Ibid.*, s. 21(2).

Budget and Financial Statements

The proposed budget must cover a 12-month period commencing on the first day of the month following the first AGM. The information to be contained in the budget and financial statement is set out in the regulations.[1] The requirements for the first annual budget are effectively the same as for all future budgets of the strata corporation.[2] The financial statement provided by the developer must cover the period from the first day of the interim budget until a day that is within the six-week period before the date of the first AGM.[3]

Within eight weeks after the first AGM, the developer must provide financial statements updated to the date the first annual budget took effect or, if no budget is approved, the date of the first AGM.[4]

Business at the First AGM

Chair

The developer, or his or her agent, serves as the chair for the first AGM.[5] In reality, most developers seldom attend the first AGM. If the developer, or his or her agent, is unable or unwilling to act as chair, the eligible voters can elect an owner to serve as the chair of the meeting.[6]

---

[1] *Strata Property Regulation*, s. 3.3.
[2] *Ibid.*, s. 3.3(1). For information about the budget process, see Chapter 15, *Finances*.
[3] *Ibid.*, s. 3.3(2).
[4] *Strata Property Act*, s. 21(6).
[5] *Ibid.*, s. 19(a).
[6] *Ibid.*, s. 19(b).

Election of Council

The owners must elect the first strata council.[1] For more information about electing a strata council, see Chapter 7, *Strata Council*.

Delivery of Records

The Barrett Commission acknowledged the complaints of participants who described their many difficulties in obtaining the necessary documents from developers to respond effectively to problems, including water damage.[2] The *Strata Property Act* addresses this concern by requiring the developer to deliver copies of a wide range of records to the strata corporation at its first AGM.[3] The list of records includes:

- all plans that were required to obtain a building permit, including any amendments,

- "as-built" plans showing the actual location of any pipe, wire, chute, duct or other facility for the passage of systems or services whose location does not appear on the plans filed in support of a building permit,

- all contracts entered into by the strata corporation,

- any disclosure statement filed by the developer under the *Real Estate Act*,

- the registered strata plan from the Land Title Office,

- names and addresses of all contractors, subcontractors and the like,

---

[1] *Strata Property Act*, s. 20(1).
[2] British Columbia, *Commission of Inquiry into the Quality of Condominium Construction in British Columbia* (Victoria, Queen's Printer, June, 1998) at p. 56.
[3] *Strata Property Act*, s. 20(2).

- all warranties, manuals, service guides and the like, and

- minutes of strata corporation meetings and books of account.

If the developer fails to comply with this requirement, he or she is liable to the strata corporation for costs incurred by the corporation to obtain such materials.[1]

Budget

During the meeting, the proposed budget can be amended by majority vote before the budget itself is put to a vote.[2] The owners must approve the first annual budget by a majority vote.[3]

If the owners do not approve the budget, they must adjourn to prepare a new budget for approval at a special general meeting to be held later. Ordinarily, the special meeting must be held within 30 days; however, the members can, by 3/4 vote, agree to hold the special general meeting beyond that time.[4]

After the First AGM

Within one week following the first AGM, the developer must transfer control of the strata corporation's money to the newly-elected council.[5] Similarly, the developer must also deliver to the newly-elected council any keys, garage door openers and similar items.[6]

Within eight weeks following the first AGM, the developer must deliver updated financial statements.[7]

---

[1]*Strata Property Act*, s. 20(3).
[2]*Ibid.*, s. 21(5).
[3]*Ibid.*, s. 21(4).
[4]*Ibid.*, s. 104(1).
[5]*Ibid.*, s. 22(a).
[6]*Ibid.*, s. 22(b).
[7]*Ibid.*, s. 21(6).

For the next two years, the developer must keep all the financial records relating to the strata corporation's finances prior to the transfer in control.[1] During that time, the strata corporation may inspect those records free of charge. At its own expense, the strata corporation may also copy or audit the developer's financial records that relate to the strata corporation.[2]

---

[1] *Strata Property Act*, s. 23(1).
[2] *Ibid.*, s. 23(2).

Part III

OPERATIONS

The *Strata Property Act* governs the operation of a strata corporation by establishing procedures for meetings and regulating the corporation's affairs.

Chapter 12

MEETINGS

General Meetings

The *Strata Property Act* permits eligible voters to attend general meetings in person. The strata corporation may, by bylaw, permit a person to attend a general meeting by telephone, or by any other method, provided that everyone participating in the meeting can communicate with each other.[1] For example, a strata corporation may pass a bylaw to allow persons to attend a general meeting by video conference, or even via the Internet, as long as everyone at the meeting can communicate with each other. A person who attends by telephone or other electronic means is considered present for the purpose of the meeting.[2]

Annual General Meetings (AGM)

The strata corporation must hold an annual general meeting within two months of its fiscal year end.[3]

A new fiscal year starts on the anniversary of the date when the first annual budget took effect.[4] The first annual budget begins on the first day of the month following the date on which the eligible voters approved that budget. In most cases, a first annual budget is approved at the first AGM.

After that, the strata corporation may only change its fiscal year by a 3/4 vote.[5]

---

[1] *Strata Property Act*, s. 49(1).
[2] *Ibid.*, s. 49(2).
[3] *Ibid.*, s. 40(2).
[4] *Ibid.*, s. 21(1).
[5] *Ibid.*, s. 102.

Waiving the AGM

Eligible voters may waive holding the AGM. To do so, all eligible voters must consent, in writing, before the last day on which the meeting must be held to waive the event. They must also consent, in writing, to resolutions approving the budget for the upcoming year, electing a council and carrying out any other business.[1] If two or more persons share a single vote, the Act requires each of them to consent to the waiver and to the proposed resolutions.[2]

Special General Meetings

A special general meeting is any general meeting other than the mandatory AGM.

The strata corporation may call a special general meeting any time by giving notice.[3] In practice, the strata council exercises this power on behalf of the strata corporation by calling a special general meeting when needed.[4]

In addition, persons holding at least 25 per cent of the strata corporation's votes may demand, in writing, that the strata corporation hold a special general meeting to consider a resolution or other matter.[5] Each person making the demand must sign the request.[6] The strata corporation must hold the special meeting within four weeks after receiving the demand.[7] Bearing in mind the need to give 20 days' written notice for a general meeting, the strata corporation must respond quickly to the demand.[8]

---

[1] *Strata Property Act*, s. 41(1).
[2] *Ibid.*, s. 41(2).
[3] *Ibid.*, s. 42.
[4] *Ibid.*, ss. 4 and 26.
[5] *Ibid.*, s. 43(1).
[6] *Ibid.*, s. 43(2).
[7] *Ibid.*, s. 43(3).
[8] For information about giving notice for a general meeting, see the section below on Notice.

At the meeting, the resolution or other matter specified in the demand must be the first item on the agenda. The meeting must deal with the resolution or other matter before consideration of any other item about which notice has been given.[1] This effectively prevents the strata council, or the membership at the meeting, from inserting other matters into the agenda so that the contentious matter is heard last when attendance at the meeting is falling off.

If the corporation fails to hold the meeting, the persons who made the demand may themselves hold the special general meeting.[2]

Waiving Special General Meetings

Eligible voters may also waive a special general meeting. To waive the meeting, all eligible voters must, in writing, waive the holding of the meeting and consent to the proposed resolution.[3] If two or more eligible voters share a single vote, the Act requires each of them to consent to the waiver and to the proposed resolution.[4]

Setting the Agenda

The strata council sets agendas for general meetings.[5] Individual members cannot insert matters on the agenda. The *Strata Property Act*, however, permits persons holding 25 per cent of the strata corporation's votes to put resolutions or other matters on the agenda of an annual or special general meeting.[6] The necessary number of persons must first, in writing, demand that a particular resolution or other matter be included in the notice of the meeting and, later, in the meeting's agenda.[7] Presumably, they must

---

[1]*Strata Property Act*, s. 43(5).
[2]*Ibid.*, s. 43(6).
[3]*Ibid.*, s. 44(1).
[4]*Ibid.*, s. 44(2).
[5]*Ibid.*, s. 46(1).
[6]*Ibid.*, s. 46.
[7]*Ibid.*, s. 46(1), (2).

deliver their demand to the strata corporation reasonably in advance of the issuance of the notice for the relevant meeting.

Notice

The *Strata Property Act* requires a strata corporation to give written notice of an annual or special general meeting to every owner, regardless of whether the notice must also be sent to the owner's mortgagee or tenant.[1]

In addition, the strata corporation must notify each tenant who is entitled to exercise the rights of his or her landlord.[2]

Any lender who takes a mortgage over a strata lot is entitled to deliver a Mortgagee's Request for Notification (Form C) to the strata corporation.[3] The form is found among the forms in the regulations. Where the lender has delivered such a Request, the strata corporation must notify the lender of each general meeting, in addition to notifying the strata lot owner.[4]

In the case of an AGM, the notice to the lender must also include the budget proposed for the next fiscal year and its supporting financial statement.[5] If a strata corporation meets certain criteria, it may provide a financial summary with the notice, rather than the actual financial statements.[6] The regulations set out the information that must appear in the budget and the financial statement.[7]

---

[1] *Strata Property Act*, s. 45(1).
[2] *Ibid.*, s. 45(1)(c). For information about the circumstances in which a tenant may exercise a vote in respect of a strata lot, see Chapter 14, *Voting*.
[3] *Ibid.*, s. 60.
[4] *Ibid.*, ss. 45(1)(a), (b).
[5] *Ibid.*, ss. 45(4) and 103(2). For information about financial statements, see Chapter 15, *Finances*.
[6] *Strata Property Regulation*, s. 6.7 (3)-(5).
[7] *Ibid.*, ss. 6.6 and 6.7.

Notice Given by Strata Corporation

The *Strata Property Act* sets out the various methods that a strata corporation can use to give notice to a person entitled to receive notice under the Act.[1]

If the person has provided the strata corporation with an address that is outside the strata plan, the strata corporation can either leave it with the person or mail it to the address provided.

If the person has not provided an address outside the strata plan, the strata corporation can:

- leave it with the person,

- leave it with an adult occupant of the person's strata lot,

- put it under the door of the person's strata lot,

- mail it to the person,

- put it through a mail slot or in a mailbox used by that person, or

- fax it to a fax number provided by the person.

If the strata corporation delivers a notice to a person in any way other than by leaving it with that person, the notice, "is conclusively deemed to have been given 4 days after it is left with an adult, put under the door, mailed, put through a mail slot or in a mail box or faxed."[2] This deeming provision does two things for the strata corporation:

[1]*Strata Property Act*, s. 61.
[2]*Ibid.*, s. 61(3).

1. If the strata corporation used one of the methods set out in the *Strata Property Act*, other than leaving it with the person, the strata corporation does not need to make further enquiries to ensure that the person actually received the notice.

2. The *Strata Property Act* deems that receipt of the notice occurs after four days. This means that if the strata corporation relies on the deeming provision, it must add four days to any notice period.

Provided that the strata corporation has made a reasonable attempt to comply with the Act's notice requirements, failure to give a person proper notice does not invalidate a vote taken at the meeting.[1]

Notice Given to a Strata Corporation

Sometimes a person wishes to give notice to a strata corporation. For instance, a mortgagee who wishes to receive information about general meetings must first deliver a Request to the corporation in the prescribed form, as described above.

The *Strata Property Act* provides that a person must give notice to a strata corporation by:[2]

- leaving it with a council member,

- mailing it to the corporation at its most recent address filed at the Land Title Office,

- faxing it to the corporation using the corporation's fax number, or a fax number provided by a council member for that purpose, or

---

[1] *Strata Property Act*, s. 47.
[2] *Ibid.*, s. 63(1).

- putting it through the mail slot or mail box, used by the corporation for receiving notices or other documents.

If the person delivers a notice to a strata corporation in any way other than by leaving it with a council member, the notice is "conclusively deemed to be given 4 days after it is mailed, faxed or put through the mail slot or in the mail box."[1]

The *Strata Property Act* requires every strata corporation to ensure that its correct mailing address is filed at the Land Title Office.[2] A strata corporation may add a fax number to its address information. If a corporation wishes to change its mailing address on file at the Land Title Office, the corporation must file a Strata Corporation Change of Mailing Address (Form D).[3] The form is found among the forms in the regulations. In the case of a strata corporation whose strata plan was filed before July 1, 2000, when the *Strata Property Act* came into force, these address requirements did not apply until January 1, 2002.[4]

Notice Periods

The strata corporation must give at least 20 days' written notice in advance of an annual or special general meeting to every person entitled to receive notice.[5]

Section 45 of the *Strata Property Act* requires "at least two weeks written notice" of a general meeting.[6] According to the *Interpretation Act*, the phrase "at least" requires that we calculate this two-week notice period by excluding the first and last days.[7] For example, if the strata corporation wishes to give an owner notice on the

---

[1]*Strata Property Act*, s. 63(2).
[2]*Ibid.*, s. 62.
[3]*Ibid.*, s. 62(3) and Strata Corporation Change of Mailing Address (Form D).
[4]*Strata Property Act*, s. 2(1) and *Strata Property Regulation*, s. 17.4.
[5]*Strata Property Act*, ss. 45(1) and 61(3).
[6]*Ibid.*, s. 45(1).
[7]*Interpretation Act*, R.S.B.C. 1996, c. 238, s. 25(4).

first day of the month, the strata corporation must not count that day as part of the two-week period because the first day must be excluded. Instead, the strata corporation looks to the next day, being the second day of the month, and then adds two weeks (being 14 days) from that date, which brings us to the 15th day of the month. Since the last date is also excluded, the soonest the meeting could be held would be on the day after that, being the 16th day of the month.

However, as noted above, if a strata corporation uses a method of giving notice which includes mailing, faxing, giving it to an adult occupant other than the person who is required to receive notice, or putting it under a strata lot's door or in a strata lot's mail box, the Act deems that notice has not been given for four days.[1] Since these methods are often used to notify persons about a meeting, the strata corporation must add four days to the 16 days. This means that the strata corporation should allow at least 20 days (e.g., 16+4=20) between giving notice and the date of the meeting.

Amending Matters to be Voted On

The notice must include a description of the matters to be voted upon at the meeting, including the proposed wording of any resolution requiring a 3/4 or unanimous vote.[2] If the proposed resolution is substantially changed by an amendment at the meeting, and then passed in amended form, the court may strike the resolution down for lack of proper notice.

Brown v. Strata Plan NW 3304[3] is a good example.

---

[1] *Strata Property Act*, s. 61(3).
[2] *Ibid.*, s. 45(3).
[3] *Brown v. Strata Plan NW 3304* (1993), 32 R.P.R. (2d) 143; [1993] B.C.J. No. 1381 (S.C.).

Case Study

The Browns owned a unit in a strata complex.

The strata council sent the Browns and every other owner a notice of a special general meeting. The relevant provision of the Condominium Act required the strata corporation to describe the general nature of any special business to be considered at the meeting. The notice said, in part:

1. Purpose: The purpose of the meeting is to receive the Strata Council's reports and to consider two Special Resolutions regarding:

   amend the bylaws; . . .

The notice came with an attachment setting out the wording of two proposed new bylaws. One of the proposed bylaws said, in part,

19.1 The exclusive use, occupation and enjoyment of a strata lot is restricted according to unit size, to not more than five adult persons, unless otherwise approved in writing by the Strata Council . . .

At the general meeting, a motion was received from the floor to amend proposed bylaw 19.1 by inserting the words "of age 45" after the words "five adult persons" to read, in part, as follows:

19.1 The exclusive use, occupation and enjoyment of a strata lot is restricted according to unit size, to not more than five adult persons <u>of age 45</u>, unless otherwise approved in writing by the Strata Council . . . . (Emphasis added)

> *The owners voted to adopt the new bylaw, as amended, and the strata corporation filed the new bylaw at the Land Title Office. The Browns successfully sued the strata corporation to strike down the new bylaw for lack of notice.*

Although they had received the notice, the Browns argued that it was insufficient because it lacked any reference to an age restriction. The court agreed. Even though the *Condominium Act* set a fairly low standard for notice, the notice should alert owners to the significant features of a proposed bylaw. In this case, the notice failed to alert owners that the proposed bylaw might involve an age restriction, which is a significant matter.

This case suggests that if, during a general meeting, amendments from the floor significantly change the character of a proposed bylaw, the proper course is to adjourn the meeting to properly notify all the owners before putting the bylaw, as amended, to a vote.

The *Strata Property Act* also addresses this problem. The Act permits amendments, at the meeting, to the wording of proposed resolutions requiring a 3/4 vote. An amendment is allowed *if the change is not substantial* and the members approve it by a 3/4 vote before the resolution itself is put to a vote.[1]

Waiving Notice of a General Meeting

A person entitled to receive notice may waive, in writing, his or her right to notice of a general meeting. Similarly, that person can also revoke the waiver by doing so in writing.[2]

If the strata corporation fails to give notice of a general meeting as required, eligible voters may still vote on matters at the meeting if every person entitled to receive

---

[1]*Strata Property Act*, s. 50(2).
[2]*Ibid.*, s. 45(2).

notice waives, in writing, his or her right to notice. If two or more persons share one vote with respect to a strata lot, then each of them must, in writing, waive their right to notice.[1]

Quorum

There must be a quorum before the strata corporation can conduct any business at a general meeting.[2] If a quorum is not present within one-half hour from the time appointed for the meeting, the meeting stands adjourned to the same place and time the following week, unless the bylaws provide otherwise.[3] If, on the next occasion, the necessary quorum is still not present within one-half hour, the Act provides the eligible voters present in person or by proxy shall constitute a quorum, unless the bylaws provide otherwise.

Any business conducted without the presence of a quorum of eligible voters is not legally effective.[4] For instance, if a general meeting loses its quorum because a large number of eligible voters leave, any business conducted after the loss of a quorum is not legally effective.

Subject to the bylaws of the strata corporation, the Act sets the quorum at 1/3 of the strata corporation's votes, either present in person or by proxy.[5]

If there are fewer than four strata lots or fewer than four owners then, subject to the bylaws, a quorum consists of eligible voters holding 2/3 of the votes, either present in person or by proxy.[6]

---

[1] *Strata Property Act*, s. 45(5), (6).
[2] *Ibid.*, s. 48(1).
[3] *Ibid.*, s. 48(3).
[4] *Ibid.*, s. 48(1).
[5] *Ibid.*, s. 48(2).
[6] *Ibid.*, s. 48(2).

Order of Business

A strata corporation's bylaws may dictate the order of business at general meetings. For instance, the Standard Bylaws set out the following order of business for annual and special general meetings:

- certify proxies and corporate representatives and issue voting cards,

- determine that there is a quorum,

- elect a person to chair the meeting, if necessary,

- present to the meeting proof of notice of meeting or waiver of notice,

- approve the agenda,

- approve minutes from the last general meeting,

- deal with unfinished business,

- at an annual general meeting, receive reports of council activities and decisions since the last AGM,

- ratify any new rules,

- report on insurance coverage,

- at an AGM, approve the budget for the coming year,

- deal with new business,

- at an AGM, elect a council, and

- terminate the meeting.[1]

---

[1] *Strata Property Act, Schedule of Standard Bylaws*, s. 28. For information about the *Schedule of Standard Bylaws* and amending bylaws, see Part IV, *Bylaws and Rules*.

Strata Council Meetings

A strata corporation's bylaws may specify procedures for strata council meetings.[1] For example, the Standard Bylaws under the *Strata Property Act* set out the following procedures for council meetings. Any council member can call a council meeting with one week's notice, or with less notice by consent or in an emergency. The member must specify the reason for the meeting in the notice, but it does not have to be in writing.[2] Meetings may be held by electronic means as long as all council members and other participants can communicate with each other during the meeting.[3] If a council meeting is held by electronic means, council members are deemed to be present in person.[4] The Standard Bylaws do not restrict a council to any particular method of electronic communication, such as a telephone. Any electronic means is permissible, so long as it allows everyone at the meeting to communicate with each other.

If an owner or tenant requests, in writing, a hearing at a council meeting, council must hold the hearing within one month. If the purpose of the hearing is to seek a decision, council must give a written decision within one week of the hearing.[5] The regulations define a hearing as an opportunity to be heard in person at a council meeting.[6]

Owners may attend council meetings as observers, except where meetings deal with hearings into bylaw violations, hearings into requests for exemptions from rental restrictions, or where observers would, in council's opinion, interfere with an individual's privacy.[7]

---

[1] See, for example, the statutory bylaws in the *Condominium Act*, ss. 119-122.
[2] *Schedule of Standard Bylaws*, s. 14.
[3] *Ibid.*, s. 17.
[4] *Ibid.*, s. 17(2).
[5] *Ibid.*, s. 15.
[6] *Strata Property Regulation*, s. 18.1.
[7] *Schedule of Standard Bylaws*, s. 17.

Ordinarily, every strata council member has a vote at council meetings. However, if all the owners are on strata council, each strata lot has one vote at council meetings.[1]

According to the Standard Bylaws, strata council decisions are by majority vote and council must record the results of all votes in the minutes.[2] If a strata corporation's bylaws fail to state the voting threshold for council decisions, the *Interpretation Act* dictates that decisions be made by majority vote.[3]

Section 19 of the Standard Bylaws requires the strata council to inform the owners of the minutes of all council meetings within two weeks of the meeting, whether or not the minutes have been approved.

The Standard Bylaws do not specify the manner in which the council must inform the owners. The *Strata Property Act* suggests, however, that council may leave the minutes at a location designated by the strata corporation for that purpose.[4]

No Proxy Voting at Council Meetings

Neither the *Strata Property Act* nor the regulations permit a council member to assign his or her vote as a council member to someone else. Since the eligible voters elected the council member, or the strata council appointed that person to council, only that individual may exercise his or her vote as a council member at council meetings.

Minutes

The strata corporation must prepare minutes of every general meeting and every strata council meeting, including

---

[1]*Strata Property Act*, s. 29(4).
[2]*Schedule of Standard Bylaws*, s. 18.
[3]*Interpretation Act*, s. 18(1).
[4]See, for example, *Strata Property Act*, s. 65. Although this section does not directly apply, its provisions serve as a useful guide.

the results of all votes.[1] The strata corporation must keep copies of all meeting minutes for at least six years.[2] See Appendix B, Sample Strata Council Minutes, for a template that may also be used to prepare minutes of general meetings.

When preparing records and providing information, strata council members must comply with the standard of care in section 31 of the *Strata Property Act*, which requires them, among other things, to act honestly and in good faith, and to exercise the care of a reasonably prudent person.[3]

The strata corporation's minutes should always be accurate and clear. The minutes should never contain false information. The strata corporation's minutes are the record of its proceedings and may later be used as evidence in court or arbitration proceedings. As a general rule, strata corporation minutes should always contain the following:

- The name of the strata corporation.

- The type of meeting held (e.g., strata council, AGM, special general meeting, maintenance committee).

- The date, time and location of the meeting.

- The names of persons present. If a member of the meeting arrives late or leaves early, the minutes should record the point at which that person arrived or departed.

- The essential elements of the meeting. The minutes should provide enough information to provide a context for understanding any decision made or action taken.

---

[1]*Strata Property Act*, s. 35(1)(a).
[2]*Ibid.*, s. 35(1)(a) and *Strata Property Regulation*, s. 4.1(3).
[3]*Strata Property Act*, s. 31. For information about a strata council member's standard of care, see Chapter 7, *Strata Council*.

- Each resolution together with the results of any vote. Section 35(1)(a) of the *Strata Property Act*, and sections 18 and 27(4) of the Standard Bylaws require the strata corporation to record the results of each vote. In a general meeting, section 27(4) of the Standard Bylaws requires the voting results to include information about the number of votes for and against a resolution, if a precise count was requested.

- If a member of the meeting discloses his or her conflict of interest in a matter, the minutes must fully record the disclosure, whether the person abstained from voting on the matter, and whether that person left the meeting or otherwise abstained from discussion of the matter.

- Whether confidential matters were discussed *in camera,* and, if so, whether the record of those discussions is omitted from the minutes.

Strata Council's Duty to Avoid Misrepresentation

A strata council must ensure its minutes are accurate because the council knows that others will reasonably rely on those minutes. The strata council members may be liable for misrepresentation if they provide inaccurate or misleading information to someone who suffers a loss because he or she reasonably relies on it. Even if the information is accurate on its face but reasonably leads the person to whom it is given to misinterpret it, the strata council may be liable.

For example, suppose that a strata council decides to omit important information from the minutes of its meetings, such as references to defects in the building envelope. Filtering the minutes will mislead the owners about their respective investments in their strata units.

Similarly, purchasers who typically rely on such minutes will likely be misled.

Alternatively, in appropriate cases, if the strata council wishes to treat the building envelope discussions as confidential, council must insert an appropriate warning in the minutes to alert readers that council discussed confidential matters concerning the building envelope *in camera*. To be sufficient, the warning must adequately inform the reader that the strata council discussed the particular subject in confidence.

Defamation

A strata council should ensure that minutes of all meetings of the strata corporation, including council minutes, are not defamatory.

In general, a remark is defamatory if it is a false statement about someone else that tends to lower that person's reputation in the community. A defamatory statement may be express or implied and may occur by innuendo.[1] When defamation occurs in writing it is called libel.

As a guideline, a strata council should ensure that every statement in the minutes is accurate and verifiable. Although the case did not involve a defamation claim, in *McGowan v. Strata Plan NW1018*[2] the court made the following recommendation concerning council minutes:

> **The fact that the petitioner's position is that of a distinct minority does not relieve the strata owner-ship or the Council from a careful and respectful consideration of the views that that minority has put forward. It does appear from some of the minutes of Council meetings that occasionally comments tending**

---

[1] See, for example, J.G. Fleming, *The Law of Torts*, 5th ed. (Agincourt: The Carswell Co. Ltd., 1977) at 528-533.

[2] *McGowan v. Strata Plan NW1018*, [2002] B.C.J. No. 959 at para. 69, 2002 B.C.S.C. 673 at para. 69 (S.C.).

> to personalize the debate with those of different
> views are allowed to be included. <u>In my view,
> comments that can be taken as critical or
> derogatory of individuals within the organization
> tend to detract from a sense of professional
> management and only add to antagonisms. The
> minutes should be carefully vetted to ensure that no
> such comments are included.</u> (Emphasis added)

In the author's experience, most strata corporation insurance policies exclude coverage for defamation claims against strata council members. A strata council may wish to check with its insurance agent whether coverage exists for a defamation claim.

Chapter 13

RECORD KEEPING

What Records?

Section 35(1) of the *Strata Property Act* says a strata corporation must prepare all of the following records:

- Minutes of general meetings and council meetings, including the results of any vote.

- A list of council members.

- A list of owners with their strata lot addresses; mailing addresses if different; strata lot numbers as shown on the strata plan; parking stall numbers, if any; and unit entitlements.

- A list of names and addresses of mortgagees who have filed Mortgagee's Request for Notification (Form C) under section 60 of the Act.

- A list of names of tenants.

- A list of assignments of voting or other rights by landlords to tenants under sections 147 and 148 of the Act.

- Books of account showing money received and spent and the reason for the receipt or expenditure.

- Any other records required by the regulations.

Among other things, the regulations require that the strata corporation also keep a record of each council member's telephone number, or some other method by which the council member may be contacted at short notice, as long as the method is not prohibited in the bylaws.[1]

In addition, the strata corporation must keep a lengthy list of other records for all the periods set out in the regulations.[2] Appendix B contains a list of all the records a strata corporation must keep, together with the minimum periods of time they must be kept.

Access

Owners, certain tenants, purchasers and mortgage lenders have access to the strata corporation's records.

Owners, Certain Tenants and Authorized Delegates

Section 36(1) of the *Strata Property Act* guarantees access to virtually all of the strata corporation's records to:

- an owner;

- a tenant who has received an assignment of a landlord's right to inspect and copy records under sections 147 or 148 of the Act; and

- people authorized in writing by owners or tenants of the type described immediately above.

Upon request by an owner, tenant with access rights, or delegate authorized in writing, the strata corporation must make the records available for inspection and provide copies of them. Section 36(3) of the *Strata Property Act* and section 25 of the *Interpretation Act*, when read together, require the strata corporation to comply with the request within 15 days, unless the request

---

[1]*Strata Property Regulation*, s. 4.1.
[2]*Strata Property Act*, s. 35(3) and *Strata Property Regulation*, s. 4.1.

is for access to the bylaws and rules, in which case the corporation has eight days to comply.[1]

In addition, a strata corporation must promptly supply a copy of the corporation's financial statements in the following circumstances. Normally, a strata corporation must provide a copy of its financial statements in prescribed form when giving notice of an annual general meeting (AGM). If, however, a strata corporation meets certain requirements, it may instead provide a summary of its financial information with the notice.[2] If the strata corporation has issued a financial summary, instead of the actual financial statements, with the notice, any person entitled to receive notice of the AGM may, before the meeting, request a copy of the financial statements. In that case, the strata corporation must immediately give a copy of the actual financial statements to that person.

The strata corporation must not charge any fee to an owner, a tenant with access rights, or an authorized delegate, for inspecting the strata corporation's records.[3] Although the strata corporation can charge such persons for photo-copies, the corporation must not charge more than 25 cents per page.[4] The strata corporation may refuse to supply copies until the copy fee is paid.[5]

A strata manager who represents a strata corporation is bound by the same restrictions. The strata manager must not charge an owner, a tenant with access rights, or an authorized delegate, any fees in excess of those permitted by the Act. If the strata manager wishes to recover any costs associated with this service, the manager must build that charge into the management fee that the manager charges to the strata corporation.

[1] *Interpretation Act*, R.S.B.C. 1996, c. 238, s. 25.
[2] For information about notice for an AGM, see Chapter 12, *Meetings*.
[3] *Strata Property Act*, s. 36(4) and *Strata Property Regulation*, s. 4.2(2).
[4] *Strata Property Act*, s. 36(4) and *Strata Property Regulation*, s. 4.2(1).
[5] *Strata Property Act*, s. 36(4).

Access to Legal Opinions

Among other things, an owner, a tenant with access rights, or an authorized delegate, has access to the strata corporation's legal opinions.[1] These provisions pose a special problem for strata corporations. Normally, these opinions are subject to solicitor-client privilege, which belongs to the strata corporation.

In some cases, the strata council best serves the strata corporation's interests by keeping its communications with the corporation's lawyers confidential among strata council members without releasing the information to the owners collectively, at least for a period of time. Although sections 35(2)(h) and 36(1) of the *Strata Property Act*, without referring to solicitor-client privilege, guarantee an owner, a tenant with access rights, or an authorized delegate access to the strata corporation's legal opinions, a court would likely uphold the privilege that attaches to legal opinions if the strata corporation wishes to keep the document confidential. Given the importance of solicitor-client privilege, the court would likely require the legislature to insert specific language in the statute removing the privilege before allowing the legislation to deprive the strata corporation of its right to keep communications with its lawyer confidential.

If an owner, a tenant with access rights, or an authorized delegate, requests access to any of the strata corporation's legal opinions, the strata council should immediately consult the corporation's lawyer for advice. In the meantime, the strata council should tell the person who made the request that, since the legal opinion may be subject to solicitor-client privilege, council has sought legal advice.

If the strata corporation's lawyer advises the strata council to decline the request for access to a legal opinion

---

[1]*Strata Property Act*, ss. 35(2)(h) and 36(1).

because it is subject to solicitor-client privilege, the strata council should follow that advice. The strata council should explain to the person who made the request the reasons for refusing to provide access to the legal opinion. Since the legal opinion and its solicitor-client privilege belong to the strata corporation, the members collectively at a general meeting still retain the right, by a majority vote under section 27(1) of the *Strata Property Act,* to direct council to provide the opinion to the person who made the request.

Legal Opinions in Lawsuits Involving Owners

If an owner is involved in a lawsuit with the strata corporation, the *Strata Property Act* prohibits the owner from access to the strata corporation's legal opinions or other information relating to the lawsuit.[1] Nor is the owner entitled to attend those portions of general meetings or strata council meetings at which the lawsuit is discussed.[2]

Purchasers

Purchasers are not yet owners, so they are not members of the strata corporation. As such, purchasers do not have direct access to the strata corporation's records.

Who is a Purchaser?

Section 1 of the *Strata Property Act* defines the term "purchaser:"

> **1. (1) "purchaser" means a person . . . who enters into an agreement to purchase a strata lot or to acquire a strata lot lease in a leasehold strata plan . . . but to whom the strata lot or strata lot lease has not yet been conveyed or assigned.**

---

[1]*Strata Property Act*, s. 169(1)(b).
[2]*Ibid.*, s. 169(1)(c).

This definition is broad. It does not require the buyer of a strata lot to have an unconditional Contract of Purchase and Sale before he or she qualifies as a purchaser under the *Strata Property Act.* For example, a purchaser typically enters a Contract of Purchase and Sale for a strata lot subject to, among other things, approval of the strata corporation's bylaws. The contract at that point is conditional because it depends on the purchaser removing the subject clause by approving the bylaws, or otherwise waiving this requirement. Even though the buyer's contract is conditional, the buyer is still a purchaser under the Act.

Purchasers obtain access to the strata corporation's information two ways: formally and informally.

Formal Access

Purchasers typically take advantage of opportunities under the *Strata Property Act* to require a strata corporation to certify particular information. Purchasers usually obtain the following certificates.

Information Certificates

Section 59 of the *Strata Property Act* entitles an owner, a purchaser, or a person authorized by an owner or purchaser, to request an Information Certificate from the strata corporation in Form B, being the form required by the regulation. The form is found among the forms in the regulations. The certificate must disclose all of the following concerning the strata corporation, and the strata lot for which the request is made, as at the date of the certificate:

- the monthly strata fees payable by the owner;

- any amount the owner owes the strata corporation, other than disputed amounts paid into court or to the strata corporation in trust under section 114 of the Act;

- any agreements under which the owner takes responsibility for expenses relating to alterations to a strata lot, the common property or the common assets;

- any amount the owner is obligated to pay in the future for a special levy that has already been approved, and the date by which the payment is to be made;

- any amount by which the expenses of the strata corporation for the current fiscal year are expected to exceed the expenses budgeted for the fiscal year;

- the amount in the contingency reserve fund (CRF) minus any expenditures which have already been approved but not yet taken from the fund;

- any amendments to the bylaws that are not yet filed in the Land Title Office;

- any resolution passed by a 3/4 or unanimous vote that is required to be filed in the Land Title Office but that has not yet been filed in the Land Title Office;

- any notice that has been given for a resolution that has not been voted on, if the resolution requires a 3/4 or unanimous vote, or deals with an amendment to the bylaws;

- any court proceeding or arbitration in which the strata corporation is a party, and any judgments or orders against the strata corporation;

- any notices or work orders received by the strata corporation that remain outstanding for the strata lot, the common property or the common assets;

- the number of strata lots in the strata plan that are rented;

- any other information required by the regulations.

The strata corporation must attach copies of its rules, the current budget, and the developer's Rental Disclosure Statement, if any, to the Information Certificate (Form B).

Section 59(1) of the *Strata Property Act* and section 25 of the *Interpretation Act*, when read together, require the strata corporation to comply with the request for an Information Certificate (Form B) within eight days.

The strata corporation must not charge more than $35 for an Information Certificate (Form B), including the required attachments, plus the cost of photocopying up to 25 cents per page.[1]

A strata manager who represents a strata corporation is bound by the same restrictions. The strata manager must not charge an owner, or purchaser, or an authorized delegate, any fees in excess of those permitted by the Act. If the strata manager wishes to recover any costs associated with this service, the manager must build that charge into the management fee charged to the strata corporation.

A strata corporation must ensure the accuracy of the information in the Information Certificate (Form B). If the strata corporation is unable to verify the accuracy of any information in the certificate, the corporation should alert the person who requested the certificate with an appropriate written warning accompanying the certificate. Sections 59(5) and (6) of the *Strata Property Act* make the information in the certificate binding on the strata corporation in its dealings with a person who reasonably relies on the certificate, unless the Supreme Court otherwise relieves the strata corporation of the consequences of an inaccuracy.

The Information Certificate (Form B) replaces the former Section 36 Certificate under the *Condominium Act*.

---

[1]*Strata Property Act*, s. 59(7) and *Strata Property Regulation*, s. 4.4.

Certificates of Payment

Section 115 of the *Strata Property Act* entitles an owner, a purchaser, or a person authorized by an owner or purchaser, to request a Certificate of Payment (Form F), being the form prescribed by the regulations. The form is found among the forms in the regulations. The certificate certifies that the owner of a strata lot does not owe money to the strata corporation or, alternatively, that the funds owed to the corporation have been paid into court or trust under the Act, or that satisfactory arrangements have been made to pay the money owing.

Section 115(1) of the *Strata Property Act* and section 25 of the *Interpretation Act*, when read together, require the strata corporation to comply with the request for a Certificate of Payment (Form F) within eight days if the following conditions are met:

- the owner does not owe money to the strata corporation, or,

- if the owner does owe money, he or she has:

  ➢ paid any disputed funds into court or to the strata corporation in trust, or

  ➢ made satisfactory payment arrangements with the corporation.

The certificate certifies that the owner meets these conditions. In completing the certificate, the strata corporation may include money owing for any of the following:

- strata fees;

- special levies;

- reimbursement of the cost of work done by the strata corporation following the owner's failure to comply with a work order from a public or local authority under section 85 of the Act;

- the strata lot's share of a judgment against a strata corporation;

- fines;

- costs charged by the strata corporation for remedying a contravention of a bylaw or rule.

The certificate must not include any damage claims against the owner that have not been determined by a court or arbitration.

The strata corporation must not charge more than $15 for a Certificate of Payment (Form F).[1] A strata manager who represents a strata corporation is bound by the same restriction. The strata manager must not charge an owner, purchaser, or authorized delegate, any fees in excess of those permitted by the Act. If the strata manager wishes to recover any costs associated with this service, the manager must build that charge into the management fee charged to the strata corporation.

The Registrar of Land Titles cannot register any conveyance, lease, assignment of a lease, or agreement for sale of a strata lot unless accompanied by a Certificate of Payment (Form F).[2] The need for a Certificate of

---

[1] *Strata Property Act*, s. 115(3) and *Strata Property Regulation*, s. 6.10.
[2] *Strata Property Act*, s. 256.

Payment (Form F) most commonly occurs when an owner sells his or her strata lot. The lawyer or notary public representing the purchaser usually requests a Certificate of Payment (Form F) shortly before the completion date of the sale. Once issued, the Certificate of Payment (Form F) is current for 60 days.[1]

The Certificate of Payment (Form F) replaces the former Form A under the *Condominium Act*.

Informal Access

A purchaser can indirectly obtain access to the strata corporation's records by borrowing the seller's access rights. Section 36(1) of the *Strata Property Act* entitles the owner, or his or her delegate authorized in writing, to inspect and obtain copies of virtually all of the strata corporation's records. If an owner authorizes a purchaser, in writing, to inspect the strata corporation's records or obtain copies of them, the corporation must allow the purchaser to inspect and copy the records specified.

In any case where an owner has authorized the purchaser, or the purchaser's real estate salesperson, to inspect and copy the strata corporation's records, the strata corporation must treat the purchaser, or his or her real estate salesperson, like an owner. This means that the strata corporation must not charge the purchaser, or his or her real estate salesperson, any fee for inspecting the records.[2] Although the strata corporation can charge them for photocopies, the corporation must not charge more than 25 cents per page for copies of the strata corporation's records.[3] The strata corporation may refuse to supply copies to the purchaser, or his or her real estate salesperson, until the copy fee is paid.[4]

---

[1]*Strata Property Act*, s. 115(2).
[2]*Strata Property Act*, s. 36(4) and *Strata Property Regulation*, s. 4.2(2).
[3]*Strata Property Regulation*, s. 4.2(1).
[4]*Strata Property Act*, s. 36(4).

Votes Per Strata Lot

The general rule is that each strata lot has one vote unless voting rights are otherwise set out in a Schedule of Voting Rights in the strata plan.[1]

In an exclusively residential strata development, each strata lot has only one vote.[2] In such a case, a Schedule of Voting Rights will not be deposited in the Land Title Office unless the strata plan has been subsequently amended to create a non-residential strata lot in the development.

A non-residential strata lot may have more or less than one vote if a Schedule of Voting Rights provides for it.[3] A Schedule of Voting Rights must be deposited in the Land Title Office with the strata plan to give more or less than one vote to a non-residential strata lot.

Who Votes at General Meetings?

To vote at a general meeting, one must be the owner of a strata lot, unless the owner has otherwise assigned the right to vote to a tenant or mortgagee.[4] If two or more persons share one vote with respect to a strata lot, only one of them may vote on a given matter.[5] If two or more people who share one vote cannot agree on how to vote, then the chair must not count their vote in respect of that matter.[6]

---

[1]*Strata Property Act*, s. 53(1).
[2]*Ibid.*, ss. 53(1), 247 and 248.
[3]*Ibid.*, ss. 247 and 248.
[4]*Ibid.*, s. 54.
[5]*Ibid.*, s. 57(1).
[6]*Ibid.*, s. 57(2).

Tenants

There are three ways that a tenant may acquire an assignment of an owner's right to vote. First, a tenant who leases a residential strata lot from the owner under a lease for a set term of three years or more is automatically assigned the powers and duties of his or her landlord, including the right to vote. The residential tenant must notify the strata corporation, in writing, of this assignment before the tenant can exercise the landlord's powers.[1]

Second, if an owner rents his or her strata lot to a family member, within the meaning of the term family in the regulations, the *Strata Property Act* automatically assigns the owner's powers and duties to the tenant.[2] See Chapter 7, *Strata Council* for a discussion of family tenants.

Third, an owner, in his or her capacity as a landlord, may assign some or all of the owner's powers and duties to a tenant whose lease is for a term less than three years.[3] The assignment is not effective until the owner, as landlord, gives the strata corporation a written notice setting out the particulars of the assignment, including the powers and duties that have been assigned.[4] This feature is available to owners of residential and non-residential strata lots.

Mortgagee

In limited circumstances, a lender with a mortgage (called a "mortgagee") over a strata lot may vote in place of the owner. The mortgage document must give the lender the right to vote. The lender must also give the strata corporation at least three days' written notice of his or her intention to vote. The lender can only vote in respect of insurance, maintenance, finance or other matters affecting the security of the mortgage.[5]

---

[1] *Strata Property Act*, s. 148(2), (3).
[2] *Ibid.*, ss. 142(3) and 148.
[3] *Ibid.*, s. 147(1).
[4] *Ibid.*, s. 147(2).
[5] *Ibid.*, s. 54(c). For information about giving notice to a strata corporation, see Chapter 12, *Meetings*.

Voter Lacks Legal Capacity

If an eligible voter who is an owner, a tenant or mortgagee lacks legal capacity for a reason other than being under 16 years old, his or her right to vote may only be exercised by someone who is legally authorized to act for that person with respect to the strata lot.[1] In simple terms, a person has legal capacity if he or she is 19 years or older, sane and sober.[2] Legal authorization to act on behalf of someone without legal capacity usually takes the form of a court order, or a power of attorney or, more recently, a representation agreement.[3]

Guardian

If a person who is entitled to vote is under 16 years old, he or she may only exercise voting rights through a parent or guardian.[4]

Owners in Arrears

A strata corporation may pass a bylaw prohibiting an eligible voter from exercising his or her right to vote in respect of a strata lot, except in matters requiring a unanimous vote, if the strata corporation is entitled to register a lien against that strata lot for arrears. In that case, the person's vote must not be counted for the purposes of determining a quorum.[5]

---

[1] *Strata Property Act*, s. 55(2).

[2] The specific degree of mental capacity required to make a legally effective decision depends on the particular transaction. See, for example, C.S. Theriault & J. Breeze, "*Representation Agreement Act*: Capacity Issues" (Adult Guardianship – New Legislation, Continuing Legal Education Society of BC, Vancouver, February 11, 2000) at p. 5.1.

[3] *Representation Agreement Act*, R.S.B.C. 1996, c. 405, as amended.

[4] *Strata Property Act*, s. 55(1).

[5] *Ibid.*, s. 53(2), (3).

This means that a bylaw, for example, may prohibit an owner from voting, except in matters requiring a unanimous vote, if the owner is in arrears for any of the following matters, being those for which the strata corporation is entitled to file a lien:[1]

- strata fees;

- special levies;

- a reimbursement for the cost of work carried out by the strata corporation because the owner failed to carry out a work order; or

- the strata lot's share of a judgment against the strata corporation.

Note that a bylaw cannot prohibit an owner from voting on the grounds that he or she owes money to the strata corporation for a fine, or for money representing the strata corporation's costs to remedy a contravention of the bylaws or rules, because the *Strata Property Act* prohibits filing a lien for either of these matters.[2] In addition, a strata corporation must first comply with various requirements before it is entitled to file a lien under the Act. The strata corporation cannot enforce a bylaw that prohibits voting because of arrears until the corporation has complied with all of the prerequisites for filing a lien. For information about the requirements for filing a lien, see Chapter 15, *Finance*.

---

[1] *Strata Property Act*, s. 116(1).
[2] *Ibid.*, s. 116(3).

Proxies

An eligible voter may vote in person or by proxy.[1] Subject to the regulations, any person can be a proxy.[2] A proxy must be in writing, signed by the person giving it,[3] and may be revoked at any time.[4]

A proxy stands in the place of the person appointing the proxy and, with some exceptions, can do anything that person may do, including vote, propose and second motions and participate in the discussion, unless otherwise limited in the appointment document.[5]

All proxies are not equal. A proxy may be general, or for a specific meeting, or for a specific resolution.[6]

The regulations contain a suggested form of Proxy Appointment (Form A). This is an optional form that a strata corporation may adopt for proxies.

Property Managers and Strata Employees

The *Strata Property Act* restricts persons who provide strata management services to a strata corporation, or the corporation's employees, from serving as proxies, except as permitted by the regulations.[7] The regulations, however, do not contain any provision that permits either a strata manager or an employee to hold a proxy. Until the province changes the regulations, neither property managers serving a strata corporation nor the corporation's employees may serve as proxies at a general meeting of the corporation.

---

[1] *Strata Property Act*, s. 56(1).
[2] *Ibid.*, s. 56(3).
[3] *Ibid.*, s. 56(2).
[4] *Ibid.*, s. 56(2).
[5] *Ibid.*, s. 56(2), (4).
[6] *Ibid.*, s. 56(2).
[7] *Ibid.*, s. 56(3).

Passing Resolutions

Most decisions at a general meeting require a majority vote, a 3/4 vote, or a unanimous vote, depending on the circumstances. In rare instances, a strata corporation's bylaws may permit a different voting threshold for non-residential strata lots in certain situations. Appendix C contains tables that list the various matters for which the *Strata Property Act*, the regulations, and in some cases the Standard Bylaws, require particular voting thresholds. The appendices list items by subject matter and type of vote respectively.

Majority Vote

Matters at general meetings are decided by majority vote unless the *Strata Property Act*, the regulations, or the bylaws require, or permit, a different voting threshold.[1] In other words, the majority vote is the default vote required in all situations, except where otherwise required by the Act, the regulations, or the bylaws.

The Act defines the term majority vote as a vote in favour of a resolution by *more than one-half* of the votes cast by eligible voters who are present in person or by proxy at the time the vote is taken and who have not abstained from voting.[2] The inclusion of the phrase "at the time the vote is taken" is critical. Suppose, for example, that at 7 pm when the general meeting starts there are 80 eligible voters present, in person or by proxy. By the time the vote is taken at 10 pm, half of the eligible votes have left the meeting. How many votes are necessary to pass a majority vote? Half plus one of the 80 votes present when the meeting began, or half plus one of the 40 votes present at the time the vote is taken? In this example, the *Strata Property Act* dictates that 21 votes

---

[1]*Strata Property Act*, s. 50(1).
[2]*Ibid.*, s. 1(1) (definition of "majority vote").

are needed, being a majority of the 40 votes present at the time the vote is taken.

In the definition of majority vote, the phrase "and who have not abstained" is also important. When counting votes, this means where one or more eligible voters abstain from a vote, the number of abstentions must be subtracted from the number of otherwise eligible votes present, either in person or by proxy. For instance, suppose the strata corporation consists entirely of residential units. Each strata lot has one vote. The table below calculates the number of votes necessary to pass a resolution by majority vote if 80 eligible votes are present, with and without abstentions:

Calculating a Majority Vote, With and Without Abstentions

Eligible Votes Present in Person or by Proxy for the Vote	Abstentions	Net Eligible Votes	Votes Necessary for Majority Vote
80	0	80	41
80	10	70	36

Note how the presence of 10 abstentions reduces the threshold for majority approval from 41 to 36 votes.

3/4 Vote

Similarly, the Act defines the term 3/4 vote as one in favour of a resolution by *at least 3/4 of the votes* cast by eligible voters who are present in person or by proxy at the time the vote is taken and who have not abstained from voting.[1] Once again, the inclusion of the phrase "at

---

[1]*Strata Property Act*, s. 1(1) (definition of "3/4 vote").

the time the vote is taken" is important. The time at which to tabulate the votes is the time the vote is taken. Similarly, the phrase "and who have not abstained from voting" is also significant. This means that the number of abstentions must be subtracted from the number of eligible votes present, whether in person or by proxy. For example, suppose again that a strata corporation consists entirely of residential units. Each strata lot has one vote. The table below calculates the number of votes necessary to pass a resolution by a 3/4 vote if 80 eligible votes are present, with and without abstentions:

Calculating a 3/4 Vote,
With and Without Abstentions

Eligible Votes Present in Person or by Proxy for the Vote	Abstentions	Net Eligible Votes	Votes Necessary for 3/4 Vote
80	0	80	60
80	10	70	53

In this example, note again how the presence of 10 abstentions reduces the threshold for passage of a 3/4 vote from 60 to 53 votes.

Reconsideration of a Resolution

The *Strata Property Act* provides that, in some circumstances, the strata corporation must wait one week before implementing a resolution requiring a 3/4 vote.

The strata corporation must wait one week if the persons who passed the resolution at a general meeting hold less than 50 per cent of the strata corporation's votes.[1]

---

[1] *Strata Property Act*, s. 51.

For instance, suppose a residential strata complex contains one hundred units. Although each strata lot has one vote, in this example only 64 eligible votes are present in person or by proxy. Forty-nine votes are cast in favour of the resolution, which passes. The following table calculates whether the strata corporation must wait one week before putting the resolution into effect. In this case, the strata corporation must wait one week because persons holding less than 50 per cent of the strata corporation's votes passed the resolution requiring a 3/4 vote.

**Calculating Votes Necessary
to Force Reconsideration of a 3/4 Resolution**

All of the Strata Corporation's Votes	50% of the Strata Corporation's Votes	Votes Present in Person or by Proxy	Votes in Favour of Resolution	Did the 3/4 Vote Pass? 49/64 = 77%	Did persons voting in favour hold less than 50% of strata corporation's votes? 49 votes< 50 votes
100	50	64	49	Yes	Yes–Wait One Week

During the one-week waiting period, persons holding at least 25 per cent of the strata corporation's votes may, by written demand, require the strata corporation to hold a special meeting to reconsider the resolution. The demand must be signed by each person making it.[1]

The strata corporation may only refrain from waiting and act immediately where it is reasonably necessary to ensure safety or prevent significant loss or damage.[2]

---

[1]*Strata Property Act*, s. 51(3), (4).
[2]*Ibid.*, s. 51(2), (5).

Unanimous Vote

The *Strata Property Act* defines the term *"unanimous vote"* as a vote in favour of a resolution by *all the votes of all the eligible voters.*[1] This definition effectively requires every eligible vote, not just those who are present at the time of the vote.

The definition of unanimous vote does not appear to permit abstentions. In addition, the absence of wording similar to that used in the definitions of majority vote and 3/4 vote, respectively, suggests abstentions are not subtracted from the number of eligible voters in unanimous votes. Otherwise, the legislature would have used the same wording as in the other definitions. If abstentions are not subtracted, then each strata lot, in effect, has a veto. This means that if even one eligible voter abstains from voting, the result cannot be unanimous.

Judicial Passage of Failed Resolutions

If a strata corporation meets certain criteria, the Act provides that where a resolution requiring a unanimous vote fails for lack of a few votes, the strata corporation can, with the support of a 3/4 vote, apply to the Supreme Court for an order judicially passing the failed resolution. This option is only available if the corporation meets the following conditions.[2]

First, the strata corporation must have 10 or more strata lots.[3]

Second, the unanimous resolution must be supported by all of the strata corporation's votes except:

---

[1]*Strata Property Act*, s. 1(1) (definition of "unanimous vote").
[2]*Ibid.*, s. 52. For information about legal proceedings, see Part VI, *Court Actions and Arbitration*.
[3]*Ibid.*, s. 52(1).

- the vote in respect of one strata lot, in a strata corporation with at least 10 strata lots, or

- the votes of more than one strata lot if those votes, when taken together, represent less than five per cent of the strata corporation's votes.[1]

For example, suppose again that a residential strata complex contains 100 units. Suppose also that the members wish to vote on a unanimous resolution. If the unanimous vote fails, the following table shows how many positive votes are necessary to permit the strata corporation to apply for judicial passage of the motion.

Calculating Votes Needed
to Seek Judicial Passage of a Nearly Unanimous Vote

All of the Strata Corporation's Votes	Votes Necessary to Pass a Unanimous Resolution at a General Meeting	Votes That Represent Less Than 5% of the Strata Corporation's Votes (Using Whole Numbers) 5% of 100 votes = 5 Next Lowest Whole Number = 4	What is the Minimum Number of Positive Votes Necessary, by Persons Present in Person or by Proxy, Who Support the Resolution, so That if it Fails, They can Apply for Judicial Passage? 100 - 4 = 96
100	100	4	96

In this example, the strata corporation needs at least 96 votes in favour of the failed unanimous motion to permit the strata corporation to apply for judicial passage. So, if there are fewer than 96 votes, in person or by proxy, the unanimous vote will fail and the strata corporation will *not* be able to ask the court to approve the motion instead.

---

[1]*Strata Property Act*, s. 52(2).

On the other hand, suppose there are 98 votes present in person or by proxy, out of which 96 are in favour, and two are against the motion.

The following table calculates whether the strata corporation may apply to the court to pass the failed unanimous resolution.

Example Showing When a Strata Corporation Could Seek Judicial Passage of a Nearly Unanimous Vote

Votes Necessary to Pass a Unanimous Resolution at a General Meeting	Maximum Votes That Represent Less Than 5% of the Strata Corporation's Votes (Using Whole Numbers)	Votes Present or by Proxy	Votes in Favour of Resolution	Unanimous Vote Passed?	Did the Vote Fail by Less Than 5% of the Strata Corporation's Votes? 100 -96 = 4 4 votes < 5% of the Strata Corporation's Votes
100	4	98	96	No	Yes

In this case, the strata corporation could, with the support of the appropriate resolution, proceed to the Supreme Court. Recognizing that litigation is expensive, the *Strata Property Act* requires the eligible voters to pass a 3/4 vote authorizing the strata corporation to apply to court for approval of the matter which required a unanimous vote.

When a strata corporation seeks judicial approval of a failed unanimous resolution, the court may order that the resolution proceed as if the dissenting voter or voters had no vote, if the court is satisfied that passage of the resolution is in the best interest of the strata corporation and would not unfairly prejudice the dissenting voters.[1] In making such an order, the court may include any other order it considers just, including an order that the strata corporation offer to purchase, at fair market value, the strata lot owned by a dissenting voter, or that the strata corporation compensate that person by some other means.[2]

Non-Residential Strata Lots

In some cases, the *Strata Property Act* permits a strata corporation to amend its bylaws to set a voting threshold at a level other than a majority, 3/4 or unanimous vote. For instance, the Act contemplates that, in a strata plan containing non-residential strata lots, the corporation may have a bylaw that sets a different voting threshold among the non-residential lots for approving amendments to the bylaws.[3]

---

[1] *Strata Property Act*, s. 52(3).
[2] *Ibid.*, s. 52(3), (4).
[3] *Ibid.*, s. 128(2).

Chapter 15

FINANCES

The Funds

Every strata corporation must have two funds: an operating fund and a contingency reserve fund (CRF).[1] The strata corporation must account for each fund separately.[2] All owners must contribute to the funds through their strata fees.[3]

The Operating Fund

The corporation must establish an operating fund to pay for common expenses that usually occur one or more times each year.[4] Common expenses are those relating to the common property and common assets of the strata corporation, or in some cases, to limited common property (LCP) or which are otherwise required to meet the corporation's obligations.[5]

Contingency Reserve Fund (CRF)

The strata corporation must also establish a CRF to pay for common expenses that usually occur less often than once per year or not at all.[6] The CRF is, in effect, a fund for the strata corporation's unusual expenses.[7]

---

[1]*Strata Property Act*, s. 92.
[2]*Ibid.*, s. 95(1).
[3]*Ibid.*, s. 92.
[4]*Ibid.*, ss. 91 and 92(a).
[5]*Ibid.*, s. 1(1) (definition of "common expenses") and the *Schedule of Standard Bylaws*, ss. 2 and 8.
[6]*Strata Property Act*, ss. 1(1) (definition of "contingency reserve fund") and 92(b).
[7]*Ibid.*, ss. 12(5) and 92.

Investing

The strata corporation must invest the money in the CRF in investments permitted by the regulations or within insured accounts at savings institutions in the province.[1] Appendix E sets out the investments permitted by the regulations.

Initially, the *Strata Property Act* allowed a strata corporation to invest CRF funds in an investment permitted under section 15 of the *Trustee Act* as an alternative to investing in an insured account at a savings institution.[2] Effective February 28, 2003, the province amended the *Strata Property Act* by removing the reference to the *Trustee Act* and instead citing the regulations.[3] At the same time the province added a new section 6.11 to the *Strata Property Regulation*, which contains, as at the date of publication, a list of permitted investments that is virtually identical to those previously found in section 15 of the *Trustee Act*.[4]

The transition provisions in the regulations recognize that before July 1, 2000, some strata corporations may have invested CRFs in investments no longer permitted by the *Strata Property Act*. If so, the regulations permit the strata corporation to retain its investment. When the strata corporation liquidates some or all of its investment, however, the corporation may only reinvest the funds in an investment permitted by the *Strata Property Act*.[5]

Interest

The *Strata Property Act* requires all interest or other income earned on money in the CRF to stay in that fund.[6]

---

[1] *Strata Property Act*, s. 95(2).
[2] *Trustee Act*, R.S.B.C. 1996, c. 464, s. 15.
[3] *Trustee Investment Statutes Amendment Act, 2002*, S.B.C. 2002, c. 33, s. 21; in force February 28, 2003 per B.C. Reg. 34/2003.
[4] B.C. Reg. 33/2003.
[5] *Strata Property Regulation*, s. 17.5 and *Strata Property Act*, s. 95(2).
[6] *Strata Property Act*, s. 95(3).

In the past, many strata corporations treated the interest accruing from their CRF investments as part of the corporations' annual revenue. For instance, at the start of a new fiscal year, a strata corporation would transfer all of its interest income earned in the previous fiscal year from its CRF investments to the operating fund. By paying its CRF interest income into the operating fund, the strata corporation could keep strata fees lower. The *Strata Property Act* prohibits this practice.

Shortfalls in the Operating Fund

In the past, many strata corporations used their CRFs to cover short-term cash flow shortages. For example, while monthly revenue from maintenance fees is the same through the year, some months are more expensive than others. This usually happens in months when the corporation has large expenses that occur once per year, like insurance premiums. In those months, a corporation would lend itself money from the CRF to cover the shortfall. In the CRF, the corporation recorded the sum due in repayment as a receivable. Typically, any sums borrowed were repaid to the CRF by the end of the fiscal year.

The *Strata Property Act* only allows a strata corporation to lend money from the CRF to its operating fund to the extent permitted by the regulations.[1] The regulations allow a strata corporation to lend money from its CRF to the operating fund to cover temporary shortages in the operating fund caused by the irregular billing of expenses set out in the budget, provided the loan is paid back by the end of that fiscal year of the strata corporation.[2]

---

[1] *Strata Property Act*, s. 95(4).
[2] *Strata Property Regulation*, s. 6.3.

Financial Statements

The regulations state that a strata corporation's financial statements must contain:[1]

- the opening and current balances in the operating fund;

- the opening and current balances in the CRF;

- details of the corporation's income from all sources, except special levies;

- details of expenditures out of the operating fund, including details of any unapproved expenditures;

- details of expenditures out of the CRF, including details of any unapproved expenditures; and

- income and expenditures, if any, by special levy.

A financial statement must be prepared and distributed with the notice of the annual general meeting (AGM).[2] A strata corporation may, however, pass a bylaw to permit the corporation to provide a financial summary with the notice, instead of the actual financial statements.[3] If a strata corporation with the necessary bylaw has issued a financial summary with the notice, any person entitled to receive notice of the AGM may, before the meeting, request a copy of the financial statements. In that case, the strata corporation must immediately give that person a copy of the actual financial statements.

Since the AGM occurs very near to the fiscal year-end, the Act recognizes that it is not possible to have the financial statements for the full year prepared and distributed in advance. The financial statements to be distributed with the notice of the AGM must be prepared

---

[1] *Strata Property Regulation*, s. 6.7.
[2] *Strata Property Act*, s. 103.
[3] *Strata Property Regulation*, s. 6.7 (3)-(5).

for the fiscal year as of a day that is within the two-month period before the date of the AGM.[1]

The strata corporation must prepare a financial statement updated to the end of the fiscal year within eight weeks after the end of the fiscal year.

The Budget

The regulations state that the following information must be contained in the budget:[2]

- the opening balances in the operating fund and the CRF;

- the estimated income from all sources other than strata fees, itemized by source;

- the estimated expenditures out of the operating fund, itemized by category of expenditure;

- the total of all contributions to the operating fund;

- the total of all contributions to the CRF;

- each strata lot's monthly contribution to the operating fund;

- each strata lot's monthly contribution to the CRF;

- the estimated balance in the operating fund at the end of the fiscal year;

- the estimated balance in the CRF at the end of the fiscal year; and

- any contributions allocated to a portion of strata lot owners as a result of LCP repair and maintenance costs, costs allocated by type, or arising as a result of the repair and maintenance of portions of strata lots.[3]

---

[1]*Strata Property Regulation*, s. 6.7.
[2]*Ibid.*, s. 6.6.
[3]For information about the circumstances in which certain expenses may be allocated only to some, rather than all, of the owners, see Part V, *Repairs*.

At each AGM, the owners must approve the budget for the next fiscal year. The proposed budget must be accompanied by the financial statements and distributed with the notice of the AGM.[1]

When preparing the budget, note that the *Strata Property Act* requires a 3/4 vote before a strata corporation may acquire or dispose of personal property with a value over $1,000, unless the strata corporation has a bylaw permitting the acquisition or disposition of personal property beyond the $1,000 limit in the Act.[2] As a result, if the strata corporation wishes to acquire or dispose of personal property over the limit established by the Act or the corporation's bylaws, that matter cannot simply be approved as part of a the budget process, which requires only a majority vote. Instead, a 3/4 vote must be taken for that matter in the budget.[3]

During the AGM, the owners may amend the proposed budget by majority vote before the budget itself is put to a vote.[4] A majority vote is necessary to approve the budget.[5] Within two weeks of passing the budget, the strata corporation must inform owners of any changes to their strata fees resulting from the new budget.[6]

At the end of the fiscal year, if there is a deficit, the *Strata Property Act* requires the strata corporation to eliminate the deficit during the next fiscal year.[7]

If there is a surplus of operating funds at the end of the fiscal year, the Act requires the surplus to be dealt with in one of the following ways, unless the owners determine otherwise by a 3/4 vote at a general meeting. The surplus may be:

---

[1] *Strata Property Act*, s. 103(2).
[2] *Ibid.*, s. 82.
[3] *Ibid.*, s. 82.
[4] *Ibid.*, s. 103(4).
[5] *Ibid.*, s. 103(1).
[6] *Ibid.*, s. 106.
[7] *Ibid.*, s. 105(2).

- transferred into the CRF;

- carried forward as part of the operating fund, as a surplus; or

- used to reduce the total contribution to the next fiscal year's operating fund.[1]

If the owners fail to approve a budget at an AGM, the strata corporation must, within 30 days, prepare a new budget and place it before a special general meeting for approval by a majority vote.[2] The owners can allow the strata corporation more than 30 days to prepare a new budget, with a 3/4 vote.[3]

If a fiscal year to which a budget relates ends before a new budget is approved, the owners must continue to pay the same monthly strata fees to the strata corporation that they were required to pay under the previous budget.[4] Similarly, and pending approval of a new budget, the strata corporation may only spend operating funds in a manner consistent with the previous budget.[5]

Budget Contributions

Every owner must contribute to the strata corporation's operating and contingency reserve funds, respectively.[6] The Act refers to this contribution as "strata fees,"[7] although many people informally refer to their contribution as "maintenance fees." The annual budget establishes the total contribution to both funds required for the fiscal year.

---

[1] *Strata Property Act*, s. 105(1).
[2] *Ibid.*, s. 104(1).
[3] *Ibid.*, s. 104(1).
[4] *Ibid.*, s. 104(2).
[5] *Ibid.*, s. 104(3).
[6] *Ibid.*, s. 99.
[7] *Ibid.*, s. 99(1).

Who Contributes: Some or All?

Under the *Strata Property Act*, the general rule is that all of the owners must contribute to the operating fund and the CRF, as the case may be, according to the schedule of unit entitlement in the strata plan.[1] A schedule of unit entitlement determines the share payable for each strata lot in proportion to the total contribution required. Section 99 of the Act describes the general rule with this formula for calculating a strata lot's contribution:[2]

$$\frac{unit\ entitlement\ of\ strata\ lot}{total\ unit\ entitlement\ of\ all\ strata\ lots} \quad \text{x} \quad total\ contribution$$

Despite the general rule, the Act and regulations create a few exceptions that require a strata corporation to allocate certain expenses to only some, rather than all of the owners. Since these exceptions often occur in connection with repairs, readers will find an explanation of these provisions in Chapter 26, *Paying for Repairs*.

How to Use a Schedule of Unit Entitlement

The following example illustrates how to use a schedule of unit entitlement to calculate strata fees for a particular strata lot. Bear in mind that, in some cases, the *Strata Property Act*, the regulations or the bylaws might require the strata corporation to allocate specific expenses out of the operating fund to a particular strata lot.[3] The following example is a general one that does not take into account such special considerations.

---

[1] *Strata Property Act*, ss. 99 and 108(2). For information about the operating fund, the CRF, a special levy, or using a schedule of unit entitlement, see Chapter 15, *Finances*.
[2] *Ibid.*, ss. 99 and 108(2).
[3] For information about the circumstances in which certain expenses may be allocated only to some, rather than all, of the owners, see Part V, *Repairs*.

Suppose the annual budget requires a total contribution of $10,000, taking into account the requirements of the operating fund and a contribution to the CRF. Suppose also that the strata plan consists of six strata lots whose unit entitlements are set out below:

Strata Lot Number	Schedule of Unit Entitlement
1	10
2	10
3	15
4	15
5	25
6	25
6 strata lots	100

The contribution of Strata Lot 2, for example, is calculated as follows:

$$\frac{\text{unit entitlement of Strata Lot 2}}{\text{total unit entitlement of all strata lots}} \times \text{total contribution} = \text{strata lot's total contribution for the fiscal year.}$$

$$\frac{10}{100} \times \$10,000 = \$1,000 = \text{The total contribution due from Strata Lot 2 for the fiscal year.}$$

Strata Lot 2's monthly contribution for strata fees is as follows:

$$\frac{\text{Strata Lot 2's total annual contribution}}{12 \text{ months}} = \text{Strata Lot 2's monthly payment}$$

$$\frac{\$1,000}{12} = \$83.33 \text{ per month} = \text{Strata Lot 2's monthly payment}$$

Operating Fund

Each strata lot owner's monthly contribution to the operating fund must be set out in the budget.[1] Generally, an owner will pay a proportionate share of the common expenses based on the unit entitlement for his or her unit.[2]

Under certain circumstances, however, only *some* owners may be required to contribute to a particular operating expense.[3] The regulations provide that if a contribution to the operating fund relates to and benefits only limited common property (LCP), the contribution is shared only by owners of the strata lots entitled to use the LCP.[4] Additionally, if a contribution to the operating fund relates to and benefits only one type of strata lot, where the bylaws identify types of strata lots, that contribution is only shared by the owners of strata lots of that type.[5]

If a strata corporation has, by bylaw, taken responsibility for the maintenance of specified portions of some but not all of the strata lots, a contribution to the operating fund in respect of the repair or maintenance of those portions is shared only by the owners of the strata lots to which the contribution relates.[6]

Contingency Reserve Fund (CRF)

Every year, a strata corporation must evaluate its contingency reserve fund. If the amount in the CRF has fallen below a certain level, the corporation must contribute funds to the CRF to restore it. Alternatively, if the amount in the CRF exceeds certain minimum requirements, the corporation has the option to contribute more money to the CRF. Once the amount in the CRF exceeds a certain maximum level,

---

[1]*Strata Property Regulation*, s. 6.6.

[2]*Strata Property Act*, s. 99.

[3]For information about the circumstances in which certain expenses may be allocated only to some, rather than all, of the owners, see Part V, *Repairs*.

[4]*Strata Property Regulation*, s. 6.4(1).

[5]*Ibid.*, s. 6.4(2).

[6]*Ibid.*, s. 6.5.

however, the corporation is prohibited from contributing any more money to the CRF unless the eligible voters agree otherwise by a 3/4 vote.

The *Strata Property Act* requires each strata corporation to determine its annual contribution to the CRF according to the regulations.[1] The regulations provide that at the end of any fiscal year after the first AGM:[2]

- If the amount of money in the CRF is less than 25 per cent of the total annual budgeted contribution to the operating fund for the fiscal year that has just ended, the corporation's annual contribution to the CRF must be at least 10 per cent of the total contribution to the operating fund for the current year. The former *Condominium Act* required a minimum annual CRF contribution equal to five per cent of the total annual budget.[3]

- If the amount of money in the CRF is at least 25 per cent, but less than 100 per cent, of the total annual budgeted contribution to the operating fund for the fiscal year that has just ended, the corporation's annual contribution to the CRF may be of any amount.

- If the amount of money in the CRF is equal to or greater than 100 per cent of the total annual budgeted contribution to the operating fund for the fiscal year that has just ended, the eligible voters must approve any additional contribution by a 3/4 vote.

---

[1] *Strata Property Act*, s. 93.
[2] *Strata Property Regulation*, s. 6.1.
[3] *Condominium Act*, ss. 35 and 117(j).

How to Calculate a CRF Contribution

When a strata corporation prepares the CRF portion of its budget each year, the corporation needs two pieces of information to decide whether, in the new fiscal year, a CRF contribution is mandatory, optional or prohibited (unless the owners otherwise agree by a 3/4 vote to override the prohibition). Both pieces of information come from the fiscal year that has just ended, or which is about to end.

1. The strata corporation needs to know the amount of money in the CRF as at the last day of the fiscal year that just ended, or the anticipated amount in the case of a fiscal year that is about to end.

2. The strata corporation must determine the total annual budgeted contribution to the operating fund for the fiscal year that has just concluded, or which is about to conclude. In other words, the strata corporation needs to know how much it budgeted for operating expenses in the last fiscal year.

Once the strata corporation has these two pieces of information, it must compare them. If, for example, the amount in the CRF at the end of the last fiscal year was less than 25 per cent of the total amount budgeted for operating expenses in the last fiscal year's budget, the strata corporation *must* make a contribution in the new fiscal year. In addition, the mandatory contribution must never be less than an amount equal to 10 per cent of the budgeted operating expenses in the new fiscal year.

The following table illustrates how, using the two pieces of information noted above, a strata corporation may determine its CRF contribution.

Calculating if a Contribution to the CRF is Required

Total Annual Budgeted Contribution to the Operating Fund in the Last Fiscal Year	Amount in the CRF at the End of the Last Fiscal Year	Percentage of Amount in the CRF When Compared to the Operating Budget in the Last Fiscal Year	Is a Contribution to the CRF Mandatory in the New Fiscal Year?
$100,000	$20,000	20%	Yes, we must contribute an amount equal to *at least 10%* of our total contribution to the operating fund in the new fiscal year.
$100,000	$30,000	30%	No. However, we may contribute to the CRF if we want to, in any amount.
$100,000	$110,000	110%	No. We first need the approval of the members by a 3/4 vote before we can make any additional contribution to the CRF.

How a Developer Calculates a CRF Contribution for the First AGM

When a developer prepares the CRF portion of a first annual budget for the first AGM, the same requirements apply, with a few necessary modifications. To calculate the relevant percentages described above, the developer must compare the amount of money in the CRF at the time of the first AGM against the estimated operating expenses for the 12-month period set out in the developer's interim budget.[1]

---

[1] *Strata Property Regulation*, s. 3.4

No CRF Return to Owners Who Sell

Sometimes, owners who sell their strata lots ask the strata corporation to return some or all of the owner's contributions to the CRF. The *Strata Property Act* states that the seller is not entitled to a return of contributions to the CRF upon a sale of the strata lot.[1]

Depreciation Reports

A depreciation report estimates the life expectancy of major items and the ultimate cost of their repair or replacement. When preparing a budget, a strata corporation may create a depreciation report to determine the appropriate amount to contribute to the CRF for certain unusual expenses.[2]

For instance, a strata council's treasurer might approach several roofing contractors to determine how long the roof will last, the cost of replacing the roof today, and the cost of replacing the roof at the end of its life.

Suppose, in this example, the roof will need to be replaced in 15 years. Replacement cost, in current dollars, is estimated at $100,000; in 15 years, $150,000. The treasurer's depreciation report might suggest that the corporation should contribute $10,000 to the CRF every year for the next 15 years, for roof replacement.

The regulations contain guidelines for the preparation of a depreciation report.[3] The legislative provisions that permit a depreciation report do not authorize the creation of a distinct fund. Rather, a depreciation report is merely a budgeting tool.[4]

---

[1] *Strata Property Act*, s. 101.
[2] *Ibid.*, s. 94.
[3] *Strata Property Regulation*, s. 6.2.
[4] *McGowan v. Strata Plan NW1018*, [2002] B.C.J. No. 959 at para. 75, 2002 B.C.S.C. 673 at para. 75 (S.C.).

Preparing a depreciation report does not relieve a strata corporation of any of its CRF obligations under the *Strata Property Act*.[1]

More About a Schedule of Unit Entitlement

Every strata plan must contain a schedule of unit entitlement. In a strata plan deposited at a Land Title Office before July 1, 2000, the schedule of unit entitlement is typically found among the last sheets (or back pages) of the plan itself. In the case of a strata plan deposited on or after July 1, 2000, under the *Strata Property Act*, the schedule of unit entitlement is found with the strata plan in a separate document called the Schedule of Unit Entitlement (Form V).

The schedule of unit entitlement is a table that assigns to each strata lot a certain number of units of entitlement. As described above, the schedule of unit entitlement determines each strata lot's share of certain expenses and liabilities. In particular, the schedule is used to calculate each strata lot's contribution to common expenses. In most cases, each strata lot must contribute to the operating fund, the contingency reserve fund, or a special levy in the proportion that the unit entitlement of that strata lot bears to the total unit entitlement of all of the strata lots. Unit entitlement also determines an owner's share, as a tenant in common, in the common property and common assets.[2] In addition, unit entitlement determines each owner's share of any judgment against the strata corporation.[3]

The *Strata Property Act* dictates how a developer must calculate unit entitlement when depositing a strata plan under the Act.

---

[1]*Strata Property Regulation*, s. 6.2(4).
[2]*Strata Property Act*, s. 66.
[3]*Ibid.*, s. 166.

1. If a strata lot is residential, the unit entitlement must be:

    a) a whole number based on the habitable area in square metres. In this case, the term *habitable area* means, "the area of a residential strata lot which can be lived in, but does not include patios, balconies, garages, parking stalls or storage areas other than closet space."[1]

    b) a whole number that is the same for all of the residential strata lots, or

    c) a number that is approved by the Superintendent on a basis that fairly allocates a portion of the common expenses to the owner of the strata lot.

2. If a strata lot is non-residential, the unit entitlement must be:

    a) a whole number based on the area in square metres,

    b) a whole number that is the same for all of the non-residential strata lots, or

    c) a number that is approved by the Superintendent on a basis that fairly allocates a portion of the common expenses to the owner of the strata lot.

3. If a strata lot is a bare land strata lot, the unit entitlement must be:

    a) a whole number that is the same for all of the strata lots, or

    b) a number that is approved by the Superintendent on a basis that fairly allocates a portion of the common expenses to the owner of the strata lot.

---

[1] *Strata Property Regulation*, B.C. Reg. 43/2000, s. 14.2.

4. In a development that contains both residential and non-residential strata lots, the Superintendent must approve the schedule of unit entitlement to ensure that it fairly distributes the common expenses between the owners of the residential and non-residential strata lots respectively.

Can Unit Entitlement Be Changed?

Depending on the prevailing statute, a schedule of unit entitlement may be altered.

Condominium Act

The former *Condominium Act* permitted a strata corporation to change its schedule of unit entitlement by passing a resolution to amend the schedule with a 75% vote and then submitting a revised schedule of unit entitlement, together with the resolution, to the Superintendent of Real Estate for acceptance. Following approval by the Superintendent, the Act required the strata corporation to deposit the revised schedule of unit entitlement in the Land Title Office.[1]

The *Condominium Act* was repealed when the *Strata Property Act* came into force and these procedures are no longer available.

Strata Property Act

By contrast, the *Strata Property Act* directly provides at least three ways to change unit entitlement.

First, in the case only of a residential strata lot, the eligible voters may pass a unanimous resolution under section 261 of the *Strata Property Act* to alter the unit entitlement of a strata lot to reflect a change in its habitable area. After passing the unanimous resolution, the strata corporation must apply to the Registrar of Land

---

[1]*Condominium Act*, s. 113 and *Strata Plan NW 195 v. British Columbia (Registrar of Land Titles)*, [1987] B.C.J. No. 334 (S.C.).

Titles to amend the schedule of unit entitlement by providing a new schedule together with a Certificate of Strata Corporation (Form E). The new schedule of unit entitlement must comply with certain requirements.[1]

Second, in the case only of a residential strata lot, where the unit entitlement of a strata lot is based on habitable area, an owner may apply to the Supreme Court of British Columbia under section 246 of the *Strata Property Act* to amend the schedule of unit entitlement if the unit entitlement does not match the habitable area of the strata lot.[2] This remedy is only available if:[3]

(a) **the actual habitable area or square footage of a strata lot is at least 10% greater than, or 10% less than, the habitable area or square footage used to determine the unit entitlement of the strata lot; or**

(b) **the actual habitable area or square footage of a strata lot is at least 20 square metres greater than, or 20 square metres less than, the habitable area or square footage used to determine the unit entitlement of the strata lot.**

In *Kranz v. The Owners, Strata Plan VR 29,*[4] our Court of Appeal rejected an owner's request under section 246 of the Act to reduce his unit entitlement because he did not meet the threshold test. The owner failed to establish a difference greater than 10 per cent between the actual habitable area of his strata lot and the square footage figure used to calculate the unit entitlement of his strata lot. The owner attempted to characterize a large portion of his strata lot as a storage area. The definition of

---

[1]*Strata Property Act*, s. 261.
[2]*Strata Property Act*, s. 246(7) and *Strata Property Regulation*, s. 14.13.
[3]*Strata Property Regulation*, s. 14.2.
[4]*Kranz v. The Owners, Strata Plan VR 29,* [2004] B.C.J. No. 358, 2004 B.C.C.A. 108 (C.A.) aff'g (2003), 8 R.P.R. (4th) 268, [2003] B.C.J. No. 248, 2003 B.C.S.C. 183 (S.C.).

habitable area excludes storage areas, other than closet space.[1] If the court would allow the owner to deduct the area of his alleged storage space from his habitable area, the owner could meet the mathematical threshold required by the regulations. The appellate court adopted the same conclusion as the court below,[2]

> **Given that conclusion, unless the so-called "storage" area is also deducted from the total square footage of strata lot A, Mr. Kranz does not meet the threshold test of establishing that the square footage used to determine the unit entitlement of lot A is 10% greater than the square footage of the habitable area of strata lot A.**
>
> **At this point, it is important to consider the definition of "habitable area" utilized for the purposes of s. 246 of the SPA. Notably, Regulation 14.2 refers not to the portion of a residential strata lot which is lived in but rather that which "can be lived in."**
>
> **To put it bluntly, I do not accept Mr. Kranz's characterization of a portion of strata lot A as being uninhabitable because it is a "storage" area. It is not storage area in the sense that certain condominiums have designated stalls or cubicles in storage rooms or basement areas of their buildings. No evidence was put before me to suggest that the so-called storage area could only be used for that purpose. Indeed, it was the evidence of Mr. Kapri Tennant, one of the Owners, that he knew of no reason why all of strata lot A was not a habitable area. In saying that, I expect, Mr. Tennant overlooked the fact that a portion of strata lot A is a garage area with five parking spaces. However, it is not reasonable to expect the Owners to deduct a large area of square footage from strata lot A for the purpose of determining its habitable area just because Mr. Kranz chooses not to develop a portion of strata lot A. If Mr. Kranz were allowed to dictate the habitable area of his own strata lot, similarly, any strata lot owner could do the same to reduce her or his unit entitlement. In that context, Regulation 14.2 of the _Strata Property Regulations_ makes very good sense.**

(Emphasis added)

---

[1]*Strata Property Regulation*, s. 14.2.
[2]*Kranz v. The Owners, Strata Plan VR 29*, [2003] B.C.J. No. 248 at paras. 14-16.

Third, if an owner can establish an error in a registered strata plan, section 14.12 of the regulations permits an owner to apply to the Registrar of Land Titles to correct the error.[1] For the purposes of this regulation, a registered strata plan includes the strata plan, a schedule of unit entitlement, a schedule of voting rights, the mailing address of the strata corporation, and any bylaws deposited with the strata plan that differ from the standard bylaws.[2] The Registrar may direct the applicant to give notice of the application to any other person(s) so that others may make submissions before the Registrar decides the matter.

Land Title Act

Arguably, section 106 of the *Land Title Act* also permits the Registrar of Land Titles to correct an error in a strata plan in an appropriate case. Section 106 of the *Land Title Act* permits the Registrar to correct a plan where, "it appears . . . on the filing of satisfactory evidence, . . . that there is an error, defect or omission in a deposited plan . . .".[3] According to the *Land Title Practice Manual*, satisfactory evidence of an error might, for example, be a surveyor's statutory declaration that explains the error and asks the Registrar to correct the plan. The Registrar may also serve notice upon, or require consents from, the owners of parcels that may be affected.[4]

In addition, the Registrar's power to correct an error may only exist where the error may be corrected without prejudicing rights acquired in good faith and for value.[5] Even if section 106 permits the Registrar, in theory, to correct an error in a schedule of unit entitlement, in many cases the Registrar will not be able to change the schedule

---

[1]*Strata Property Regulation*, s. 14.12.

[2]*Strata Property Regulation*, s. 14.12(1) (definition of "registered strata plan") and *Strata Property Act*, s. 245.

[3]*Land Title Act*, R.S.B.C. 1996, c. 250, s. 106.

[4]W.J. Mackay, R.S. Alexander, K.D. Jacques, J.P.M. McAvity & M.A. Waldron eds., *Land Title Practice Manual*, looseleaf (Vancouver, Continuing Legal Education Society of BC, 2000) at 7-87.

[5]*Land Title Act*, s. 383(1).

if the correction could adversely affect the rights of other owners who purchased their strata lots without any knowledge of the alleged error.

Finally, although a strata plan is certainly a form of plan used under the *Land Title Act*, it may be questionable whether the reference to a plan in section 106 includes a schedule of unit entitlement in a strata plan deposited under the *Strata Property Act*. Effective July 1, 2000, when the *Strata Property Act* came into force, the schedule of unit entitlement consisted of a separate document called a Schedule of Unit Entitlement (Form V).[1]

An Indirect Way to Change Unit Entitlement

In *The Owners, Strata Plan No. VR 1767 v. Seven Estate Ltd. et al.*,[2] the Supreme Court of British Columbia effectively created a fourth method for changing unit entitlement. The court used its powers under section 164 of the *Strata Property Act* to remedy a significantly unfair act by ordering the amendment of the schedule of unit entitlement.

In the *Seven Estate* case, the condominium complex consisted of a wooden building over top of a concrete garage that was used as a parking lot. The strata plan contained 28 strata lots. In the strata plan, the parking lot was a single strata lot. In addition to the parking lot, there were 25 residential strata lots and two commercial ones. Seven Estate Ltd. (the "owner") owned the parking lot.

The unit entitlement figure for the parking lot was 4030 in the schedule of unit entitlement in the strata plan. As the result of a mistake made by the developer when he first prepared the schedule of unit entitlement, the unit entitlement figure for the parking lot was at least four times greater than the entitlement of any other single strata lot.

---

[1] *Strata Property Act*, s. 245(a) and *Strata Property Regulation* (Form V).
[2] *The Owners, Strata Plan No. VR 1767 v. Seven Estate Ltd. et al.* (2002), 49 R.P.R. (3rd) 156, [2002] B.C.J. No. 755, 2002 B.C.S.C. 381 (S.C.).

From the start, the owner complained that the unit entitlement for the parking lot was a mistake and that it should be changed. In 1989, the strata corporation passed a resolution at a general meeting to reduce the parking lot's unit entitlement from 4030 to 2015 and to reduce the voting rights for the parking lot from five to two. From that time onward the strata corporation used the revised 2015 figure to calculate the owner's contribution to ordinary operating expenses. The resolution, however, was never recorded at the Land Title Office, as was then required by the *Condominium Act* to formally change a schedule of unit entitlement.[1]

As it turned out, the building was a leaky condo whose building envelope needed repair. The strata corporation approved four separate special levies to raise money for the repairs. Instead of assessing the owner on the basis of the revised 2015 unit entitlement figure, the strata corporation relied on the 4030 unit entitlement figure in the strata plan to claim that the owner owed approximately $126,912 for its share of the repairs.

The strata corporation then filed a lien against the owner's title and sought a forced sale of the strata lot. The owner sued the strata corporation for an order relieving the owner from contributing to the special levies.

Without explicitly saying so, the court concluded that the repairs to the building envelope were a common expense. That meant the owner must contribute to the levies according to the schedule of unit entitlement which, in this case, meant using the 4030 figure. Could the schedule of unit entitlement, however, be changed?

Although the *Condominium Act* permitted a strata corporation to amend its schedule of unit entitlement,[2] the court found that the corporation's failure to implement the

---

[1]Although the reasons for judgment do not explicitly state that the resolution was not recorded at the Land Title Office, the reasons say at paragraph 32 that, "the resolution was never implemented." Legal counsel for the strata corporation has confirmed to the author that the resolution was not recorded at the Land Title Office.
[2]*Condominium Act*, s. 113.

resolution by recording it at the Land Title Office in compliance with that Act meant that the 4030 unit entitlement figure in the strata plan still governed. Presumably, time ran out at the Land Title Office to record the resolution that reduced the unit entitlement to 2015 in accordance with the *Condominium Act* when that Act was repealed on July 1, 2000.[1]

The *Strata Property Act* contains several ways to amend a schedule of unit entitlement, but none of the methods applied in this case.

First, even if the 1989 resolution was passed unanimously and steps could be taken today under section 261 of the *Strata Property Act* to amend the schedule of unit entitlement, that section applies only to a *residential* strata lot. The strata lot in question was a parking lot.

Second, the court's authority to change unit entitlement under section 246 of the *Strata Property Act* is also restricted to a *residential* strata lot.

Third, the court in the *Seven Estate* case held, "that regulation 14 does not allow for the amendment of (unit entitlement)."[2] The court did not explain why this was the case. We assume that the court was referring to Regulation 14.12, which provides,

> **14.12 (1) In this section:**
>
> **"error" means any erroneous measurement or error, defect or omission in a registered strata plan;**
>
> **"registered strata plan" includes any document, deposited in the land title office, that**
>
> **(a) is referred to in section 245 (a) or (b) of the Act,**

---

[1] *Strata Property Act*, s. 294.
[2] *The Owners, Strata Plan No. VR 1767 v. Seven Estate Ltd. et al.*, 2000, B.C.S.C. 381 at para. 53.

>   (b) **forms part of a strata plan under the** ***Condominium Act*****, R.S.B.C. 1996, c. 64 or a former Act, or**
>
>   (c) **amends or replaces a document referred to in paragraph (a) or (b).**
>
> (2) **If it appears to the registrar that there is an error in any registered strata plan, the registrar may give notice or direct that notice be given to any person, in the manner and within the time determined by the registrar, and the registrar, after considering submissions, if any, and examining the evidence, may correct the error.**

Since the definition of *registered strata plan* includes any document referred to in section 245(a) of the *Strata Property Act* or one that amends such a document, and because section 245(a) of that Act expressly refers to a schedule of unit entitlement, one would think that the Registrar of Land Titles has the authority to correct an error in a schedule of unit entitlement in appropriate circumstances. It is not clear why in the court's view this remedy was not available to the owner in the *Seven Estate* case. Perhaps there was something in the peculiar circumstances of the *Seven Estate* case that took the owner beyond the reach of the Registrar's powers, but to which the court did not expressly refer in its written decision.

Unless the owner could establish oppression under the *Condominium Act*, or a significantly unfair action under the *Strata Property Act*, the general rule applied and the owner must contribute based upon the unit entitlement figure of 4030 in the strata plan.

The court found that if any remedial provision applied, it would be the power to remedy a significantly unfair action under section 164 of the *Strata Property Act*. The court reasoned that since the strata corporation sought judgment against the owner for the amount owing together with an order to enforce the lien by selling the parking lot under the *Strata Property Act*, the same statute should apply to any remedy claimed by the owner.

The court concluded that it would be significantly unfair, in this case, to require the owner to pay based on the unit entitlement figure of 4030 in the strata plan. The court took into account that for many years the strata corporation had allocated expenses to the owner on the basis of the 2015 unit entitlement figure in the 1989 resolution, and there was no longer any direct way under the *Strata Property Act* to change the 4030 figure in the schedule unit entitlement.

Given that section 164 of the *Strata Property Act* permits the court to make any order necessary to prevent or remedy a significantly unfair action, the court directed that the strata plan at the Land Title Office be amended to change the unit entitlement of the parking lot from 4030 to 2015. The court ordered that the owner must contribute to the special levies on the basis of a 2015 unit entitlement figure, not 4030. The court also directed the strata corporation to remove its lien upon payment by the owner of the special levies calculated on that basis.

Special Levies

The *Strata Property Act* permits a strata corporation to raise money by special levies against the owners.[1] In essence, a special levy serves as a "cash call" by the strata corporation to the owners.

Depending on the way a special levy is applied against the owners, either a 3/4 or unanimous vote is required with one exception.[2] Where a special levy is necessary to

---

[1] *Strata Property Act*, s. 108(1).
[2] *Ibid.*, s. 108(2).

cover an insurance deductible to repair or replace damaged property in certain circumstances, section 158 of the Act dispenses with the necessity of prior approval by the eligible voters.[1] A 3/4 vote is necessary if the strata corporation intends to collect contributions to the special levy according to the schedule of unit entitlement. On the other hand, if the corporation intends to seek contribution on some other basis that is a fair division of expenses, a unanimous vote is necessary.

In each case, the resolution to approve the special levy must set out:

- the purpose and total amount of the levy;

- the method used to determine each strata lot's share of the levy;

- the amount of each strata lot's share; and

- the date by which the levy must be paid or, if payable by installments, the dates of the installment payments.[2]

The strata corporation must use the money collected for the purpose set out in the resolution. Afterwards, the corporation must inform the owners about how the money was spent.[3]

If the amount collected exceeds the amount required, the strata corporation must return the surplus money to the owners in amounts proportional to their contributions. However, if none of the owners would receive more than $100, the corporation may deposit the excess in the CRF rather than returning the surplus funds to the respective owners.[4]

If a strata corporation has, by bylaw, taken responsibility for the maintenance of some specified portions of some

---

[1]*Strata Property Act*, s. 158(3).
[2]*Ibid.*, s. 108(3).
[3]*Ibid.*, s. 108(4).
[4]*Ibid.*, s. 108(5), (6).

but not all of the strata lots, a special levy in respect of the repair or maintenance of those portions is shared only by the owners of the strata lots to which the special levy relates.[1]

Who Contributes: Some or All?

Under the *Strata Property Act*, the general rule is that all of the owners must contribute to a special levy according to the schedule of unit entitlement in the strata plan.[2] Despite the general rule, the Act and the regulations create certain exceptions that require a strata corporation to allocate a special levy among only some, rather than all, of the owners. Since these exceptions often occur in connection with repairs, readers will find an explanation of these provisions in Chapter 26, *Paying for Repairs*.

Special Levies During Purchase

Sometimes, a special levy arises after an owner agrees to sell his or her strata lot but before the sale completes. Some, or all, of the special levy may be payable on a date that falls *after* the sale is scheduled to complete. Depending on the wording of the resolution authorizing the special levy, or the terms of the seller's contract with a purchaser, the seller may have to pay the whole amount of the levy in respect of the strata lot. This result may occur for one of several reasons.

1. The wording of the resolution authorizing a special levy often permits owners to pay their respective contributions to the special levy over time by installments. In such cases, the resolution usually contains

---

[1] *Strata Property Regulation*, s. 6.5. For information about the circumstances in which certain expenses may be allocated only to some, rather than all, of the owners, see Part V, *Repairs*.
[2] *Strata Property Act*, ss. 99 and 108.

an acceleration clause. If a strata lot is sold before that strata lot's contribution to the special levy is paid in full, the acceleration clause typically makes the whole outstanding balance of the special levy in respect of that strata lot immediately payable. If a seller fails to pay the whole amount due under an acceleration clause, the strata corporation may file a lien against the seller's strata lot. To provide clear title to the purchaser, the seller must pay off the strata corporation's lien.

2. The Contract of Purchase and Sale between the seller and the purchaser may obligate the seller to pay the entire special levy. The purchaser of a strata lot may negotiate a term in the Contract of Purchase and Sale by which the seller agrees that if a special levy is approved before the sale completes, the seller will pay the contribution to the special levy due in respect of the strata lot, including any portion due after the completion date that the purchaser, as the new owner, might otherwise be obligated to pay.

3. The *Strata Property Act* may also affect the seller's position. If the strata corporation approves a special levy before the sale of a strata lot completes, the *Act* requires the seller and purchaser to allocate the special levy between them. In effect, the Act makes the completion date of the sale the date for allocating this liability. Section 109 of the Act provides:

> **109. If a special levy is approved before a strata lot is conveyed to a purchaser,**
>
> > **(a) <u>the seller owes</u> the strata corporation the portion of the levy that is payable before the date the strata lot is conveyed, and**

(b) <u>the purchaser owes</u> the strata corporation the portion of the levy that is payable on or after the date the strata lot is conveyed.[1]

(Emphasis added)

The wording of the special resolution that authorized the special levy is very important. If the resolution requires the seller to pay the unpaid balance of the levy *before* the seller conveys his or her strata lot, the whole amount is payable before the strata lot is conveyed. In that case, the seller must pay the whole special levy.

On the other hand, if the resolution lacks any requirement for the seller to pay the unpaid balance *before* conveying his or her strata lot, the wording may make a portion of the levy "payable on or after the date the strata lot is conveyed." If so, the buyer will likely be liable to the strata corporation for the portion of the special levy payable on or after the date of the conveyance. In that case, the purchaser will have to pay the amount due, unless his or her contract with the seller requires the seller to pay that portion of the special levy on the buyer's behalf.

Recovery of Proceeds Payable to a Strata Corporation: Excess Special Levy Funds

The following information concerns *only* the recovery of proceeds that represent the return of excess special levy funds. This information does not necessarily apply, for example, to the recovery of CRF funds, to the distribution of income earned by a strata corporation or of a windfall gain, such as a monetary lottery prize.

In some circumstances, for instance, a strata corporation may receive funds to offset damages as a result of defective construction, including water penetration. The

---

[1] *Strata Property Act*, s. 109.

funds may come from a judgment or settlement, or an insurance or warranty claim. In some cases, a previous owner may have contributed to a special levy to fund the repairs, or the litigation, or both. Typically, the special levy that funded the endeavour ultimately produces the strata corporation's recovery of a judgment, or settlement, or insurance, or warranty proceeds. By the time the strata corporation receives the proceeds, however, the owner who previously contributed to the special levy may no longer be an owner within the meaning of the *Strata Property Act.*

If a special levy is the ultimate source of the money recovered, the strata corporation *must* return any excess funds to the owners, with one exception. A special levy is the ultimate source of funds where the levy paid for endeavours that have now produced the recovery of money.

Section 108(5) of the *Strata Property Act* governs the return of excess special levy funds, as follows:

> **108. (5) If the amount collected exceeds that required, or for any other reason is not fully used for the purpose set out in the resolution, the strata corporation must return the money to the owners in amounts proportional to their contributions.**

Section 108(5) requires that the money be returned to the "owners." The *Strata Property Act* defines an *owner* as a person shown in the register of a land title office as the owner of the fee simple estate; that is, the registered owner.[1]

In other words, the *Strata Property Act* requires that if the money collected for a special levy exceeds the amount required, the excess funds must be returned to the *registered* owners in amounts proportional to their contribution. An exception applies, however, where none of the owners would receive more than $100. In that case,

---

[1] *Strata Property Act*, s. 1.

instead of returning the money to the owners, the corporation may deposit the excess in the contingency reserve fund, as described earlier in this chapter.[1]

To further complicate matters, additional issues may develop when the strata corporation actually returns excess special levy funds to the registered owners at the successful conclusion of settlement negotiations or a lawsuit. The funds may be paid to the persons who were owners on the date the settlement was reached or judgment was rendered. Alternatively the funds may be paid to the persons who are owners at the time the funds are available for payout. There may be a considerable period of time between when the settlement or judgment arose and when the funds are available for payout. Determining which owners are eligible to receive the funds may depend on the wording of the strata corporation resolution that authorized the litigation in the first place, or alternatively a settlement. If the resolution does not address this issue, the strata corporation may have to determine the record date for payment; that is, to decide on what date must a person be a registered owner to qualify to receive a portion of the excess funds (e.g., the date judgment was rendered or the date the corporation actually receives the money).

Where a Strata Lot Has Been Sold

Once a strata lot has been sold, if excess special levy funds are to be returned, the question might arise whether a strata corporation may return the funds to a previous owner of a strata lot who paid the levy, rather than to the current registered owner.

Although the courts have not yet considered this issue, the prevailing legal view is that the strata corporation must return any excess special levy to the person who is

---

[1]*Strata Property Act*, s. 108 (5), (6).

the registered owner of the strata lot *at the time the funds are returned to the corporation.*

Agreement to Pay the Seller Future Funds

Where an owner reasonably expects the strata corporation in the near future to recover excess funds, but in the meantime plans to sell the owner's strata lot, the owner may wonder how to later collect the owner's portion of that recovery if the strata lot is sold. Since the strata corporation must pay excess special levy proceeds to the registered owners, the corporation must pay any share in respect of that strata lot to its new registered owner. Depending on the certainty of the anticipated future recovery, the seller likely has several options.

Where Future Recovery is Known for Certain

Suppose a strata corporation has reached a settlement in litigation, or with an insurance or warranty provider, or a judgment is rendered, but the corporation states that it will pay the funds to owners who are registered owners *at the time* the funds are received by the strata corporation. In such a case, the amount of the settlement or judgment is known, but the owners have to wait for the funds.

In such a case, the seller and purchaser can take this factor into account when negotiating the purchase price of the strata lot. Alternatively, they can enter a written agreement in which the purchaser, as the new registered owner, agrees to either pay the seller once the funds are received, or in the future to direct the strata corporation to pay the funds that are due to the purchaser, as the new registered owner, to the seller.

Where Future Recovery is Uncertain

Suppose, however, the seller does not know for certain whether there will be a future recovery. Insurance or warranty claims may only recently have been filed; litigation may be underway.

The seller may factor the uncertain recovery of funds into the asking price, but in many cases this may not be practical. The likelihood of the return of funds may be too uncertain to be quantified. Alternatively, it may increase the asking price for the strata lot beyond what the market will reasonably bear. As a result, the seller may want to negotiate an agreement with the purchaser that any funds that are recovered through the strata corporation will be paid to the seller.

An agreement of this type is legally very complex. There are many factors to consider. In the author's view, the legal skills necessary to properly prepare such an agreement are in most cases beyond the training of a real estate licensee. In the author's view, a seller should not expect a REALTOR to draft such an agreement. Instead, the seller should engage a lawyer who is familiar with strata matters to prepare the agreement.

For instance, if additional funds are required to fund the endeavour, the agreement should provide that the purchaser agrees to vote in favour of, and to pay, any related future special levies, and the seller agrees to reimburse the purchaser for those special levies. The agreement should obtain the purchaser's consent to sign future releases, if required, in any settlement proceedings and should clearly provide under what circumstances the purchaser will be liable to pay funds in the future to the seller. The agreement must also provide that if the purchaser sells his or her interest in the strata lot, then the purchaser will require their purchaser to be bound by an agreement containing the same obligations to the seller.

Note that any agreement that is entered into between the purchaser and seller is a contractual arrangement between only those two parties. The strata corporation is *not* a party to the agreement. While the strata corporation may be advised of the agreement and may, as a result, be asked to pay the funds to the seller, the strata corporation cannot be obligated to pay the funds to anyone but a registered owner.

Expenditures

A strata corporation must meet various conditions before it can spend money from its operating fund or CRF. Similarly, there are prerequisites before a section may spend money from its operating fund or CRF.

Operating Funds

The strata corporation can only spend funds from the operating fund if:

- the expenditure is consistent with the purpose of the fund, *and* the eligible voters have authorized it in the budget;

- the eligible voters have approved it by a 3/4 vote at a general meeting;

- the expenditure falls within a discretionary spending power in a bylaw or, alternatively under the Act, to spend without prior approval;

- the fiscal year has ended without approval of the next annual budget; or

- there is an emergency.[1]

---

[1] *Strata Property Act*, ss. 97, 98 and 104(3).

The *Strata Property Act* permits a strata corporation to create a bylaw allowing the strata council to spend operating funds, *without* prior approval, up to a pre-set limit. If the bylaws are silent on this subject, the Act permits the council to spend operating funds, without prior approval, up to an amount equal to five per cent of the total contribution to the operating fund for the current fiscal year, or $2,000, whichever is less.[1]

Under the former *Condominium Act*, many strata corporations passed bylaws that permitted their respective strata councils to spend operating funds, without prior approval, up to certain limits.[2] However, councils typically ignored the cumulative effect of such expenditures, provided that each one fell below the spending limit. The *Strata Property Act* requires strata councils to regulate these expenditures on a cumulative basis so that the total of all such expenditures within the same fiscal year falls within the spending limit.

Re *Blunt and Strata Corporation VR 45*[3] illustrates the need to ensure the strata council stays within its spending powers.

Case Study

In April 1976, the owners approved the strata corporation's budget at the annual general meeting. The budget did not contain any provision for painting the building.

At the time, the relevant section of the Strata Titles Act provided, in part:

---

[1] *Strata Property Act*, s. 98(2), (4).
[2] *Condominium Act*, s. 49.
[3] *Blunt and Strata Corporation VR 45* (1977), 2 B.C.L.R. 248, (S.C.).

> 27. **Unless otherwise authorized by a bylaw, . . . a strata council shall not, except in emergencies, authorize an expenditure exceeding five hundred dollars <u>which was not set out in the annual budget</u> without authorization by special resolution of the strata corporation.**
> (Emphasis added)

In the absence of an amended bylaw, the council's unapproved spending authority under the Act was $500.

In June 1976, the strata council hired a painter to paint the building's exterior. After the painter completed the work, the strata council authorized payment of $2,400 to the painter.

Except for Mr. Blunt, all the other owners paid their respective contributions towards the cost of painting. Mr. Blunt refused to pay and sued the strata corporation for a mandatory injunction requiring the corporation to call a general meeting to consider the expenditure.

In the meantime, the strata corporation apparently fined Mr. Blunt for failing to contribute towards the painting costs.

The court agreed with Mr. Blunt. Since the $2,400 expenditure was not approved in the budget, nor within council's $500 unapproved spending authority, the owners needed to approve this expenditure by a special resolution.[1] In the circumstances, the court also found no basis in law for the fines levied against Mr. Blunt. The court declined to order the injunction, however, because the strata corporation offered, during the court proceedings, to hold the necessary meeting. If the strata corporation failed

---

[1] A "special resolution" under the *Strata Titles Act* is roughly equivalent to a 3/4 vote under the *Strata Property Act*.

to hold the meeting as promised, Mr. Blunt could reapply for an injunction.

Contingency Reserve Funds

The strata corporation can only spend funds from the CRF if:

- the expenditure is consistent with the purpose of the fund, *and* the owners have approved it by a 3/4 vote;

- there is an emergency; or

- the expenditure is necessary to cover an insurance deductible under section 158(3) of the Act.[1]

In *McGowan v. Strata Plan NW1018*,[2] a strata corporation passed a special resolution (sic) at an extraordinary general meeting (sic) on April 17, 2002, when the *Strata Property Act* was in force, that appeared to endorse discretionary CRF expenditures without first consulting the eligible voters. The resolution endorsed "the existing practice of maintaining the painting and roofing fund as a revolving fund, being expended at the discretion of the elected council." Since the painting and roofing fund appeared to be part of the corporation's CRF, the court observed that the Act does not permit a strata council to make discretionary expenditures on the basis set out in the resolution.

Emergencies

The Act permits the strata council to spend money from the operating fund or the CRF without prior approval from the owners if there are reasonable grounds to believe that

---

[1]*Strata Property Act*, ss. 96, 98 and 158(3).
[2]*McGowan v. Strata Plan NW1018*, [2002] B.C.J. No. 959 at para. 75, 2002 B.C.S.C. 673 at para. 75 (S.C.).

an immediate expenditure is necessary to ensure safety or prevent significant loss or damage, whether physical or otherwise.[1]

In an emergency, the strata council may only spend the *minimum* amount necessary to ensure safety or avoid loss.[2]

The council must also inform the owners as soon as feasible about the emergency expenditure.[3]

Sections

In some cases, a strata corporation may spend funds that benefit only the strata lots within a particular section. Similarly, a section may spend money from its own operating fund, CRF, or special levy.

Strata Corporation Expenditures

When a strata corporation spends operating funds or money from the CRF for matters that relate solely to a section, as a general rule those expenses are shared by the owners of strata lots in that section. Each strata lot's share of expenses is determined according to the strata lot's unit entitlement, in proportion to the unit entitlements of the other strata lots in that section, unless the owners have unanimously agreed to change the basis of their contributions.[4]

Despite the general rule, the Act and the regulations create certain exceptions that require a strata corporation to allocate an expenditure among only some, rather than all, of the owners in the section. Since these exceptions often occur in connection with repairs, readers will find an explanation of these provisions in Chapter 26, *Paying for Repairs.*

---

[1] *Strata Property Act*, s. 98(3).
[2] *Ibid.*, s. 98(5).
[3] *Ibid.*, s. 98(6).
[4] *Ibid.*, s. 195.

Section Expenditures

A section has the same powers and duties as the strata corporation to establish its own operating fund and CRF for matters that relate solely to that section. Similarly, a section may budget and require section owners to contribute to a special levy for expenditures authorized by the section.[1]

The *Strata Property Act* also suggests that the same spending requirements that govern a strata corporation also regulate spending by a section.[2] In addition, the Act suggests that the same provisions that regulate whether all, or only some, owners must contribute to the operating fund, the CRF, or a special levy in the strata corporation, also apply to a section, subject to necessary modifications. Since these considerations often occur in connection with repairs, readers will find an explanation of these provisions in Chapter 26, *Paying for Repairs*.

Borrowing

A strata corporation may borrow money to exercise its powers and duties, if the eligible voters approve the transaction by a 3/4 vote at a general meeting.[3]

When borrowing money, the *Strata Property Act* permits a strata corporation to give a lender security for the loan by way of a mortgage, the assignment of unpaid strata fees or special levies, or a negotiable instrument.[4] Note, however, that the Act prohibits the strata corporation from giving a mortgage over common property.[5] If, on the other hand, the strata corporation is the registered owner of a strata lot in the strata plan, the strata lot is a common asset over which the corporation may give a

---

[1]*Strata Property Act*, s. 194(2)(a), (b).
[2]*Ibid.*, ss. 194 and 195.
[3]*Ibid.*, s. 111(1).
[4]*Ibid.*, s. 111(2).
[5]*Ibid.*, s. 81.

mortgage. This might occur, for example, where a strata corporation owns a strata lot that serves as a caretaker's suite.

Collecting Money

A strata corporation's most important responsibility is to manage and maintain the common property and common assets of the corporation for the benefit of the owners.[1] To carry out those responsibilities, it is often necessary for the strata corporation to collect money due to the corporation from owners and other persons.

Depending on the circumstances, a strata corporation may enforce payment of money due to the corporation by:

- interest on arrears;

- fines for late payments;

- demand notices;

- liens against the title of a strata lot;

- withholding a Certificate of Payment (Form F);

- court actions; or

- arbitration.

Fines and Interest

Section 1 of the Standard Bylaws makes strata fees payable on or before the first day of the month to which the strata fees relate.[2] The regulations provide that if a strata corporation created under previous legislation lacks a bylaw establishing a schedule for the payment of strata fees, that

---

[1]*Strata Property Act*, s. 3.
[2]*Ibid., Schedule of Standard Bylaws*, s. 1.

corporation automatically acquired section 1 of the Standard Bylaws effective July 1, 2000.[1]

Since failure to pay strata fees on time amounts to a contravention of a strata corporation's bylaws, a strata corporation may, among other things, fine the owner for late payment.[2]

Additionally, the *Strata Property Act* provides that a bylaw that sets a schedule for paying strata fees may also set out a rate of interest for late strata fees.[3] The Act provides that the interest forms part of the strata fees when a Certificate of Lien is registered.[4]

The regulations limit the amount of interest that can be charged for the late payment of strata fees to 10 per cent per annum, compounded annually.[5]

Demand Notice

The *Strata Property Act* requires the strata corporation to give two weeks' written notice demanding payment and indicating that action may be taken before suing or arbitrating against an owner or tenant.[6] Similarly, the strata corporation must also give two weeks' written notice demanding payment and indicating that a lien may be registered before filing a lien against the owner's strata lot.[7] The legislation does not specify any particular form of written notice. Any form of written notice will likely suffice if it reasonably conveys the necessary information to the reader. For example, an invoice from a strata corporation to an owner or tenant is likely sufficient written notice if it makes it plain that failure to pay the amount due may result in court proceedings to collect the

---

[1] *Strata Property Regulation*, s. 17.9.
[2] *Strata Property Act, Schedule of Standard Bylaws*, s. 23.
[3] *Ibid.*, s. 107(1).
[4] *Ibid.*, s. 107(2).
[5] *Strata Property Regulation*, s. 6.8.
[6] *Strata Property Act*, s. 112(1).
[7] *Ibid.*, s. 112(2).

debt, or the registration of a lien against title to the strata lot where a lien is allowed.

If the owner's lender has given the strata corporation a Mortgagee's Request For Notification, and the strata corporation is required to deliver a written demand to an owner or tenant, as described above, the corporation must also deliver a copy of the demand to the lender.[1] The requirements for delivering a notice are described in Chapter 12, *Meetings*.

If the owner or tenant disputes the debt, he or she may pay the disputed amount into court where permitted by the rules of court. Alternatively, the owner or tenant may pay the disputed amount to the strata corporation in trust, pending resolution of the dispute.[2]

When considering how the amount may be collected, the strata corporation must consider the reason the funds are owed.

Certificate of Lien

The strata corporation may also file a Certificate of Lien against the owner's strata lot in the Land Title Office.[3] However, before registering the Certificate of Lien, the strata corporation must give the owner at least two weeks' written notice demanding payment *and* advising that a lien may be registered if payment is not made within the two weeks.[4] The lien may cover the owner's indebtedness for:[5]

- strata fees and any interest owing,

- special levies,

---

[1] *Strata Property Act*, s. 113.
[2] *Ibid.*, s. 114(1).
[3] *Ibid.*, s. 116(1).
[4] *Ibid.*, s. 112(2).
[5] *Ibid.*, ss. 116(1) and 118.

- reimbursement for work done to the owner's strata lot by the strata corporation for which the owner is responsible,

- the strata lot's share of a judgment against the strata corporation, and

- the reasonable legal costs and disbursements for filing the lien. Reasonable legal costs are restricted to an amount equivalent to the taxable party and party costs for registering and enforcing the lien.[1]

The strata corporation cannot file a lien if the owner has paid the disputed amount into court, or into trust with the strata corporation, or has otherwise made satisfactory arrangements with the corporation to pay the money.[2] Note also that a lien cannot be filed for fines owing to the strata corporation or for the cost of remedying a contravention of the bylaws or rules.[3]

If the developer owns a strata lot, the strata corporation can also file a lien against the developer's lot for money owing by the developer for:[4]

- a shortfall in the interim budget and any related penalty,[5]

- a penalty for failing to call the first AGM,[6] or

- reimbursement to the strata corporation for the cost of obtaining a document that the developer was supposed to provide.[7]

---

[1]*Canada Trustco Mortgage Company v. Gies*, (2001), 93 B.C.L.R. (3rd) 73, [2001] B.C.J. No. 1597, 2001 B.C.S.C. 1016.

[2]*Strata Property Act*, s. 116(3).

[3]*Ibid.*, s. 116.

[4]*Ibid.*, ss. 18 and 116(2). For information about the liabilities of a developer who fails to comply with certain requirements, see Chapter 11, *Developer*.

[5]*Ibid.*, s. 14(4), (5).

[6]*Ibid.*, s. 17(b).

[7]*Ibid.*, s. 20(3).

If the developer owns two or more strata lots, the strata corporation may only file the lien against one of the lots.[1]

Once registered, the strata corporation's lien ranks ahead of every other lien or registered charge except:[2]

- to the extent that the corporation's lien is a lien for the strata lot's share of a judgment against the strata corporation;

- a lien in favor of the Crown and which is not a mortgage; or

- a charge under the *Builders Lien Act*.[3]

In *Hammerberg & Co. v. Margitay*,[4] an owner who reimbursed a strata corporation for its actual legal expenses in lien proceedings was entitled to ask the court to review the lawyers' invoices. If a strata corporation won a lawsuit against an owner for money due, a bylaw allowed the corporation to also recover its actual legal costs from the owner. When an owner failed to pay his portion of a special levy, the strata corporation retained a law firm to file a lien against the owner's title and obtain an order for the sale of the owner's strata lot. The owner paid the amount due. In the meantime, the strata corporation's lawyers invoiced the corporation approximately $4,937 for their services in the matter. Citing the bylaw, the strata corporation then compelled the owner to reimburse the corporation that amount for its actual legal costs. When the owner applied to the Supreme Court of British Columbia to review the lawyers' accounts for which he had reimbursed the strata corporation, the lawyers objected to the owner's standing to apply for a review. The lawyers argued that only their client, the strata

---

[1]*Strata Property Act*, s. 116(2).
[2]*Ibid.*, s. 116(5).
[3]*Builders Lien Act*, S.B.C. 1997, c. 45.
[4]*Hammerberg & Co. v. Margitay* (2001), 94 B.C.L.R. (3d) 158, [2001] B.C.J. No. 2034, 2001 B.C.S.C. 1312 (S.C.).

corporation, could ask for a review. Citing the *Legal Profession Act*, the court held that the owner could seek a review of the lawyers' accounts.[1] The court then reviewed the invoices and ordered the lawyers to refund approximately $788 to the owner. The lien serves as notice of the strata corporation's claim for the amount owing. In many cases, a lien remains on title until the owner needs to refinance his or her mortgage or sell the strata lot. In these instances, the owner is effectively forced to deal with the problem because he or she cannot refinance or sell without discharging the lien from title. The owner may pay the debt or dispute it. If the owner disputes the strata corporation's claim, the strata corporation will normally agree to discharge the lien upon payment of the disputed funds into court or into trust with the strata corporation.

If the strata corporation wants to promptly enforce its lien without waiting, the corporation must sue the owner for a judicial determination of the amount owing under the lien and an order to sell the owner's strata lot.[2] It is not necessary to first authorize the enforcement proceeding by a resolution passed by a 3/4 vote at an annual or special general meeting.[3] Typically, the corporation retains a lawyer for the enforcement proceeding.

The court will first determine the sum properly owing to the strata corporation and enter judgment for that amount, plus prejudgment interest and costs against the owner.

Sometimes an owner contests a lien on the ground that he or she was entitled to withhold payment of strata fees, or a contribution to special levy, to complain about some wrong done to them. An owner might argue, for instance, that she has stopped paying strata fees until the strata

---

[1] *Legal Profession Act*, S.B.C. 1998, c. 9, s. 70.
[2] *Strata Property Act*, s. 117.
[3] *The Owners, Strata Plan VR 1008 v. Oldaker et al.*, [2004] B.C.J. No. 74, 2004 B.C.S.C. 63.

corporation repairs her balcony. Another owner might claim that he is entitled to offset his claim against the strata corporation for damages for negligence against his obligation to pay a special levy, and so on. None of these complaints relieve owners from their financial obligations under the legislation to pay strata fees, a special levy, and so on.[1] If an owner is unhappy about the management of the corporation, or the conduct of an owner or tenant, that owner has other options. First, the unhappy owner may have a political remedy such as demanding a general meeting where the eligible voters may pass a majority vote to direct or restrict the council in its activities. Alternatively, there may be suitable legal remedies. An owner may arbitrate against or sue the strata corporation, the strata council, an owner, or a tenant to enforce compliance with the *Strata Property Act.*[2]

After entering judgment in favour of the strata corporation the court will order the defaulting owner to pay the amount owing within a specific period of time. The payment period is set at the court's discretion. In most cases, this serves as a standstill period in which nothing happens to the property while the owner exercises his or her last chance to pay the debt and escape the lien proceedings. Usually, the court allows a payment period of 30 days, although the court has the discretion to make the period shorter or longer. Failing payment by the deadline, the strata corporation may list the strata lot for sale.

The strata corporation typically lists the owner's strata lot for sale with a real estate agent. After a buyer is found, the court must approve the sale. In accordance with the court order, the sale proceeds are applied to the real estate commission, if any, the amount owing to the strata

---

[1]See, for example, *Richard Bedford Oldaker v. Strata Plan VR 1008* (13 September 2002), Vancouver L003498 (B.C.S.C.); *Taychuk v. The Owners, Strata Plan LMS 744* (2002), 7 R.P.R. (4th) 302, [2002] B.C.J. No. 2653, 2002 B.C.S.C. 1638, (S.C.).

[2]*Strata Property Act*, ss. 164 and 165. For information about legal proceedings and arbitration, see Part VI, *Court Proceedings and Arbitration*.

corporation under the lien, including certain legal costs, and then to mortgagees and other charge holders on title.

Certificate of Payment (Form F)

In some circumstances, a strata corporation can encourage payment of arrears by refusing to provide a Certificate of Payment (Form F) pending payment or other satisfactory arrangements.

An owner, purchaser or authorized person may obtain a Certificate of Payment (Form F) if the owner does not owe money to the strata corporation, or the money owed has been paid into court or to the strata corporation to hold in trust, or the owner has made satisfactory arrangements to pay the money owing.[1]

The Certificate of Payment (Form F) is necessary to register any conveyance, lease or agreement for sale of the strata lot, because the Registrar of Land Titles will not register any of these transactions without it.[2] The strata corporation can charge for the certificate, but the fee must not exceed the amount set out in the regulations.[3] The maximum fee that a strata corporation can charge for a Certificate of Payment (Form F) is $15.[4]

Because a Certificate of Payment (Form F) is needed before a conveyance, lease or agreement for sale can be registered, an owner who wishes to complete his or her sale to a purchaser must either pay the strata corporation the amount owing, or make satisfactory arrangements with the strata corporation for those amounts. The need for the certificate forces an owner to address the issue of money owing to the strata corporation, including money owing for fines. Until an owner, however, wishes to register a conveyance, lease or agreement for sale, the

---

[1]*Strata Property Act*, s. 115. For information about a Certificate of Payment (Form F), see Chapter 13, *Record Keeping*.

[2]*Ibid.*, s. 256(1).

[3]*Ibid.*, s. 115(3).

[4]*Strata Property Regulation*, s. 6.10.

Certificate of Payment (Form F) is not a useful tool to force an owner to pay amounts owing to the strata corporation.

In a Certificate of Payment (Form F), a strata corporation may include money owing for:[1]

- strata fees, including interest if permitted by a bylaw,

- special levies,

- reimbursement for work done to the owner's strata lot by the strata corporation for which the owner is responsible,

- the strata lot's share of a judgment against the strata corporation,

- fines or other costs for remedying a contravention of the bylaws or rules,[2] and

- an amount due from the developer, as the owner of a strata lot, for a shortfall in the interim budget and any related penalty, the penalty for failure to hold the first AGM, or reimbursement for the cost of obtaining copies of documents which the developer should have delivered at the first AGM.

In the Certificate of Payment (Form F), the strata corporation must not include any claim for damages against the owner which have not been determined by a court or arbitration.[3]

---

[1] *Strata Property Act*, s. 115(4).
[2] See also *Canada Trustco Mortgage Company v. Gies* (2001), 93 B.C.L.R. (3rd) 73, [2001] B.C.J. No. 1597, 2001 B.C.S.C. 1016.
[3] *Strata Property Act*, s. 115(5).

Court Action

The strata corporation may sue an owner for a variety of matters including money owing to the strata corporation.[1] The court proceeding must be authorized by a 3/4 vote unless the strata corporation is suing in Small Claims Court and has a bylaw that dispenses with the need for authorization from the owners.[2]

As previously indicated, the corporation cannot file a Certificate of Lien for money owing for a fine or the cost of remedying the owner's contravention of a bylaw or rule.[3] In both of these cases, it appears that the strata corporation must first sue the owner to recover the fine or reimbursement for remedying a contravention. If the strata corporation succeeds in court, the corporation can register its judgment against title to the owner's strata lot.

Depending on the circumstances, the strata corporation may also pursue other collection remedies to enforce its judgment, such as garnishment. For more information about enforcing payment of fines for breach of a bylaw or rule, see Part IV, *Bylaws and Rules*.

Arbitration

The strata corporation may refer a dispute, including a dispute over money owing for fines, to arbitration.[4] The arbitrator's decision and order for costs may be filed in either the Supreme Court of British Columbia or the Provincial Court of British Columbia: Small Claims Division, depending on the amount of the award and other factors. Once the decision is filed, it has the same effect as if it was an order of that court. A strata corporation can then proceed to enforce the judgment.[5]

---

[1] For information about legal proceedings, see Part VI, *Court Actions and Arbitration*.
[2] *Strata Property Act*, s. 171(4).
[3] *Ibid.*, s. 116(3).
[4] *Ibid.*, s. 177(3). For information about arbitration proceedings, see Part VI, *Court Actions and Arbitration*.
[5] *Strata Property Act*, s. 189.

Distribution of a Strata Corporation's Property Upon Dissolution

A building strata plan deposited at the Land Title Office before July 1, 2000, under the former *Condominium Act* contains a schedule of interest upon destruction. A schedule of interest upon destruction is typically found together with the schedule of unit entitlement among the last sheets (or back pages) of the plan itself.

If a building was destroyed, section 64 of the *Condominium Act* permitted the owners to decide by special resolution not to rebuild their structure. The schedule of interest upon destruction determined the share of each owner in the strata corporation's property and assets if the owners adopted a special resolution under section 64 of the former Act declaring the building destroyed.[1]

The *Strata Property Act* abandons the requirement for a schedule of interest upon destruction in a strata plan filed on or after July 1, 2000. Instead where a strata plan is cancelled and the strata corporation wound up, the Act requires a schedule called a *conversion schedule* or an *interest schedule*, depending on how the corporation is dissolved.[2] In each case, the schedule allocates an owner's proportionate interest, as a tenant in common, in the strata corporation's property according to the most recent property tax assessment values, as follows:

> **most recent assessed value of an owner's strata lot**
> _____
> **most recent assessed value of all the strata lots in the strata plan, excluding any strata lots held by or on behalf of the strata corporation**

---

[1] *Condominium Act*, ss. 4(g) and 64; *Condominium Act Regulations*, B.C. Reg. 534/74, Form 2.

[2] *Strata Property Act*, ss. 273, 278.

If there is no assessed value for a strata lot, the strata corporation may substitute an independent appraised value that is approved by a 3/4 vote.[1]

What happens where a strata corporation that was created before July 1, 2000, is dissolved and its strata plan cancelled? In that case, the *Strata Property Act* provides that the schedule of interest upon destruction in the strata plan determines each owner's interest in the property of the strata corporation.[2]

---

[1]*Strata Property Act*, ss. 273, 278.
[2]*Ibid.*

Chapter 16

INSURANCE

This chapter provides a fairly comprehensive overview of the insurance aspects of condominium living. Of course, there will be issues peculiar to particular situations and these should be discussed with qualified service providers, lawyers, accountants, insurers, insurance brokers or agents and consultants, depending on the circumstances.

Since strata bylaws usually contain no reference to insurance, except that owners should receive a copy of the policy on request, it is necessary to look almost exclusively to the legislation for guidance on insurance requirements.

According to section 149(1) of the *Strata Property Act*, the strata corporation must obtain and maintain *property* insurance on the common property, including any buildings shown on the strata plan, the common assets and any fixtures built or installed on a strata lot by the developer as part of the original construction of that strata lot.

The strata corporation must also maintain insurance against *liability* for property damage and bodily injury.[1]

Every year, the strata corporation must review the adequacy of its coverage and report about it to the owners at the annual general meeting (AGM).[2]

In addition, the strata corporation has the option of buying other forms of insurance.[3]

Owners, too, can buy insurance to augment or increase the corporation's coverage for their own strata lots.[4]

---

[1] *Strata Property Act*, s. 150(1) and *Strata Property Regulation*, s. 17.4. If a strata corporation was created before July 1, 2000, when the *Strata Property Act* came into force, the corporation did not have to comply with this requirement until January 1, 2002.

[2] *Strata Property Act*, s. 154.

[3] *Ibid.*, s. 152.

[4] *Ibid.*, s. 161.

Property Insurance

This is mandated by the Act and insures direct loss to common property, common assets, and buildings shown on the strata plan.[1]

The strata corporation must also insure fixtures built or installed on each strata lot if the developer built or installed the fixtures as part of the original construction of the strata lot.[2] The regulations define fixtures as, "items attached to a building, including floor and wall coverings and electrical and plumbing fixtures . . ." The definition specifically excludes "refrigerators, stoves, dishwashers, microwaves, washers, dryers or other items" if they can be removed without damage to the building.[3]

Coverage should be for full replacement value of all major perils as set out in the regulations and the bylaws.[4] The regulations define major perils as, "fire, lightning, smoke, windstorm, hail, explosion, water escape, strikes, riots or civil commotion, impact by aircraft or vehicles, vandalism and malicious acts."[5] Earthquake is not included in the definition but most strata corporations purchase earthquake coverage and, in BC, all should be protected from earthquake loss.

Covered

Although the Act does not specify coverage for individual strata lots, all strata insurance policies include strata lots.

The coverage for each strata lot usually includes all originally-installed fixtures and fittings, as well as appliances, floor and window coverings. Owners' improvements and betterments are not normally insured by the strata policy.

---

[1] *Strata Property Act*, ss. 149(1)(d) and 149(2).
[2] *Ibid.*, s. 149(1)(d).
[3] *Strata Property Regulation*, s. 9.1.
[4] *Strata Property Act*, s. 149(4)(a), (b) and *Strata Property Regulation*, s. 9.1(2).
[5] *Strata Property Regulation*, s. 9.1(2).

Not Covered

Owners' Improvements

Sometimes owners improve their strata lots by adding things like marble finishes, hardwood flooring and mirrored walls. They are then surprised to learn that these improvements are not included in the strata policy and, after a loss, the cost to replace or repair them rests with the owners.

Section 161 of the *Strata Property Act* permits owners to obtain additional insurance for these improvements. This should be done either through the strata policy insurer, if available, or the owner's own policy.

This additional insurance can also be valuable to owners who purchase their strata lots during inflationary markets. Sometimes the purchase price exceeds the insured value and owners can protect their investments with such coverage.

Personal Property

Strata corporation policies do not include coverage for the *personal property* or *contents* of individual strata lots, such as furniture, clothing, jewellery and other personal items belonging to owners or tenants. Condominium dwellers should purchase tenants' or unit owners' policies for this purpose. It is helpful to buy the insurance from the strata policy insurer to avoid disputes between insurers after a loss. Such disputes can take time to resolve and, in the meantime, owners and tenants are left to fend for themselves.

Rentals

Protection against loss of rental income should be purchased by the strata corporation *only* if the corporation relies on income from property which is rented out. This is often not the case. Even when strata corporations are in a position to rent building space, the rentals are infrequent, insignificant, do not contribute to the budget in any meaningful way and need not be insured.

On the other hand, owners who rent out their strata lots should definitely purchase this coverage as part of their unit owners' insurance.

Replacement Value

As required by the Act, most strata insurance policies are written on a replacement cost basis. This means the full amount of the repair or replacement cost is insured and the problem of determining depreciation is eliminated.

Valuation

To ensure adequate insurance, most strata corporations obtain a regular appraisal of the property. This should be an independent evaluation conducted by a qualified appraiser. It is not appropriate for the strata council or strata manager to estimate the insurable value. During low inflationary periods, strata councils may cut costs by reducing the frequency of appraisals, but the risk of doing so may be substantial because guessing can lead to uninsured losses.

Co-Insurance Clauses

Strata corporations that do not obtain proper appraisals should be aware that many strata policies contain co-insurance clauses that effectively reduce the insurers' contribution to loss. An 80 per cent co-insurance clause permits underinsurance of up to 20 per cent without penalty. This provides a cushion in periods when values are rapidly increasing. Ninety per cent co-insurance permits underinsurance of 10 per cent without penalty.

These clauses are rarely applied because insurance companies insist on appraisals and, provided appraisals are obtained, policies contain "stated amount" co-insurance clauses. These clauses remove the need to prove insurance to value at the time of loss making the replacement cost easier to calculate and the policy clearer. Their real purpose is to protect two or more insurers on the same risk from insureds who try to minimize premiums by buying less than full replacement cost.

Loss Payees

The insurable interests of mortgage and other financial lenders are protected by a "loss payee" clause or endorsement. Essentially, such a clause or endorsement makes the mortgagee, or other lenders, beneficiaries of the proceeds of the insurance, to the extent of their interest, in the event of a loss. Preferred is the "standard mortgage" clause that also gives the mortgagee the right to be notified if the policy is about to lapse and, if it is a broad form, to collect on a loss even if the insured is in violation of the policy terms.

Perils Insured

Most policies provide protection against all risks of direct physical loss or damage except as excluded. This is obviously better than a named perils policy but is usually subject to a long list of exclusions.

Exclusions

Temperature Extremes, Leaks, Explosions and Faults

Among the risks excluded are loss or damage caused by dampness or dryness of atmosphere and extremes of temperature, leakage, corrosion or rot, normal settling, explosion, collapse, faulty material, workmanship or design, and pollution, except where these things occur as a result of an insured peril, such as fire. Since the regulations define perils to include explosion and water escape, strata corporations should check their policies to ensure that these perils are covered.[1]

Below the Basement

Anything below the basement is also usually excluded. Since many strata properties have facilities, equipment and other items on levels that may or may not be considered to be part of the basement, insurers should confirm that these are *in* the basement, *not below* the basement, and are covered. If there is any doubt about this, the strata council should obtain a "foundations, footings and below ground coverage" endorsement.

Motor Vehicles

Some strata properties, especially those situated near bodies of water, are subject to minor flooding from time to time. Cars and other vehicles parked or stored in or below the basement may be insured under the Insurance Corporation of British Columbia's (ICBC) comprehensive general liability policy. However, ICBC could try to recover significant damage payments from the strata corporation, and this should be discussed with an insurance agent or consultant.

Similarly, owners are responsible for loss and damage caused to their vehicles by theft and vandalism. While many strata corporations engage security services, the Act does not require them to do so.

---

[1] *Strata Property Regulation*, s. 9.1(2).

Deductibles

Deductibles are used to prevent dollar swapping with insurers, to obtain premium savings and to reduce administration. Deductibles should be set high enough to eliminate numerous small losses while protecting the strata corporation from catastrophic loss. In any event, strata corporations that buy small deductibles and then rely on the insurance to constantly fix minor problems are quickly forced to take a higher deductible or look elsewhere for coverage.

Commonly occurring deductibles are $500 to $1,000 generally; $1,000 to $5,000 for water damage; $2,500 to $10,000 for flood; $500 for glass; and, five per cent for earthquake.

Earthquake

Earthquake deductibles of five per cent are typical on policies insuring small values. However, at five per cent of the sum insured, earthquake deductibles can be very onerous on policies insuring higher values, particularly for strata property consisting of a number of separate buildings with combined high values.

In a recent insurance review, a strata corporation with five buildings, and a total value of $60 million, was horrified to learn that the five per cent earthquake deductible meant that owners would have to contribute the first $3 million on each earthquake loss to any one building.

Strata councils in this situation should negotiate a reduced deductible or have the insurer agree to separate valuations and deductibles for each building with one maximum aggregate deductible, should there be earthquake damage to more than one building simultaneously.

Aggregate

Although insurers cannot apply more than one deductible to one loss, each loss will trigger separate deductibles. To limit the total number of deductibles payable when a multiplicity of losses occurs at the same time, ensure that strata policies contain a maximum aggregate deductible per policy period, or an endorsement to this effect.

Payments

Section 158 of the *Strata Property Act* characterizes insurance deductible payments on the strata corporation's insurance as a common expense, to be funded by strata fees. Moreover, approval is not required for a special levy or for an expenditure from the CRF for a deductible to repair or replace damaged property.[1] In addition, the strata corporation can sue an owner to recover the deductible if the owner is responsible for the loss or damage that gave rise to the claim.[2]

Strata councils deal with deductibles in a variety of ways depending on their bylaws or, if silent, on the circumstances of each case.

Generally, if a strata lot sustains damage as a result of an insured peril in the strata corporation's policy, the strata corporation pays the deductible. So, if the roof leaks and damages the ceiling and floors in a strata lot, the strata corporation pays the deductible.

Whether the strata corporation is also responsible to pay the deductible on the owners' policy, to repair or replace personal property, is an interesting point. Gerry Fanaken, in his book *Understanding and Improving the Condominium Concept: An Authoritative Guidebook,*[3] is adamant that the

---

[1] *Strata Property Act*, s. 158(3).
[2] *Ibid.*, s. 158(2).
[3] Gerry Fanaken, *Understanding and Improving the Condominium Concept: An Authoritative Guidebook* (Vancouver, Vancouver Condominium Services Ltd., 1994) at p. 131-132.

strata corporation is liable for such loss and should compensate owners in this situation. He also condemns the practice of some strata corporations that insist owners carry their own coverage for flood insurance deductibles, which have increased dramatically in recent years.

Glass is an exception in that most strata policies cover glass breakage and repair. If the window of a strata lot is broken, most often you will find that the claim is paid by the strata corporation's insurance, subject to the owner paying the deductible in accordance with the bylaws.

If an owner or tenant causes damage to common property, common assets, or another strata lot, the owner of the strata lot causing the damage may be required to pay the deductible under the strata corporation's insurance and the other owners' insurance, as the case may be.

The recent case of *Strata Corp. VR 2673 v. Comissiona*[1] is authority for this:

Case Study

When water leaking from certain owners' units caused damage to common property and other owners' units, the strata corporation claimed from the owners of the units causing the damage, payment of the deductible under the strata corporation's insurance.

The issue was whether in law or under the legislation, bylaws, rules and regulations, the strata corporation had such a claim against the unit owners causing the damage.

---

[1] *Strata Corp. VR 2673 v. Comissiona* (2000), 80 B.C.L.R. (3rd) 350, [2000] B.C.J. No. 1681, 2000 B.C.S.C. 1240.

After reviewing previous cases, the court found that there is no legal bar to such a claim by the strata corporation and the fact that the unit owner causing the damage is also a named insured in the strata policy does not create such a bar.[1]

Considering the legislation, both past and present, the court had this to say about section 158(2) of the *Strata Property Act*:[2]

> **Section 158(2) does not create a right in the strata corporation to sue an owner; rather, it does not limit the capacity of the strata corporation to do so. Section 158(2) does not change the law . . . Whether a strata corporation can maintain such an action must be determined by all of the provisions of the applicable statute and the bylaws, rules and regulations of the strata corporation.**

The rules and regulations of this particular strata corporation expressly provided that, "any damage to common property caused by negligence of the owner, occupants of his strata lot, or his guests, will be charged to the owner of the strata lot." There was no provision dealing with damage to another owner's lot and since the court was not asked to decide the issue, it did not. Nevertheless, in considering the case law, the court said it was very clear under the law that an owner is liable for the damages caused to both common property and other owners' units.

---

[1]Specifically, the court distinguished this case from the earlier case of *Lalji-Samji v. Strata Plan VR 2135*, on the basis that in *Lalji-Samji*, the strata's claim against the negligent owner was for an uninsured loss to the common property. The case did not deal with the liability of an owner for the deductible portion of an insured loss to the common property.

[2]*Strata Corp. VR 2673 v. Comissiona*, [2000] B.C.J. No. 1681 at para. 22 per Levine, J.

Conditions

All insurance policies are subject to conditions and strata policies are no exception. There are two types of conditions: statutory and general.

Statutory

Statutory conditions are mandated by legislation and all policies must include them.

The most important statutory conditions in the property insurance:

- void the coverage affected if there is a material misrepresentation by the insured,[1]

- void that part of the policy affected if there is a material change not promptly notified to the insurer,

- make the insurer pay losses within 60 days after the insured files proof of loss, and

- require legal actions against the insurer to be brought within one year after loss or damage.

General

General conditions are at the discretion of the insurer and, although many have become standard to most policies, some can be changed, sometimes for an additional premium. Most often, these require:

- the strata corporation to notify the insurer of any problem with the fire detection system, including the cancellation of any contract for their maintenance or monitoring,

---

[1]A material misrepresentation is a representation which, had the insurer known about it, would have caused the insurer to decline coverage, add an exclusion or charge a higher premium. For example, misrepresenting your previous claims history would be considered material.

- the strata corporation to take reasonable steps to recover a loss,

- the strata corporation to give immediate notice of a claim to the insurer and cooperate with the insurer in the investigation of a loss, and

- the insurer to reinstate the amount of insurance after a loss is paid, for the remainder of the policy period.

Usually, vacancies in excess of 60 days in individual strata lots need not be reported to the strata insurer.[1] However, reporting is necessary if the entire premises, or a substantial portion of the premises, as a whole, is vacant.

Boiler and Machinery Insurance

Although not mandated by the *Strata Property Act*, boiler and machinery coverage is certainly essential for any strata property with a boiler or other mechanical or electrical equipment.

The Coverage

It insures direct damage to strata property and property in the strata's care, custody and control, caused by explosion of boilers and other types of pressure vessels. It also insures accidental breakdown of boilers, mechanical and electrical equipment.

The full amount of the insured property value should be available, subject, of course, to a deductible, usually of around $500 per accident.

---

[1] Significant vacancies, of 30 to 60 days or more, in individual strata lots must be reported to the unit owner's or tenant's insurer.

Combined

Although it is unlikely that a loss under this insurance will cause total destruction of all insured locations, boilers can explode with tremendous force causing major damage. As a result, insurance that combines the property and boiler and machinery coverages and amounts, ensures adequate protection and avoids disputes between insurers that can occur when the property insurance is underwritten by a different insurer.

Extra Expense

The insurer will also pay an additional amount, generally up to $50,000, for extra expenses and expediting charges to reduce the duration of a breakdown. In fact, up to $100,000 may be available if these coverages are stated separately. Although they duplicate each other somewhat, retaining or combining them for $100,000 is preferred. They are extremely valuable for the extra cost of temporary repairs and for expediting charges like overtime labour costs and rapid means of transportation. Increased costs occasioned by laws, bylaws and regulations should also be covered.

Specific Losses

Separate sub-amounts of insurance often apply to specific types of losses, such as ammonia contamination of refrigerated items and water damage from hot water pipes, heat exchangers and air-conditioning units.

Additional Services

Strata councils should ask the insurer to conduct a survey of locations to determine what should be insured and to clarify what will not be covered by the insurer's standard form. On occasion, this can expose a critical, though not necessarily expensive, piece of equipment that is impossible to repair or replace quickly and ought to be covered.

Also, for no additional premium, boiler insurers often provide excellent loss control services that can eliminate separate fees for inspections.

Definitions

Object

Standard boiler policies insure only objects that are in use or connected ready for use. However, losses do occur while machinery is being repaired, dismantled or assembled. Although it is unlikely the insurer will agree to cover installation and testing of *new* machinery, coverage for *existing* objects in a state of disuse, disrepair, dismantling or assembly can and should be obtained.

Accident

To be covered, breakdowns must be sudden and accidental with simultaneous physical damage. Some policies permit discovery of damage at times of regular maintenance or repair of unrelated problems. This can be important when damage to expensive equipment is not detected until long after it has occurred.

If this is a concern, strata councils should approach their insurers or agents for occurrence-based coverage. This will respond to a loss occurring during the period of the policy irrespective of the date of discovery of the loss and even if discovered years after the expiry of the policy.

Exclusions

Usually excluded are losses caused by or resulting from fire and water, explosion outside the object, pollution and clean up, flood, earthquake, wind and indirect losses. Accidents caused by vandalism should be covered.

Conditions

Accidents must be brought to the attention of the insurer promptly, and no repairs undertaken or evidence removed without the insurer's approval, except to preserve property. Disagreements over the amount of loss will be settled by appraisers, appointed by the parties, and legal action against the insurer must be commenced within specified time frames.

Crime Insurance

Good procedural controls, including separating sensitive job duties, are the most effective way of preventing crime. Prompt deposits of cash and cheques reduce burglary exposure—bright lights and alarms do, too.

What is Insured?

Strata policies can offer up to five varieties of crime coverages. Usually only employee dishonesty and interior and messenger robbery insurance are sufficient. Respectively, they cover loss of money, securities and other property caused by the fraudulent or dishonest act of an employee and loss of money or securities in a robbery.

The amount of insurance for employee dishonesty is usually $10,000 per employee or, if the employee cannot be identified, $10,000 per loss. For interior and messenger robbery, the amount is lower, usually $5,000. Often, there is no deductible.

The crime coverages tend to be fairly broad, covering all employees on a blanket basis, except additions created by mergers and acquisitions that must be reported within 30 days or some other specified period.

The amount of insurance, though not significant, is usually enough to cover the crime risk of strata corporations that do not keep large amounts of cash on site. Watch for seasonal or bonus periods; if these create additional risk, ensure the amount of insurance reflects this need.

Enhancements

When changing insurers, it is very important to notify the insurer on the expiring policy of any anticipated or potential losses that may have occurred during the period of the expiring policy, even though they have not materialized by the time the policy expires. This ensures their recovery from the expired insurance. A new insurance policy will not pay such a loss unless there is a "loss under prior policy" provision.

A "loss under prior policy" provision will ensure that a recently-discovered loss that would have been covered under a prior insurance policy is covered under the current policy.

In fact, the insured usually has a year or two following *termination of the policy* to discover and report losses to the insurer. Although the crime must be committed during the policy period, and coverage for an employee will be deemed cancelled immediately upon discovery of a criminal act by that employee, it is possible to obtain an extended reporting period following *termination of an employee.* This will cover additional losses, not yet discovered, arising from crimes committed by that employee prior to termination.

Definitions Creating Duplications

Strata councils should check the definition of "employee" in their crime coverage. Paid employees, including employees of strata managers, are covered while in the regular employ of the insured. This may create a duplication of coverage with the strata managers' bonding. If so, this coverage can be traded in for other coverage improvements.

What You See is What You Get

The property stolen need not be owned by the insured, and it will be replaced based on the actual cash value or with material of like kind and quality.

However, the insurer will not pay for the costs of establishing a loss; nor for consequential damages such as loss of potential income, like interest. Moreover, the insured must be able to prove the loss without computations of inventory or profit and loss.

General Liability Insurance

Liability insurance is no longer an option—the *Strata Property Act* mandates it. Strata corporations created prior to July 1, 2000 had until January 1, 2002 to comply with this requirement.[1]

Section 150 of the Act states:

> **150 (1) The strata corporation must obtain and maintain liability insurance to insure the strata corporation against liability for property damage and bodily injury.**
>
> **(2) The insurance must be of at least the amount required in the regulations.[2]**

The minimum amount of liability insurance required by the regulations is $2 million. In practice, however, most strata councils buy liability insurance of at least $5 million. The insurance covers claims by *third parties* for injury to their property or person, arising from operations usual to strata managers and owners. As such, it does not cover claims by the strata corporation for damage to common property. Nor does it apply to claims from owners for injury to themselves, their personal property or their strata lots.

---

[1] *Strata Property Regulation*, s. 17.4.
[2] *Strata Property Act*, s. 150(1), (2) and *Strata Property Regulation*, s. 9.2.

Investigation and defence costs are often provided in addition to the sum insured. This is helpful because defending a bodily injury claim can be very expensive.

There is also, usually, medical expense coverage of $2,500 per person and $25,000 for all persons, per policy year, for minor medical attention and treatment at the scene of an accident in or around the insured property.

Neither tenant's legal liability nor non-owned auto insurance is usually required by strata corporations. Tenant's legal liability is of interest to owners and their tenants; and non-owned auto, to strata corporations whose employees are expected to use their vehicles for strata business. If applicable, these matters should be discussed with the insurer or agent.

Bodily Injury and Property Damage

Strata corporation policies are not always clear about what is covered, the amounts insured or deductibles. An example is whether there is coverage for personal injury such as libel, slander and invasion of privacy. It ought to be covered, stated and defined.

Pollution Liability

Commonly, policies contain limited pollution coverage, provided the pollution is not usual to the business of the strata corporation or the owners and tenants, and that it is detected and reported to the insurer within a very short time frame, usually 120 hours. Proximity to the ocean, lakes and rivers can make this coverage especially important. Commercial owners and tenants should be made aware of the terms of the strata corporation's coverage and they, too, should carry pollution liability insurance.

Health Clubs

Health clubs pose unique liability hazards that are not covered for owners but, arguably, may be covered for tenants and are covered for guests, unless there is a specific exclusion. Strata councils should notify their insurers of the specific amenities, facilities and equipment on the property insured and obtain clarification of the coverage provided. As a loss prevention measure, strata corporations should post signs in every facility that people using the facilities and equipment do so at their own risk.

Contract Liability

Liability assumed by the strata corporation under a contract is normally excluded from coverage. However, some policies allow coverage for liability assumed under an "insured contract" as defined.

Such contracts normally include leases, sidetrack agreements, easements, municipality indemnities, elevator maintenance agreements and parts of contracts in which the legal liability of another is assumed before injury or damage. These exceptions are usually broad enough to encompass most situations in which the strata corporation assumes a liability under contract. Nevertheless, if available at little or no cost, the strata council should obtain a "blanket contractual" endorsement and, if in doubt about any particular contract, get the insurer's specific confirmation of coverage.

Liquor Liability

Some commercial owners are exposed to liquor and other unique liabilities. Strata corporations should be named, as insureds, in these owners' policies in case they are added to lawsuits against the commercial owners.

Owners Not Covered

Injury to owners and damage to property they own or occupy or to personal property in their care, custody or control is not covered. This is third party liability insurance, sometimes called "public liability" insurance.

Tenants are covered for injury to their person or property occurring on common property. Guests and others are covered everywhere. Whether owners are covered for injury or damage occurring on common property is an interesting issue discussed in Gerry Fanaken's book. He maintains they are and points to insurance settlements to owners in these circumstances.[1]

Medical Payments

Subject usually to exclusions for owners, joggers and workers, this insurance makes limited payments to third parties injured in accidents in and around the insured property. Incidental medical malpractice committed by persons ministering to injured third parties in these circumstances (other than medical practitioners) is also covered.

A word of caution: in the event of multiple accidents, the strata council may *not* want to offer medical payments, to preserve the amount of liability coverage generally. Medical payments reduce the amount of insurance and are not a legal obligation for strata corporations.

---

[1] Gerry Fanaken, *Understanding and Improving the Condominium Concept: An Authoritative Guidebook* (Vancouver, Vancouver Condominium Services Ltd., 1994), p. 133.

Conditions

The liability insurance has its own set of conditions, which include:

- prompt reporting of claims and accidents to the insurer,

- cooperating with and assisting the insurer to enforce any rights of the strata corporation,

- not making any payments or assuming any obligations without the insurer's consent, except for first aid, and

- bringing legal action against the insurer within one year of a settlement or judgment.

Most policies require that any applicable property insurance be called upon before the liability insurance responds. A "cross liability" clause ensures that the insurance responds to each insured named in the policy, but this will not increase the amount of insurance.

Directors' and Officers' Liability Insurance

Although this insurance is still optional under the legislation, strata council members are held to the same objective standard of care as that required of directors of companies and non-profit societies, regardless of their experience. Nor can they escape liability by delegating their responsibilities to an outside management company. As a result, this insurance is a necessity for strata councils.[1]

---

[1] *Strata Property Act*, s. 31. For information about a strata council member's standard of care, see Chapter 7, *Strata Council*.

What is Covered?

Directors' and Officers' Liability Insurance (D&O) covers losses arising from mismanagement by the strata council members and the strata manager.

A minimum amount of $1 million is recommended; more for larger strata corporations engaged in sizeable contracts. Deductibles of $500 per claim are common and, usually, defence costs are payable in addition to the amount insured.

This insurance is written on a claims made basis. This means claims must be reported to the current insurer, no matter when the mismanagement occurred. The claims made nature of the coverage requires that any increased amount of insurance purchased for a temporary increased exposure must be carried for as long as a risk of claims from that exposure exists.

What is Not Covered?

Most Directors' and Officers' Liability Insurance policies exclude coverage for:

- dishonesty

- bodily injury and property damage

- personal gain

- fines and penalties for failing to comply with the Act

- salaries

- breach of contract

- violation of civil rights and discrimination

There are also exclusions for loss from the purchase or sale of securities and from obtaining and maintaining insurance in amount, nature, form, and scope. The latter make it extremely important for the strata council to purchase the proper insurance and to make sure it is renewed on time each year.

Who is Covered?

The definition of insured should include the strata corporation as an entity, not just in terms of its responsibility to indemnify the directors and officers.

Employees, security, cleaning and gardening personnel, as well as committee members and volunteers, can also be added to the definition. Potentially however, this can erode the amount of insurance available to the elected officials and should be considered carefully.

Bylaws

Strata council members are entitled to be reimbursed by the strata corporation for losses they sustain in claims arising from strata council activities done in good faith, if the bylaws provide for it. Although section 22 of the Standard Bylaws excuses a council member from liability in certain circumstances, the bylaw does not require the strata corporation to indemnify a council member for expenses incurred in his or her defence. To indemnify a council member in these circumstances, a strata corporation may amend its bylaws. To ensure that the amended bylaw meets council's needs, the strata corporation should first obtain legal advice about the appropriate wording for the indemnity bylaw.

General

Sections

A section constitutes a form of mini-government within a strata corporation. The *Strata Property Act* permits a strata corporation to create sections of strata lot owners to represent the different interests of those owners.[1] A section is limited to obtaining insurance only against perils that are not insured by the strata corporation, or for amounts in excess of amounts insured by the strata corporation.[2]

Air Space Strata Plans

Agreements between air space strata corporations[3] and the owners of the supporting property should require each party to maintain the insurance specified in the Act as a minimum, and additional coverage, if appropriate. As well, the agreements must address the risk of loss of occupancy, use or enjoyment that could be caused to one party by damage to or destruction of the other's property.

Unless they are insured under a common policy, the owners of these properties must be insureds in each other's insurance policies to the extent of their interests in the property insured for access, support, utilities, maintenance and other necessary benefits. After a loss, this should be sufficient to protect their respective interests in repairing, replacing or rebuilding the property of the other should the other, for whatever reason, fail or refuse to do so.

If there is any doubt about this, the parties' interests should be recorded in the policies by endorsement. As coverage follows the insureds, not the property, and then,

---

[1]For more information about sections, see Chapter 10, *Sections*.
[2]*Strata Property Act*, s. 194(4).
[3]For more information about air space strata plans, see Chapter 4, *Strata Plan Types, Styles, and Uses*.

only for loss or damage to property *owned* by the insureds, the policies must include all parties to be insured and must specify their interests. This is critical with property that is not *owned* by them but in which they have an insurable interest.

Another reason for capturing the coverage by endorsement and not relying on the named insured provision alone is to ensure that the risks to be insured are not eliminated or limited by any other terms of the policy. For instance, it could be argued that loss of use or occupancy of an air space property caused by damage to the supporting property is not *direct physical* loss as is usually required or is *consequential* or *contractual* loss which is usually excluded from coverage. Ideally, the air space agreements should be made part of the contracts of insurance and the insurance endorsed to reference them and provide the requisite coverage irrespective of the general policy terms concerning indirect, contractual and consequential loss or damage.

Check also that the "other insurance" clause in each policy works in tandem and that any subrogation clauses are amended as required. Finally, it is a good idea to require the insurer of each policy to give at least 30 days' notice of material alteration or cancellation of the policy to all parties with an insured interest.

Outside Contracts and Contingencies

Strata councils should always check that outside contractors carry their own general liability insurance. Professionals such as construction contractors, architects, engineers, accountants, lawyers, brokers, strata managers, security personnel and other service providers should also carry professional liability or errors and omissions insurance.

The insurance should be sufficient to cover any reasonably anticipated losses. In substantial projects, one rule of thumb is $1 million minimum or an amount equal to the cost of the project, whichever is higher. Moreover, the amount should apply per project or location so it is not exhausted by claims on other projects. Alternatively, an increase to the aggregate amount of insurance may be sufficient. The strata corporation should be added, as a named insured, to the contractor's insurance for its projects. This will not require additional premiums and will ensure the strata corporation has coverage, along with the contractor, should it be named in a lawsuit for loss or damage caused by the work of the contractor.

Similarly, add the contractor to the strata corporation's property insurance, as a named insured, for the same reasons. In any event, report all new projects to the insurer or agent and obtain advice for coverage of any additional risks that may be attracted.

Strata Managers

Strata management contracts normally provide that the manager act in the best interests of the strata corporation, arrange insurance and obtain property valuations from qualified appraisers.

Strata management contracts usually also require the strata manager to carry liability insurance for property damage, bodily injury or death arising from his or her willful or negligent acts. This may be a duplication of coverage if the strata manager is a named insured on the strata corporation's policy. Since most responsible property management companies carry this insurance anyway, it is not an onerous requirement.

The most important insurance requirement of the property management company is that it carry fidelity insurance or be bonded. Although not required by the Act, bonding should be mandatory for anyone who handles strata corporation funds, including the council members. The amount of coverage should be a multiple of the strata fees and any special levies. Two signatories for cheques issued on the strata's behalf is an effective control provided use of pre-signed cheques is prohibited.

It is strongly recommended that strata managers and insurance agents carry professional liability or errors and omissions insurance, as well. This covers monetary losses caused by their negligence in performing, or failing to perform, professional services for the strata corporation. The amount of insurance should:

- be substantial,

- apply per strata corporation, and

- include a multiple aggregate per policy period.

Owners

There is a risk that owners will default on their monthly strata fees and special levies if they suffer a significant, uninsured, individual loss. Therefore, the strata corporation has an interest in ensuring that each owner, residential or commercial, is adequately protected by property and liability insurance for their own strata lot losses.

In addition to covering improvements and betterments to individual strata lots, a unit owner's insurance can also cover assessments for loss to the strata corporation's property and arising from its liability. Note, however, that this coverage may be limited where the assessment is levied to cover the cost of the deductible in the strata corporation's policy.

Although not a requirement under the Act, and often not addressed in the bylaws, strata councils should require or, at the very least, encourage owners to buy separate unit owner's insurance.

Conclusion

Insurance arranged by reputable brokers and agents will provide good, broad-form coverage, secured by well-known, established companies. It fulfills the minimal requirements of the legislation and generally protects strata corporations from the anticipated perils for reasonable premiums.

Premiums

A few brokerage houses have managed to secure a large share of condominium business and, as a result, have been able to offer their clients excellent premium reductions in recent years. This is due largely to bulk buying and also reflects the highly competitive state of the insurance market at this time.

However, strata corporations should be attentive to significant premium reductions and offers unrelated to a change in risk. Sometimes, these spell concurrent reductions in coverage, increases in deductibles or, worse, material changes in the security of the insurers underwriting the coverage.

Competition

One disadvantage of bulk buying is that it tends to limit coverage and service to a one-size-fits-all approach. This can be unresponsive to the specific needs of particular strata corporations. If this is a problem, approach other insurance brokers or agents for the extra coverage and alternate quotations on renewal. Don't expect premiums to be reduced further, but it may be possible to enhance the coverage and the security of the providers. Be sure to include a complete history and as much information as possible to new providers to avoid an uninsured loss during the changeover.

Chapter 17

COMMON PROPERTY

Definition

In a strata development, property is either part of a strata lot or part of the common property.[1]

The *Strata Property Act* defines common property as follows:

> 1. (1) "common property" means
>
> > (a) that part of the land and buildings shown on a strata plan that is not part of a strata lot, and
> >
> > (b) pipes, wires, cables, chutes, ducts and other facilities for the passage or provision of water, sewage, drainage, gas, oil, electricity, telephone, radio, television, garbage, heating and cooling systems, or other similar services, if they are located:
> >
> > > i) within a floor, wall or ceiling that forms a boundary
> > >
> > > > (A) between a strata lot and another strata lot,
> > > >
> > > > (B) between a strata lot and the common property, or
> > > >
> > > > (C) between a strata lot or common property and another parcel of land, or
> > >
> > > ii) wholly or partially within a strata lot, if they are capable of being and intended to be used in connection with the enjoyment of another strata lot or the common property;[2]

---

[1]*Strata Property Act*, ss. 1(1) (definition of "common property") and 244(2).
[2]*Ibid.*

By virtue of paragraph (b)(ii) of this definition, "pipes, wires, cables, chutes, ducts and other facilities" are common property, even if they are located, "wholly or partially within a strata lot, if they are capable of being and intended to be used in connection with the enjoyment of another strata lot or the common property." For example, in *Taychuk v. The Owners, Strata Plan LMS 744*,[1] the Supreme Court of British Columbia regarded pipes *inside* a strata lot as common property. The pipes supplied a bathtub and several sinks with badly discolored water. The court found that the relevant pipes inside the strata lot were connected to other pipes that serviced all the other units in the building. Applying this definition of *common property*, the court inferred from these circumstances that the relevant pipes inside the strata lot were intended to be used in connection with the enjoyment of another strata lot.[2] Since the pipes constituted common property, the strata corporation was responsible to repair the water problem.[3]

Common property is collectively owned by all strata lot owners, as tenants in common, with each having a share equal to the owner's proportional share of unit entitlement.[4] As an owner of the common property, an owner is permitted to use and enjoy the common property unless the use of the property has been restricted in some way.

Restrictions

There are three main ways an owner, or in some cases a tenant, may acquire the right to use common property as though it belongs to that individual.

---

[1]*Taychuk v. The Owners, Strata Plan LMS 744* (2002), 7 R.P.R. (4th) 302, [2002] B.C.J. No. 2653, 2002 B.C.S.C. 1638 (S.C.).
[2]*Taychuk v. The Owners, Strata Plan LMS 744*, 2002 B.C.S.C. 1638 at para. 28.
[3]For information about repairs, see Part V, *Repairs*.
[4]*Strata Property Act*, s. 66.

1. The developer, or later, the eligible voters, may designate the area as limited common property (LCP).

2. The strata corporation may permit an owner or tenant to exercise short-term, exclusive-use over the relevant area.

3. In the early stages of the development, a developer may take a long-term lease over a portion of the common property. The long-term lease gives the developer the exclusive right to occupy the relevant area, for example, the right to occupy the portion of common property used for parking vehicles. Later, the developer typically sells a partial assignment, or a sublease, of his or her rights under the long-term lease to the first purchaser, perhaps by selling the purchaser an assignment of the right to use a particular parking stall. Alternatively, in some cases a developer enters a licence agreement with the strata corporation instead of taking a long-term lease. In a similar fashion, the developer may later sell a sub-licence to a first purchaser.

Limited Common Property (LCP)

The *Strata Property Act* defines limited common property as follows:

> 1. (1) **"limited common property" means common property designated for the exclusive use of the owners of one or more strata lots.**[1]

The developer, or later the eligible voters, can designate common property as LCP. The only sure way to verify whether, for example, a balcony, patio, or any other feature is LCP is to check *both* the strata plan and the resolutions dealing with common property filed at the Land Title Office.

---

[1] *Strata Property Act*, s. 1(1) (definition of "limited common property"). For the definition of an "owner," see also Chapter 8, *Members*.

The LCP designation attaches to a strata lot, whoever from time to time is the owner of that lot. Because the LCP designation attaches to the strata lot, the right to use the LCP is passed to a new owner when the property is sold, or to a tenant if the property is leased.

Every owner who has the right to use LCP must allow the strata corporation reasonable access to the LCP for the strata corporation to perform its duties.[1]

Developers' LCP Designation

A developer can designate common property as LCP when he or she files the strata plan at the Land Title Office.[2] The developer's LCP designation appears on the strata plan. See Appendix A for an example of developer-designated LCP among the sample strata plan excerpts.

No uniform practice exists among developers in the way they designate common property as LCP in strata plans. In one building, for example, all of the balconies and patios may be designated as LCP in the strata plan. On the other hand, in the strata plan for the building next door, each balcony and patio may be part of its associated strata lot. Never assume that because a balcony or patio is associated with a strata lot that the balcony or patio is LCP. The only sure way to tell is by checking the strata plan and any resolutions dealing with the common property at the Land Title Office.

After depositing a strata plan, and before the first AGM, a developer may only amend the strata plan by the unanimous resolution of the eligible voters at a general meeting, subject to the exception below for parking stalls.[3]

If the eligible voters wish to remove the developer's LCP designation, they must pass a unanimous resolution to

---

[1] *Strata Property Act*, s. 77.
[2] *Ibid.*, s. 73.
[3] *Ibid.*, s. 257.

amend the strata plan to remove the LCP designation and then file a reference or explanatory plan, whichever the Registrar requires, in the prescribed form.[1] The strata corporation must also file a Certificate of Strata Corporation (Form E), being the required form, to certify passage of the necessary resolution.[2] The form is found among the forms in the regulations.

LCP Parking Stalls

The *Strata Property Act*, however, creates an exception for LCP parking stalls. At any time before the first annual general meeting (AGM), the *Strata Property Act* permits the developer to amend the strata plan to unilaterally designate existing parking stalls as LCP.[3] In doing so, the developer acts as the strata council and must act in good faith with a view to the best interests of the strata corporation.[4]

Alternatively, if certain requirements are met to ensure a minimum number of parking stalls, the developer may also designate up to a maximum of two parking stalls per strata lot as LCP.[5] In this case, the developer is not required to act in the best interests of the strata corporation.[6]

Except in certain phased developments, these LCP parking provisions are not available to a developer who deposited the strata plan before July 1, 2000, when the *Strata Property Act* came into force.[7]

Owners' LCP Designation

The eligible voters can change the designation of common property to LCP with or without amending the strata plan.[8]

---

[1] *Strata Property Act*, ss. 75(1) and 257.
[2] *Strata Property Act*, s. 257 and *Strata Property Regulation*, Form E.
[3] *Strata Property Act*, s. 258(1).
[4] *Ibid.*, s. 258(2).
[5] *Ibid.*, s. 258(3).
[6] *Ibid.*, s. 258(5).
[7] *Strata Property Regulation*, s. 17.19. For information about phased developments, see Chapter 31, *Phases*.
[8] *Strata Property Act*, ss. 73(b), (c) and 257.

Amending the Strata Plan

The eligible voters may change the designation from common property to LCP by amending the strata plan. This requires a unanimous vote at an annual or special general meeting.[1]

After passing the necessary resolution, the strata corporation must apply to the Registrar of Land Titles to amend the plan by filing a reference or explanatory plan, whichever the Registrar requires, in the prescribed form.[2] The strata corporation must also file a Certificate of Strata Corporation (Form E), being the required form, to certify passage of the necessary resolution. When the owners use this method to designate common property as LCP, the LCP designation appears in the amended strata plan in the drawing showing the particular area.

If the eligible voters want to remove an LCP designation they previously made by amending the strata plan, they must follow the same steps in reverse. The eligible voters must pass a unanimous resolution to amend the strata plan to remove the LCP designation and then file the necessary documents with the Registrar at the Land Title Office.[3]

Without Amending the Strata Plan

The eligible voters may designate common property as LCP *without* amending the strata plan with a 3/4 vote at an annual or special general meeting.[4]

After passing the necessary resolution designating common property as LCP, the strata corporation must file the resolution in the Land Title Office with a sketch, satisfactory to the Registrar, that defines the area of LCP and specifies each strata lot whose owners are entitled to exclusively use the LCP. The resolution designating

---

[1] *Strata Property Act*, s. 257(a).
[2] *Ibid.*, s. 257.
[3] *Ibid.*, ss. 75(1) and 257.
[4] *Ibid.*, s. 74.

common property as LCP is not effective until it is filed at the Land Title Office.[1]

When the eligible voters use this method to designate common property as LCP, the LCP designation does *not* show up in the drawing for that area in the strata plan because the owners have not amended the strata plan. Instead, the Registrar records the resolution changing the designation from common property to LCP among the resolutions dealing with common property.

If the eligible voters want to remove an LCP designation they previously made by 3/4 vote, they must follow the same steps in reverse. The eligible voters must pass a resolution by 3/4 vote to remove the LCP designation and then file the resolution at the Land Title Office.[2] The resolution removing the LCP designation is not effective until it is filed at the Land Title Office.[3]

Short-Term Exclusive-Use

The strata corporation may give an owner or tenant permission to exclusively use common property that is not designated LCP, or to use a common asset.[4] Instead of exclusive use, the strata corporation can also give an owner or tenant a special privilege.[5] For example, in strata plans where parking stalls and storage lockers are common property, strata corporations typically use short-term, exclusive-use arrangements to assign particular stalls and lockers to individual owners and tenants.

If the permission or privilege involves a significant change in the use or appearance of the common property, the eligible voters must first approve the arrangement by a 3/4 vote at a general meeting.[6] In all other cases, the strata

---

[1] *Strata Property Act*, s. 74(3).
[2] *Ibid.*, s. 75(2).
[3] *Ibid.*, s. 75(3).
[4] *Ibid.*, s. 76(1).
[5] *Ibid.*
[6] *Ibid.*, ss. 71 and 76.

council, on behalf of the strata corporation, may give the necessary permission or grant the privilege.

The strata corporation must not grant a permission or privilege for more than one year.[1] The strata corporation can also impose conditions on the permission or privilege.[2] Upon renewal, the strata corporation can change the period (bearing in mind the one-year maximum) and the conditions.[3]

The strata corporation can also cancel the permission or privilege at any time by giving the owner or tenant reasonable notice of the cancellation.[4]

Many owners entered short-term, exclusive-use arrangements before July 1, 2000, when the *Strata Property Act* came into force. In such cases, the regulations permit those arrangements to continue beyond July 1, 2000 in accordance with their terms. Those arrangements, however, may only be renewed in accordance with the *Strata Property Act*.[5]

In *Reid v. The Owners, Strata Plan No. LMS 2503,*[6] the superior courts in British Columbia narrowly interpreted certain privileges over common property.

In the *Reid* case, several strata lots adjoined a large entryway area that was designated as common property on the strata plan. The strata council passed a resolution under section 76(1) of the *Strata Property Act* giving two owners temporary permission to place specifically listed plants and other garden items on the common property area.

The complainant was an owner whose rear windows looked directly on to the entryway area. He complained that the owners with temporary permission had placed

---

[1] *Strata Property Act*, s. 76(2).
[2] *Ibid.*
[3] *Ibid.*, s. 76(3).
[4] *Ibid.*, s. 76(4).
[5] *Strata Property Regulation*, s. 17.7.
[6] *Reid v. The Owners, Strata Plan No. LMS 2503*, [2001] B.C.J. No. 2377; 2001 B.C.S.C. 1578 (S.C.), aff'd (2003), 179 B.C.A.C. 82, 12 B.C.L.R. (4th) 67, [2003] B.C.J. No. 417, 2003 B.C.C.A. 126 (C.A.), leave to appeal to S.C.C. dismissed without reasons 22 April 2004, [2003] S.C.C.A. No. 500.

some of their permitted shrubs directly in front of his windows, thereby obstructing his view. The complainant also argued that the same owners were using the area from time to time as a dog pen, a place to store personal belongings, a place to air out camping equipment, and as a place to host picnics, barbeques and parties where alcohol was served.

The complainant asked the court to revoke the strata council's resolution on the ground that the arrangement was significantly unfair to him, contrary to section 164 of the Act.

In the *Reid* case, the court found that the strata council's resolution only gave the other owners a special privilege, not exclusive use. The court, however, did not explain the significance of the distinction.

The placement of the shrubs across the complainant's view exceeded what the strata council's resolution authorized the owners to do. In other words, the owners went beyond their authority under the arrangement by placing the shrubs in those locations. The court advised that the council should take steps to ensure that the plants were placed elsewhere.

Similarly, there was evidence that the other owners were using the entryway area for pets, storage, the airing out of camping equipment, and social events as alleged by the complainant. The court pointed out that none of these uses were authorized by the council's resolution and that if the other owners were misusing the entryway in that fashion, the strata council should take steps to rectify the matter.

The court held, however, that the strata council's decision to permit the neighbours to place plants on the common property did not constitute the kind of burdensome or harsh conduct necessary to establish significant unfairness.[1] When the complainant later appealed against that decision, his appeal was dismissed.

---

[1] For information about an order to remedy a significantly unfair action or exercise of voting rights under section 164 of the *Strata Property Act*, see Chapter 27, *Lawsuits*.

The *Reid* case demonstrates that where a strata corporation gives an owner or tenant a special privilege or permission to use common property, a court will narrowly interpret that privilege or permission. An owner or tenant should never assume, for instance, that because a special privilege expressly allows her to do one thing, it necessarily implies that she may, in addition, do something else.

Long-Term Leases to the Developer

Some developers use a long-term lease to provide parking stalls to buyers. In those cases, the strata plan typically designates the parking stalls as common property. Before the first conveyance of any of the strata lots, the developer causes the strata corporation to lease all of the parking stalls to the developer or an affiliated company under a long-term lease, for example, for 99 years. Buyers wanting parking stalls must then purchase from the developer or the affiliated company, as the case may be, a partial assignment, or a sublease, of the developer's long-term lease for the use of particular parking stalls.

In some cases a developer enters a licence agreement with the strata corporation instead of taking a long-term lease. Although a licence is legally different from a lease, the practical effect of the developer's licence arrangement is usually the same from a purchaser's point of view.

Investigating Common Property

In a strata development the use of common property is often a cause for disputes among strata lot owners. Parking stalls, storage areas, rooftop decks, and landscaped areas around individual strata lots have generated the most difficulty.

Since the common property is available for use by all strata lot owners, an owner who wants exclusive use of a part of the common property must be able to point to some authority that gives the owner the right to use the area in question. Additionally, if an owner has a right to use some area of common property, it is important to know whether that right can pass to a subsequent purchaser, or to a tenant, if the owner leases the strata lot. The first step in determining how common property can be used is to find out whether the particular common property has been designated as LCP. Common property that is designated as LCP for a particular strata lot assures the owner of that strata lot that he or she is entitled to use that common property. This is so, regardless of whether the common property was designated by the developer, or at a later date by the strata corporation. The designation of LCP also assures subsequent owners or tenants that they too will have the right to use that particular piece of common property, subject to the designation being removed by a unanimous, or 3/4 vote as noted above.

If the particular property is not designated as LCP, it remains common property. While common property is available for use by all owners, other arrangements may have been made which permit an owner to exclusively use the relevant portion of the common property. If the property is not LCP, the second step in determining how the property can be used is to determine whether the strata corporation has granted an owner permission to exclusively use the particular common property or whether the property was leased by the developer.

A short-term, exclusive-use agreement made on or after July 1, 2000, when the *Strata Property Act* came into force, between an owner and the strata corporation that allows the owner to exclusively use common property, is limited to a maximum period of one year. Although the strata council, on behalf of the corporation, can renew the agreement, it could choose to not renew, or to renew on particular terms and conditions.[1] If an owner is using a piece of common property under the terms of an exclusive-use agreement, the owner has a less certain arrangement than if the property was designated LCP.

Since the short-term, exclusive-use agreement is granted to the owner personally and is not attached to the strata lot, the right to use the piece of common property does *not* automatically transfer to a purchaser or tenant when the owner sells the strata lot or leases the strata lot to a tenant. It is up to the purchaser or tenant to negotiate a new exclusive-use agreement with the strata council. When selling or leasing strata lots, owners who have an agreement to exclusively use common property should be careful not to promise the purchaser or tenant the use of that property.

Even though particular common property is not designated as LCP, or is not subject to an exclusive-use agreement, an owner may still be entitled to use that piece of common property as a result of the lease of the property by the developer. As a means of controlling the use of common property, the developer may have leased common property, and then assigned or subleased a portion of that common property to a first purchaser. In such cases it is necessary to look at the terms of the lease between the developer and the strata corporation, and the terms of the assignment or sublease from the developer to the first purchaser, and any further transfer of rights from the first purchaser to a subsequent purchaser, and so on, to know whether a current owner has the right to use that portion of common property, or to transfer the right to a purchaser or tenant.

Whenever there are areas such as parking stalls involved in a strata sale, the safest thing to do is check the registered strata plan and the resolutions dealing with the

---

[1] *Strata Property Act*, s. 76.

common property at the Land Title Office to identify what kind of legal interest in the parking stall the seller can pass to a purchaser.

Parking

The rights and duties of an owner, or tenant, in connection with a parking stall depend on the nature of the parking space.

To determine the nature of a strata parking stall, the governing principle is that in a strata development, property is either part of a strata lot or part of the common property. One must first examine the strata plan, the resolutions affecting common property and any other relevant documents. Only then can one identify whether the parking stall is part of a strata lot or part of the common property.

Strata Lot

In a non-residential strata development, a parking stall may be a separate strata lot on the strata plan.[1] This is no longer allowed in a residential strata plan.[2] In *rare* cases, however, in some older residential strata plans a parking stall may exist as a separate strata lot.

Alternatively, a parking stall may appear on a strata plan as part of a strata lot.

In either case, whether a parking stall is by itself a separate strata lot, or part of a strata lot, whoever is the registered owner of the strata lot is the legal owner of the parking space.

---

[1]See, for example, *The Owners, Strata Plan No. VR 1767 v. Seven Estate Ltd. et al.* (2002), 49 R.P.R. (3rd) 156, [2002] B.C.J. No. 755, 2002 B.C.S.C. 381 (S.C.).
[2]*Strata Property Act*, s. 244(2).

Common Property

Parking areas are most often common property. If a parking stall is common property, one of the following arrangements, as previously described, usually applies:

(a) The parking stall is limited common property;

(b) The strata corporation has assigned the short-term, exclusive-use of the parking stall to an individual owner or tenant; or

(c) The portion of the common property used for parking is subject to a lease in favour of the developer, or someone associated with the developer, who has sold a partial assignment of rights under that lease to a first purchaser to use the parking stall. Normally, the first purchaser will assign his or her rights under the lease to the next purchaser and so on. Alternatively, in rare cases the developer may substitute a licence scheme for a long-term lease in this model.

The use of parking areas can be further complicated by the mistaken promises of the developer. Here is what happened in *Hill v. Strata Plan NW 2477*.[1]

Case Study

The seller was the developer of a new strata complex. The buyers wanted two parking stalls with their strata unit.

In the strata plan, the area containing the parking stalls was common property.

The Contract of Purchase and Sale said, in part,

---

[1]*Hill v. Strata Plan NW 2477* (1991), 57 B.C.L.R. (2d) 263, 2 B.C.A.C. 289, 81 D.L.R. (4th) 720 (B.C.C.A.).

Vendor guarantees two parking spots with unit.

Shortly before completion, the strata corporation called its first AGM. At the meeting, the owners passed a new bylaw limiting parking stalls to one per unit. Owners wishing additional stalls would have to apply to the strata corporation and pay a set monthly fee.

When the buyers considered legal action, they learned for the first time that all of the parking stalls were the common property of the strata corporation. The developer had no authority to sell the parking stalls.

The court refused to permit the developer's promise in the contract to override the registered strata plan. Since the strata plan designated the parking stalls as common property, only the strata corporation could dispose of, or otherwise regulate, the stalls.

Despite the buyers' contract with the developer, the new bylaw governed the situation. If the buyers wanted a second parking stall, they would have to apply to the strata corporation and pay the monthly fee under the bylaw.

Presumably, the buyers would have to claim against the developer for any damages suffered as a result of the developer's failed promise to provide "two parking spots" under the contract.

To assist strata lot owners in dealing with parking stalls, the *Strata Property Act* requires the strata corporation to keep a list of owners with their strata lot addresses and parking stall numbers, if any.[1]

---

[1] *Strata Property Act*, s. 35(1)(c)(i).

Changes to Common Property

Significant Change in Use

It is possible for the members of a strata corporation to change the use or appearance of common property or common assets. For example, a strata corporation may wish to remove a hot tub, pave an area of grass to create a parking area for recreational vehicles, or turn the caretaker's suite into a woodworking room.

The *Strata Property Act* requires that to make a significant change to the use or appearance of common property or land that is a common asset the change must be approved by a resolution passed by 3/4 vote. The only exception to the need for a 3/4 vote is a situation where the change is necessary to ensure safety or prevent significant loss or damage.[1]

Alterations to Common Property

The Standard Bylaws require that before an owner makes an alteration to common property, including LCP and common assets, the written approval of the strata corporation must be obtained.[2] As noted above, if the alteration results in a significant change in the use or appearance of common property, a 3/4 vote at a general meeting is also required.

Additionally, the Standard Bylaws provide that the strata corporation may require an owner to take responsibility for any expenses relating to an alteration to common property as a condition of the strata corporation's approval.[3] For example, suppose that a wooden deck is common property or LCP. If an owner wished to install a

---

[1] *Strata Property Act*, s. 71.
[2] *Strata Property Act, Schedule of Standard Bylaws*, s. 6.
[3] *Schedule of Standard Bylaws*, s. 6. For information about the *Schedule of Standard Bylaws*, see Chapter 19, *Statutory Bylaws and the Effect of the Strata Property Act*.

vinyl coating on the deck, permission from the strata corporation would be required. Additionally, the permission may depend upon the owner's written agreement to take responsibility for additional expenses that arise as a result of the installation of the vinyl coating.

There are important legal considerations when a strata corporation enters into an agreement permitting an owner to alter common property. For information about these considerations, see Chapter 25, *Carrying Out Repair or Maintenance Work*.

Common Assets

The Act creates the term *common asset,*[1] which is property held by or on behalf of the strata corporation. The asset may be personal property, like a lawn mower, or real property. If the asset is real property, it may appear in the strata plan, in which case it must be shown as a strata lot in the plan. For example, the strata corporation may own a strata lot used as the caretaker's suite. Alternatively, the asset may be land that is not shown on the strata plan. The strata corporation may, for instance, own the parcel of land next door to the strata development.

Common Facilities

Typically, a common facility is an important amenity located on common property and which all the owners may use.

The former *Condominium Act* and the *Strata Property Act* both use the term common facilities, but the meaning of the phrase appears more restricted in the current legislation.

---

[1] *Strata Property Act*, s. 1(1) (definition of "common asset").

The *Condominium Act* defined a common facility as:[1]

> ... a facility that is available for the use of all the owners, and, without limiting this definition, may include a laundry room, playground, swimming pool, recreation centre, clubhouse or tennis court.

The *Condominium Act* did not restrict the use of the phrase *common facilities* to any particular kind of strata plan.

The *Strata Property Act* only uses the term *common facilities* in connection with phased developments.[2] For the purpose of the phasing provisions, the Act defines common facilities as,[3]

> ... a major facility in a phased strata plan, including a laundry room, playground, swimming pool, recreation centre, clubhouse or tennis court, if the facility is available for the use of the owners.

In strata plans filed on or after July 1, 2000 when the *Strata Property Act* came into force, the term *common facilities* will only be used in phased projects.

User Fees

Except as set out in the regulations, a strata corporation must not impose user fees for the use of common property or common assets by owners, tenants, occupants, or their visitors.[4] The regulations provide that user fees may be imposed for the use of common property or common assets if the fee is reasonable and is set out in either a bylaw or a rule that has been ratified at a general meeting.[5] These requirements, however, did not apply to a

---

[1]*Condominium Act*, s. 1(1) (definition of "common facility").
[2]For information about phased developments, see Chapter 31, *Phases*.
[3]*Strata Property Act*, s. 217.
[4]*Ibid.*, s. 110.
[5]*Strata Property Regulation*, s. 6.9.

strata corporation until January 1, 2002, if its strata plan was deposited before July 1, 2000, when the *Strata Property Act* came into force.[1]

Respecting Other Users

The Standard Bylaws prohibit an owner, tenant, occupant or visitor from using common property, or a common asset, in a way that causes a nuisance, creates a hazard, causes unreasonable noise, or unreasonably interferes with another person's right to use the common property, a common asset, or a strata lot.[2] Similarly, a person must not use common property or a common asset in a way that is illegal, or contrary to a purpose for which the common property or common asset is intended as shown by the strata plan.[3]

[1]*Strata Property Act*, ss. 2(1) and 110 and *Strata Property Regulation*, s. 17.4.
[2]*Schedule of Standard Bylaws*, s. 3.
[3]*Ibid.*

Part IV

BYLAWS AND RULES

A strata community regulates its affairs through bylaws and rules. Each strata corporation automatically receives a set of statutory bylaws when it is created. A strata community, however, can change those bylaws to express its own particular values. In addition, a strata council can make rules to regulate the use of common property and common assets.

Chapter 18

NEED FOR BYLAWS AND RULES

E very strata corporation must have bylaws. Rules are optional.

Bylaws

Bylaws serve as a strata corporation's constitution. They also reflect each strata community's values. A strata owner is always subject to the community interests expressed in the bylaws.

The bylaws govern how owners and tenants may use their strata lots, the common property and common assets. The bylaws also govern the administration of the strata corporation.[1]

Bylaws can have a significant influence on the operation of a strata corporation. They are also intrusive when they affect how an owner or a tenant may use his or her strata lot. For example, although we like to think that our home is our castle, in a residential strata complex the bylaws may, among other things, prohibit rentals, restrict the number of adults who may occupy a strata lot, or restrict pets.

When a strata corporation is created by the deposit of a strata plan, the corporation acquires the default bylaws contained in the statute in force at the time the strata plan was filed. The technical term for default bylaws is *standard bylaws*. However, because the default bylaws in the *Strata Property Act* are called the Standard Bylaws, the default bylaws contained in a statute will generally be referred to as the statutory bylaws.

---

[1] *Strata Property Act*, s. 119(2).

A strata corporation may change virtually everything in its statutory bylaws, subject to some legal restrictions. A corporation alters its statutory bylaws by passing a custom-made bylaw to add to, or subtract from, the statutory bylaws, or by creating a new bylaw or entirely deleting a statutory bylaw. To the extent that a custom-made bylaw deals with a particular subject in a way that differs from the statutory bylaws, the custom-made bylaw overrides the statutory bylaws.

The technical term for passing a custom-made bylaw is *amending the bylaws*. Similarly, a custom-made bylaw is called an *amended bylaw*. To be legally enforceable, an amended bylaw must be filed with the strata plan at the Land Title Office.

A strata corporation can tailor its bylaws to reflect the concerns of its members. Many strata corporations, for example, have amended their bylaws to address issues such as rental and pet restrictions. In addition to such common amendments, a strata corporation may wish to examine its operations and any areas that frequently cause disputes among strata lot owners. For example, a large strata corporation that has difficulties with the manner in which general meetings are conducted may wish to incorporate into its bylaws certain rules of order that relate to meeting procedures.

Any area that appears to be a recurring problem for the strata corporation may be resolved through a bylaw. In this way, owners know in advance how an issue is to be handled and that they have had input into determining the resolution.

The courts tend to interpret bylaws liberally, placing more emphasis on their purpose than technicalities. *Strata Plan VIS 4663 v. Little*,[1] is a good illustration.

---

[1]*Strata Plan VIS 4663 v. Little*, [2001] B.C.J. No. 850, 2001 B.C.C.A. 337.

Case Study

The court described the strata development as a very attractive village of permanently located recreational vehicles with significant improvements to most of them, including railed decks.

The bylaws established the maximum length and width for a recreational vehicle on a strata lot. The bylaws also said, in part,

> Awnings may be installed on permitted recreation vehicles **PROVIDED ALWAYS** that in no case shall awnings be enclosed with the exception of partial enclosures by transparent material. . . .

The owner made certain improvements to her strata lot, including construction of a deck adjacent to the exterior of her recreational vehicle. There was a small gap between the vehicle and the deck. The owner also built a roof over the entire deck and enclosed half the deck with siding, glass and a screen.

The strata corporation complained that the owner's new deck extended the width of her recreational vehicle beyond the maximum permitted by the bylaws. The owner apparently argued that the deck was not actually an extension because the small space separated the vehicle from the deck.

The strata corporation was prepared to characterize the new roof as an awning, but complained that the area enclosed with siding, glass and a screen breached the bylaws. The owner argued that the materials enclosing the deck were permissible because they were "transparent materials" within the meaning of the bylaws.

The Court of Appeal enforced the bylaws and upheld an earlier order requiring the owner to remove her improvements.

The Court of Appeal found that the deck extended the size of the recreational vehicle beyond the maximum permissible width, despite the gap separating the vehicle from the deck. The court also refused to characterize the materials used to enclose the deck as "transparent." The court described its reasoning, in part, as follows:[1]

> **Respect for collected governance of a community requires that bylaws be interpreted purposively, so that they accomplish the community's goals.**
>
> **In my view, the small gap is not enough reason to find that the improvement could not reasonably be regarded as an extension of the R.V. such that it now exceeds the permitted size. Moreover, the improvement the (owner) built can reasonably be regarded as not coming within the definition of an "awning." It is difficult to find that a combination of sliding door, glass and screen windows, and siding comparable to that on the R.V. constitutes a "partial enclosure of transparent material." To suggest otherwise would be to put the strata council in the straitjacket of a highly technical, literal interpretation of bylaws designed to be applied pragmatically and fairly for the good of the community.**

---

[1] *Strata Plan VIS 4663 v. Little*, [2001] B.C.J. No. 850 at paras. 21-22 per Huddart, J.A.

Rules

Rules are less formal than bylaws. They regulate the use of common property and common assets. Rules are optional; a strata corporation does not have to have them. A strata council may make rules without first consulting the owners, although the eligible voters must later ratify each new rule. Rules are not filed at the Land Title Office, but they form part of a strata corporation's records.

Sections

In some cases, the *Strata Property Act* permits a section to create bylaws respecting matters that relate solely to the section.[1] The strata corporation's bylaws apply to a section unless, in certain matters, the section has passed its own bylaw governing the matter. A section may only create a bylaw in respect of a matter that relates solely to the section.[2]

The *Strata Property Act* restricts the ability of a residential section to create bylaws before the strata corporation holds its first annual general meeting (AGM). In a residential section, and pending the first AGM, a unanimous vote by the eligible voters at a special general meeting of the strata corporation is necessary before the section may create a bylaw. This prerequisite does not apply if the section is non-residential.[3]

In addition, the executive of a section may make rules governing the use, safety and condition of land owned by the section, or limited common property (LCP) designated for the exclusive use of all the strata lots in the section.[4]

---

[1]*Strata Property Act*, ss. 194(2) and 197. For more information about sections, see Chapter 10, *Sections*.
[2]*Ibid.*, s. 197.
[3]*Ibid.*, ss. 127(4) and 197.
[4]*Ibid.*, s. 197.

The provisions of the *Strata Property Act* that govern a strata corporation's rules also apply to a section's rules.[1]

Everything concerning bylaws and rules of a strata corporation applies equally to a section, subject to the legislation and to any necessary modifications inherent in dealing with a section, as opposed to a strata corporation.

Access

The strata corporation must provide access to its bylaws and rules to every owner, tenant, or any other person authorized in writing by an owner or tenant.[2] If any of these persons ask to inspect the strata corporation's bylaws or rules, section 36(3) of the *Strata Property Act* and section 25 of the *Interpretation Act*, when read together, require the strata corporation to comply with the request within eight days.[3]

If any of these persons want copies of the relevant documents, the strata corporation may charge a fee for each copy and may refuse to provide copies until it receives payment.[4] The fee for copies must not exceed the maximum fee set out in the regulations—up to 25 cents per page.[5]

---

[1] *Strata Property Act*, ss. 197(5) and 125.
[2] *Ibid.*, s. 36.
[3] *Ibid.*, s. 36(3) and *Interpretation Act*, R.S.B.C. 1996, c. 238, s. 25.
[4] *Strata Property Act*, s. 36(4).
[5] *Strata Property Act*, s. 36(4) and *Strata Property Regulation*, s. 4.1.

Chapter 19

STATUTORY BYLAWS AND THE EFFECT OF THE STRATA PROPERTY ACT

Unless amended by a developer at the time the strata plan is filed, a strata corporation automatically receives a set of statutory bylaws. These bylaws are contained in the statute under which the strata corporation is created.

Prior to January 1, 2002, to assemble a complete set of a strata corporation's bylaws, the strata corporation combined that corporation's particular statutory bylaws with any amended bylaws filed at the Land Title Office. This method for identifying a strata corporation's statutory bylaws, however, changed effective January 1, 2002.

Identifying the Statutory Bylaws *Before* January 1, 2002

Over the years, the statutory bylaws have changed from time to time with amendments to the legislation.

Until December 31, 2001, to determine which set of statutory bylaws applied at a specific time, one had to know when the strata corporation's strata plan was deposited at the Land Title Office. Using the date the strata plan was filed, the following table identifies which statute prevailed at the relevant time and where to find the statutory bylaws in the statute.

Identifying the Statutory Bylaws *Before* January 1, 2002

Date in Force	Statute	Location of Statutory Bylaws
September 1, 1966	*Strata Titles Act,* S.B.C. 1966, c. 46	The 1st and 2nd schedule contained the statutory bylaws.
August 15, 1974	*Strata Titles Act,* S.B.C. 1974, c. 89	The 1st and 2nd schedule contained the statutory bylaws.
September 1, 1975	*Strata Titles Amendment Act,* S.B.C. 1975, c. 74	Among other things, this statute made some amendments to the prevailing statutory bylaws.
February 16, 1978	*Strata Titles Amendment Act, (No. 2),* S.B.C. 1977, c. 64	Among other things, this statute made some amendments to the prevailing statutory bylaws.
May 17, 1980	*Condominium Act,* R.S.B.C. 1979, c. 61	This statute consolidated in one document all the changes from 1974 to 1979. This Act also changed the name of the statute to the *Condominium Act.* The statutory bylaws were in Part 5 of the Act.
April 21, 1997	*Condominium Act,* R.S.B.C. 1996, c. 64	This statute consolidated in one document all the changes from 1979 to 1996. The statutory bylaws remained in Part 5 of the Act.
July 1, 2000	*Strata Property Act,* S.B.C. 1998, c. 43, as amended	The statutory bylaws are in the *Schedule of Standard Bylaws.*

For example, a strata corporation created under the former *Condominium Act* acquired the set of statutory bylaws found in Part 5 of that Act.[1] On the other hand, a strata corporation created on or after July 1, 2000, automatically inherits the statutory bylaws found in the *Schedule of Standard Bylaws* at the back of the *Strata Property Act.*[2]

---

[1] *Condominium Act*, s. 26(2).
[2] *Strata Property Act*, s. 120(1).

Identifying the Standard Bylaws *On or After* January 1, 2002

Effective January 1, 2002, the Standard Bylaws in the *Strata Property Act* are deemed to be the statutory bylaws for *every* strata corporation, no matter when the strata corporation was created.[1]

For example, consider a strata plan that was deposited while the former *Condominium Act* was in force. Until December 31, 2001, the statutory bylaws found in Part 5 of the *Condominium Act* served as the corporation's statutory bylaws. As of January 1, 2002, the statutory bylaws of the strata corporation changed. On that date, the bylaws found in the *Schedule of Standard Bylaws* at the back of the *Strata Property Act* became the strata corporation's statutory bylaws. The statutory bylaws found in Part 5 of the *Condominium Act* are no longer the corporation's statutory bylaws.

Exception for Pets

The statutory bylaws in the former *Condominium Act* were silent on the subject of pets. By contrast, section 3(4) of the Standard Bylaws in the *Strata Property Act* contains the following pet restriction:

> **3. (4) An owner, tenant or occupant must not keep any pets on a strata lot other than one or more of the following:**
>
> > **(a) a reasonable number of fish or other small aquarium animals;**
> >
> > **(b) a reasonable number of small caged mammals;**
> >
> > **(c) up to 2 caged birds;**
> >
> > **(d) one dog or one cat.**

---

[1]*Strata Property Regulation*, s. 17.11(3).

Effective January 1, 2002, every strata corporation inherited the pet restriction in section 3(4) of the Standard Bylaws, except to the extent that a corporation has already dealt with the subject of pets in an amended bylaw filed at the Land Title Office. Note, however, that the transition provisions in the regulations provide that the pet restriction does not apply to a pet living with an owner, tenant or occupant on January 2, 2002 and which continues to live there after that date.[1]

Impact of the *Strata Property Act*

The *Strata Property Act* may limit the enforceability of some bylaws and rules made before the Act came into force.[2]

In addition to the statutory bylaws that most strata corporations acquired under the previous legislation, prior to the *Strata Property Act* coming into force, most corporations also amended their statutory bylaws by filing bylaw amendments at the Land Title Office.

Although the *Strata Property Act* came into force on July 1, 2000, there was a grace period for all statutory and amended bylaws that were already in existence on that date. During the grace period, bylaws already in existence continued to operate, even if they conflicted with the Act or the regulations. The grace period ended on the last day of 2001.

Effective January 1, 2002, the following provisions governed statutory bylaws and amended bylaws that already existed when the *Strata Property Act* came into force.

---

[1] *Strata Property Regulation*, s. 17.12.
[2] For information about the impact of the *Strata Property Act* on previously existing rules, see Chapter 21, *Rules*.

Statutory Bylaws

The Standard Bylaws in the *Strata Property Act* became the statutory bylaws for every strata corporation in the province, regardless of the date the corporation was created.[1] These Standard Bylaws prevail, except to the extent that a strata corporation has already dealt with the same subject matter by previously passing an amended bylaw that is filed in the Land Title Office.

Section 1 of the Standard Bylaws is an exception to the rule that the Standard Bylaws did not apply until January 1, 2002 in strata corporations created prior to July 1, 2000. If a strata corporation created under previous legislation lacked a bylaw that established a schedule for the payment of strata fees, that corporation automatically acquired section 1 of the Standard Bylaws in the *Strata Property Act*, effective July 1, 2000.[2] That standard bylaw requires an owner to pay strata fees on or before the first day of the month to which the strata fees relate.

Amended Bylaws

Amended bylaws that were already filed at the Land Title Office when the *Strata Property Act* came into force will continue to prevail over the Standard Bylaws, with one exception.

Subject to one exception described below, in any case where such an amended bylaw conflicts with Parts 1 through 17 of the *Strata Property Act* (in other words, everything in the *Strata Property Act*, except the *Schedule of Standard Bylaws* at the back of the statute), or the regulations, the amended bylaw ceases to have any effect to the

---

[1] *Strata Property Regulation*, s. 17.11(3).
[2] *Ibid.*, ss. 17.1 and 17.9.

extent of the conflict.[1] For example, a strata corporation may have filed a bylaw that requires the corporation to approve an owner's tenant before the owner rents a residential strata lot to the tenant. The *Strata Property Act* does not permit such a bylaw.[2] Since January 1, 2002, a strata corporation cannot enforce that bylaw.

There is a narrow exception, however, for an amended bylaw that apportions contributions to the contingency reserve fund (CRF), if the bylaw meets certain criteria.[3] First, the strata corporation must have filed the amended bylaw in the Land Title Office before July 1, 2000, when the *Strata Property Act* came into force. Second, the bylaw must apportion CRF contributions according to *type* of strata lot. Last, the specific type of strata lot must be identified as a type of strata lot in the bylaws of the strata corporation or a section.[4] If the amended bylaw meets these requirements, the bylaw will continue to operate beyond January 1, 2001, even if it conflicts with the Act and regulations.

---

[1] *Strata Property Regulation*, s. 17.11.
[2] *Strata Property Act*, s. 141 (1).
[3] *Strata Property Regulation*, s. 17.11(6)
[4] For information about a type of strata lot, see Chapter 26, *Paying for Repairs*.

Chapter 20

AMENDING BYLAWS

The strata corporation may amend the statutory bylaws by changing their wording, or otherwise deleting or adding to them.[1] The *Strata Property Act* contains some restrictions on the extent to which a strata corporation may amend its bylaws.

1. Amendments to the bylaws are not enforceable if they contravene the Act, the regulations, the *Human Rights Code* or any other law.[2] For instance, the *Strata Property Act* requires every strata corporation to establish a CRF.[3] Suppose a strata corporation passes an amended bylaw prohibiting the corporation from having a CRF. The new bylaw is unenforceable because it violates the *Strata Property Act*. Nor would it make any difference if the members voted unanimously in support of the new bylaw because it still violates the statute.

2. Amendments are not enforceable if they destroy or modify certain easements under the *Strata Property Act*.[4] The Act creates various easements, among other things, to protect the vertical and horizontal support given by the strata lots to one another.[5]

3. With some exceptions, amendments are not enforceable if they prohibit or restrict the right of an owner of a strata lot to freely sell, lease, mortgage or otherwise

---

[1]*Strata Property Act*, s. 126. For information about the *Schedule of Standard Bylaws*, see Chapter 19, *Statutory Bylaws and the Effect of the Strata Property Act*.

[2]*Ibid.*, s. 121(1)(a).

[3]*Ibid.*, s. 92.

[4]*Ibid.*, s. 121(1)(b).

[5]*Ibid.*, s. 69.

dispose of his or her lot.[1] The Act, however, permits exceptions for bylaw amendments that restrict rentals, or the age of persons who can reside in the strata lot or activities governing the sale of a strata lot, such as holding open houses.[2]

Special Restrictions on Bylaw Amendments

The *Strata Property Act* specifically restricts the reach of some bylaw amendments, as follows:

- A bylaw that limits rentals must set out the procedure for administering the limit.[3] In addition, the bylaw must not require the screening of tenants, establish screening criteria, require the approval of tenants or require the insertion of terms in a tenancy agreement.[4]

- A bylaw must not prohibit or unreasonably restrict activities relating to the sale of a strata lot, including locations for posting signs and open houses.[5]

- A bylaw must not require someone to use a voluntary dispute resolution process to resolve disputes among members, tenants and the corporation, or confer on any person the authority to make a binding decision in a dispute.[6]

---

[1]*Strata Property Act*, s. 121(1)(c).
[2]*Ibid.*, ss. 121(2) and 122.
[3]*Ibid.*, s. 141(3).
[4]*Ibid.*, s. 141(1).
[5]*Ibid.*, s. 122.
[6]*Ibid.*, s. 124(2).

Procedure

If a strata corporation wishes to amend the bylaws it must do so at a general meeting.

The notice for the general meeting must properly describe the resolution to amend the bylaws. In most cases, the resolution will require a 3/4 vote to pass. The following table shows the type of vote necessary to amend a bylaw, depending on the circumstances:[1]

Type of Vote Necessary to Amend a Bylaw

Strata Use	Vote Required
Entirely residential	3/4 vote
Entirely non-residential	3/4 vote or as otherwise provided in the bylaws
Mixed residential and non-residential	Both a 3/4 vote of the residential lots and a 3/4 vote of the non-residential lots respectively, or as otherwise provided in the bylaws for the non-residential lots

If some or all of a strata development is non-residential, it is essential to first check the existing bylaws for any provision that sets a special voting threshold for amending the bylaws in the future. For instance, in a non-residential strata development it is possible to have a bylaw that says all future amendments to the bylaws must be approved by majority vote. In that case, only a majority vote is needed to approve a resolution to amend the bylaws.

If the resolution requires a 3/4 or unanimous vote, the notice for the general meeting *must* include the proposed wording of the resolution to amend the bylaws.[2]

---

[1] *Strata Property Act*, s. 128(1).
[2] *Ibid.*, s. 45.

During the general meeting, amendments may be made to the proposed wording of the resolution requiring a 3/4 vote, if the amendments do not substantially change the resolution and are approved by a 3/4 vote before the vote on the resolution.[1]

If the resolution to amend the standard bylaws requires a 3/4 vote and it passes, the strata corporation may have to wait one week before taking steps to implement the bylaw amendment, depending on voting results.[2] If the number of votes in favour of the resolution represents less than 50 per cent of all of the strata corporation's votes, the strata corporation will have to wait a week to permit eligible voters an opportunity to demand a new general meeting to reconsider the matter. For more information, see *Reconsideration of a Resolution Passed by 3/4 Vote* in Chapter 14, *Voting*.

Finally, an amendment is not legally effective until the strata corporation files the amendment at the Land Title Office with the strata plan.[3] The *Strata Property Act* requires a strata corporation to file the amendment in a prescribed form called an "Amendment to Bylaws" (Form I). The form is found among the forms in the regulations.

Under the *Strata Property Act*, an amended bylaw must be filed at the Land Title Office within 60 days of its approval.[4] In other words, if a strata corporation delays filing an Amendment to Bylaws (Form I) for more than 60 days after the approval of the bylaw amendment, the staff at the Land Title Office will not accept the amendment form. Presumably, the strata corporation would have to call another general meeting to once again approve the amendment and then file the appropriate documentation at the Land Title Office on time.

---

[1] *Strata Property Act*, s. 50(2).
[2] *Ibid.*, s. 51.
[3] *Ibid.*, s. 128(2).
[4] *Ibid.*, s. 128(3).

Amendments Contemplated by the *Strata Property Act*

Subject to the legal restrictions described above, a strata corporation may change any or all of its statutory bylaws. The *Strata Property Act* specifically contemplates that strata corporations may amend their bylaws to deal with certain matters. A table of suggested amendment subjects can be found in Appendix G.

When Does an Amended Bylaw Apply?

An amended bylaw applies as soon as the strata corporation files the amendment at the Land Title Office in the prescribed form, unless the *Strata Property Act*, the regulations or the bylaw provide otherwise.

In some cases, the *Strata Property Act* relieves certain persons and pets from the immediate consequences of an amended bylaw. These are sometimes called grandfather provisions. The Act grandfathers the following types of amendments:

Age Restrictions

A bylaw restricting the age of persons who may reside in a strata lot does not apply to someone residing there when the bylaw is passed.[1]

Pet Prohibitions

A bylaw prohibiting pets does not apply to a pet living with an owner, tenant or occupant at the time when the bylaw is passed.[2]

---

[1] *Strata Property Act*, s. 123(2).
[2] *Ibid.*, s. 123(1).

Rental Restrictions

In the case of a bylaw that restricts rentals, the Act grandfathers certain strata lots, delays the application of the bylaw to some strata lots, and creates exemptions from the bylaw. For more information, see Chapter 22, *Rental Restriction Bylaws*.

Chapter 21

RULES

To regulate the common property or a common asset, a strata corporation may pass a rule instead of a bylaw.

Under the *Strata Property Act*, the term *rules* replaces the phrase *rules and regulations* in the former *Condominium Act*. In the past, most people informally referred to rules and regulations as regulations. For simplicity, we use the term *rules*, being the phrase used in the *Strata Property Act*.

A rule or regulation created before the *Strata Property Act* came into force, and existing at that time, is deemed to be a rule under the Act.[1]

Rules may only regulate the use, safety and condition of common property and common assets.[2] A rule cannot regulate the use of a strata lot; for that, a bylaw is necessary.

Making a Rule

The strata council may make a rule. It is not necessary for the strata council to give the owners any advance notice of its intention to create a rule, or to follow any special procedure in the council's proceedings, unless the strata corporation's bylaws require it. The strata council may create a rule by majority vote, unless the bylaws governing the strata council's procedure require a different voting threshold.[3]

As soon as the strata council creates a rule, however, it must promptly inform the owners about it.[4] A rule must be set out in a written document that is capable of being photocopied, including any rule that is posted on a sign.[5]

---

[1] *Strata Property Regulation*, s. 17.10(1).
[2] *Ibid.*, s. 125.
[3] *Ibid.*, ss. 26, 50(1) and the *Schedule of Standard Bylaws*, s. 18.
[4] *Strata Property Regulation*, s. 125(4).
[5] *Ibid.*, s. 125(3).

After the strata council creates a rule, it has a limited lifespan unless a majority of eligible voters approve the rule. A rule ceases to have effect at the first annual general meeting (AGM) held after council made the rule unless the eligible voters ratify the rule by majority vote at that meeting or at an earlier general meeting.[1]

After the rule is ratified, it remains in force until it is repealed, replaced or altered.[2]

Amending a Rule

The *Strata Property Act* does not set out the procedure for altering or repealing a rule. Presumably, the same procedure for making a rule governs amendments to that rule. In other words, it appears that the strata council may alter or repeal a rule, but the change must later be ratified by majority vote at a general meeting on or before the next AGM.

When Does a Rule Apply?

When the strata council creates a rule, it is effective immediately even though the owners must later ratify the rule at the next AGM.

Restrictions

The *Strata Property Act* contains some restrictions on the extent to which a rule is enforceable.

1. A rule is not enforceable if it contravenes the *Strata Property Act*, the regulations, the *Human Rights Code* or any other law.[3] Suppose, for instance, that the strata corporation owns a strata lot in the strata plan that the corporation uses as a guest suite for the visitors of

---

[1] *Strata Property Act*, s. 125(6).
[2] *Ibid.*, s. 125(7).
[3] *Ibid.*, ss. 121(1)(a) and 125(2).

owners and tenants. The *Strata Property Act* requires the approval of the eligible voters by a 3/4 vote before the strata corporation makes a significant change in the use or appearance of land that is a common asset.[1] If the strata council passed a rule converting the unit from a guest facility to a caretaker's suite, the rule would not be enforceable. The rule violates the provision of the *Strata Property Act* requiring prior approval by the eligible voters. The owners cannot solve the problem by ratifying the rule by majority vote because the rule still violates the Act in the absence of approval by 3/4 vote.

2. A rule is not enforceable if it destroys or modifies certain easements under the *Strata Property Act*.[2] The Act creates various easements, among other things, to protect the vertical and horizontal support given by the common property to adjacent strata lots.[3]

3. The *Strata Property Act* says a rule is not enforceable if it prohibits or restricts the right of an owner of a strata lot to freely sell, lease, mortgage or otherwise dispose of his or her strata lot.[4] At first glance, this provision is hard to understand because a rule may only regulate the use of common property or a common asset, not the use of a strata lot. One can imagine, however, a rule governing "for sale" signs posted on the strata corporation's common property. The rule in this example regulates the use of common property, but the rule may affect an owner's ability to freely sell his or her strata lot.

4. If a rule conflicts with a bylaw, the bylaw prevails.[5]

---

[1] *Strata Property Act*, s. 71.
[2] *Ibid.*, ss. 121(1)(b) and 125(2).
[3] *Ibid.*, s. 69.
[4] *Ibid.*, s. 121(1)(c).
[5] *Ibid.*, s. 125(5).

Impact of the *Strata Property Act*

The *Strata Property Act* may limit the enforceability of some rules made before the Act came into force.

Although the *Strata Property Act* came into force on July 1, 2000, there is a grace period for all rules that were already in existence on that date. During the grace period, rules already in existence continue to operate, even if they conflict with the Act or the regulations. The grace period ended on the last day of 2001.[1]

Effective January 1, 2002, rules that existed when the *Strata Property Act* came into force continue to operate, with one exception. In any case where such a rule conflicts with Parts 1 through 17 of the *Strata Property Act* (in other words, everything in the *Strata Property Act*, except the *Schedule of Standard Bylaws* at the back of the statute), the regulations, or a bylaw, that rule ceases to have effect to the extent of the conflict.[2]

For instance, before July 1, 2000, when the *Strata Property Act* came into force, a strata corporation may have created a rule that imposes a daily fine for every day that a breach of a rule continues. At this time, the regulations do not permit a rule that imposes fines on a daily basis.[3] Although the corporation's rule will continue to operate during the grace period, it will not be enforceable on or after January 1, 2002 because it conflicts with the regulations.

---

[1] *Strata Property Regulation*, s. 17.10.
[2] *Ibid.*, s. 17.10(3).
[3] *Strata Property Act*, s. 132(2) and *Strata Property Regulation*, s. 7.1(3).

Chapter 22

RENTAL RESTRICTION BYLAWS

The statutory bylaws do not limit an owner's right to rent his or her residential strata lot to a tenant.[1] A strata corporation, however, may amend its bylaws to restrict rentals in residential strata lots.

Rental Disclosure Statement

If a developer intends to rent one or more residential strata lots, or to specifically designate strata lots for rental after purchasers acquire them from the developer, the *Strata Property Act* requires the developer to file a Rental Disclosure Statement (Form J) with the Superintendent of Real Estate before the first strata lot is offered for sale.[2] The developer must also give a copy of the filed Rental Disclosure Statement (Form J) to each prospective buyer before he or she purchases a strata lot.[3] The prescribed form for a Rental Disclosure Statement (Form J) is found in the regulations.

In the Rental Disclosure Statement (Form J) the developer must specify:

- The number of residential strata lots in the development,

- The number of strata lots rented at the time of the statement, and the date the rental period expires,

- The number of additional strata lots the developer reserves the right to rent, and the date the rental period expires,

---

[1]For information about statutory bylaws, see Chapter 19, *Statutory Bylaws and the Effect of the Strata Property Act.*

[2]*Strata Property Act*, s. 139(1)(a).

[3]*Ibid.*, s. 139(1)(b) and *Strata Property Regulation*, Rental Disclosure Statement (Form J).

- Whether there is a bylaw of the strata corporation which restricts rentals and, if so, the text of the bylaw.

The developer may change the number of strata lots intended for rental, the rental period for the strata lots or both in the Rental Disclosure Statement (Form J).[1] If the developer still owns all the strata lots, changing the Rental Disclosure Statement (Form J) is relatively easy. The developer does not need anyone's permission.

However, if the developer does not own all the strata lots, he or she must first obtain the prior approval of the owners by a 3/4 vote at a general meeting.[2] The developer is not eligible to vote on the resolution. Nor may persons vote if they are voting in respect of a non-residential lot or a strata lot that is already rented.[3]

If the developer changes his or her Rental Disclosure Statement (Form J), the developer must file an amended copy with the Superintendent of Real Estate. In addition, the developer must give a copy to every prospective purchaser who previously received a copy of the former Rental Disclosure Statement (Form J). The developer must also give a copy to each prospective buyer before he or she enters into an agreement to purchase a strata lot.[4]

Failure to Comply

If the developer fails to follow any of these requirements, the purchaser of a residential strata lot may cancel his or her agreement with the developer to purchase the strata lot, without penalty.[5]

---

[1] *Strata Property Act*, s. 139(2).
[2] *Ibid.*, s. 139(2)(b).
[3] *Ibid.*, s. 139(3).
[4] *Ibid.*, s. 139(4).
[5] *Ibid.*, s. 140.

Previous Condominium Legislation

Developers also filed rental disclosure statements under previous condominium legislation, including the former *Condominium Act*, whose provisions in this regard were similar to those in the *Strata Property Act*.[1] If a developer delivered a Rental Disclosure Statement to the Superintendent of Real Estate before July 1, 2000, when the *Strata Property Act* came into force, that document is deemed to be a Rental Disclosure Statement under the *Strata Property Act*.[2]

Strata Corporation May Restrict Residential Rentals

A strata corporation may only restrict the rental of *residential* strata lots in the strata plan.[3] Rental restrictions are typically found in a strata corporation's bylaws. In the case of a leasehold strata plan, rental restrictions may also be found in a schedule of restrictions filed with the leasehold strata plan at the Land Title Office.[4]

The former *Condominium Act* permitted a strata corporation to limit the number of residential strata lots that could be rented.[5] Generally speaking, the courts found that the power to *limit* was not the same as the power to *prohibit*. Though a strata corporation might limit the number of rentals to one, it could not pass a bylaw limiting rentals to zero because that amounted to a prohibition.[6]

---

[1]See, for example, *Condominium Act*, ss. 31-33.
[2]*Strata Property Regulation*, s. 17.14(1).
[3]*Ibid.*, s. 141(2).
[4]*Strata Property Act*, ss. 206 and 208.
[5]*Condominium Act*, R.S.B.C. 1996, c. 64, s. 30.
[6]*Mattiazzo v. Owners, Strata Plan VR 1144*, [1985] B.C.J. No. 1122 (S.C.); *453881 B.C. Ltd. v. Owner, Strata Plan LMS 508* (1994), 41 R.P.R. (2d) 318 (B.C.S.C.); *Cowe v. Owners, Strata Plan VR 1349* (1994), 92 B.C.L.R. (2d) 327 (S.C.) and *Marshall v. Strata Plan No. NW 2584* (1996), 27 B.C.L.R. (3d) 70; 3 R.P.R. (3d) 144; [1996] B.C.J. No. 1716 (S.C.). See contra *Von Schottenstein v. Owners, Strata Plan 730* (1985), 64 B.C.L.R. 376 (S.C.).

The *Strata Property Act* permits a strata corporation to pass a bylaw that either:

- prohibits the rental of residential strata lots, or

- limits one or more of the number or percentage of residential strata lots that may be rented, or the period of time for which they may be rented.[1]

Any bylaw which limits the number or percentage of strata lots that may be rented must set out the procedure to be followed by the strata corporation in administering the bylaw.[2] In addition, the bylaw must not require the screening of tenants, establish screening criteria, require the approval of tenants, or require the insertion of terms in a tenancy agreement.[3]

When Does a Rental Restriction Bylaw Apply?

If a strata corporation passes a bylaw restricting rentals under the *Strata Property Act,* the date the rental restriction applies may vary from strata lot to strata lot. The application of the rental restriction bylaw may be affected if the developer filed a Rental Disclosure Statement, or by a provision of the Act that delays the application of a rental restriction bylaw or otherwise exempts the owner from the bylaw.[4]

Rental Disclosure Statements

To determine whether the rental restriction bylaw applies to his or her strata lot, an owner must first determine whether

---

[1]*Strata Property Act*, s. 141(2).
[2]*Ibid.*, s. 141(3).
[3]*Ibid.*, s. 141(1).
[4]*Strata Property Act*, s. 143 and *Strata Property Regulation*, s. 17.15.

the developer filed a Rental Disclosure Statement. If a Rental Disclosure Statement applies to a residential strata lot, the *Strata Property Act* and the regulations also distinguish between a Statement filed on or after July 1, 2000, when the *Strata Property Act* came into force, and a Statement filed under the former *Condominium Act*.

To further complicate matters, the *Strata Property Act* and the regulations also distinguish between the effect of the Rental Disclosure Statement on a first purchaser versus a subsequent purchaser. The term *first purchaser* describes a person who bought his or her freehold or leasehold interest in the strata lot from the developer.[1] The term *subsequent purchaser* describes a person who bought from the first or any later purchaser. For example, if a developer sold a strata lot to Person A, who later sold it to Person B, then Person B is a subsequent purchaser.

In summary, to determine whether a rental restriction bylaw applies to his or her strata lot, an owner must verify whether the developer filed a Rental Disclosure Statement that governs the strata lot, whether the Statement was filed before or after July 1, 2000, and whether the owner is the first or a subsequent purchaser.

If the strata development is one where the developer was initially required by the *Real Estate Act* to give each purchaser a copy of a prospectus or disclosure statement (e.g., the development consisted of more than five strata lots and the developer was not exempted from delivering a prospectus or disclosure statement), an owner will typically find a copy of the Rental Disclosure Statement, if any, in that prospectus or disclosure statement.[2] If it is uncertain whether a Rental Disclosure Statement exists in connection with a strata plan, an owner may need to check for a Rental Disclosure Statement on file at the office of the Superintendent of Real Estate. Effective July 1, 2003, the fee payable to the Superintendent to obtain a copy of a

---

[1] See, for example, *Strata Property Act*, s. 1(1) (definition of "purchaser").
[2] *Real Estate Act*, Part II.

Rental Disclosure Statement, or any amendment to it, is thirty-eight dollars ($38).[1]

Determining when a rental restriction bylaw applies to a strata lot can be a complicated process under the *Strata Property Act* and the regulations. To simplify the procedure, particularly when there is a Rental Disclosure Statement, readers should see Appendix F (Charts Explaining the Application of a Rental Restriction Bylaw).

Rental Disclosure Statement Filed On or After July 1, 2000

In this case, if a strata lot is designated as a rental strata lot in a developer's Rental Disclosure Statement, the restriction does not apply until:

- the expiry of the rental period in the Rental Disclosure Statement, or

- the date on which the first purchaser conveys the property to another buyer,

whichever occurs first.[2]

First Purchaser?

If the owner is the first purchaser, the Rental Disclosure Statement (Form J) will preserve the owner's right to rent the unit for the rental period specified in the statement. If the rental period has not expired, the owner remains able to rent the strata lot, despite any rental restriction bylaw. This is so even though the rental restriction bylaw may apply to other residential strata lots. If, however, the rental period has expired, the first purchaser will no longer be able to rent the strata lot under the protection of the Rental Disclosure Statement. However, the owner must then consider whether one of the other delaying provisions, or one of the exemptions, in the *Strata Property*

---

[1] *Strata Property Act*, s. 143(2).
[2] *Strata Property Act*, s. 143(2).

Act or the regulations will postpone the application of the rental restriction bylaw as described below.

Where the Rental Period is Described as "Indefinite"

If a developer described the rental period in the Rental Disclosure Statement (Form J) as *indefinite*, the owner should obtain legal advice about the effect of the Form J on the owner's ability to rent the strata lot.

Abbas v. The Owners, Strata Plan LMS 1921, appears to be the only case to date that considers the effect of an indefinite Rental Disclosure Statement.[1] *Abbas* was an unreported, oral judgment pronounced in Chambers. The legal community was not generally aware of the *Abbas* decision until 2002 when it surfaced in a dispute.

In *Abbas*, the Rental Disclosure Statement was issued under the *Condominium Act*. The Rental Disclosure Statement stated that the developer reserved the right to lease all of the units in the building for an indefinite period. The court held that the owner could not rely on the Rental Disclosure Statement. Section 31(1)(c) of the *Condominium Act* required the developer to disclose the following information in its Rental Disclosure Statement,

> **31. (1) (a)** the number of strata lots leased by him (the owner developer) at the date the purchaser agrees to purchase his strata lot;
>
> **(b)** the number of additional residential lots he (the owner developer) intends to lease;
>
> **(c)** the <u>length of time</u> he (the owner developer) <u>intends</u> to lease the lots; . . .
> (Emphasis added)

In *Abbas*, the court found that the developer failed to comply with at least two requirements created by the *Condominium Act*[2] and the prescribed form of Rental

---

[1]*Abbas v. The Owners, Strata Plan LMS 1921*, (13 April 2000), Vancouver No. A992516 (B.C.S.C.).

[2]*Condominium Act*, s. 31(1)(c).

Disclosure Statement[1] then in use. First, the developer failed to state its *intention*, and second, *the length of time* the developer planned to lease the strata lots. Although the court did not expressly say so, the ruling implies that describing a rental period as indefinite fails to state a length of time. The court held that the owner could not rely on the Rental Disclosure Statement to rent her strata lot because the Rental Disclosure Statement did not comply with the statutory requirements.

In the *Abbas* case, it does not appear that the court had the benefit of time for research or careful reflection before judgment. Nor does it appear that any consideration was given to section 28 of the *Interpretation Act* which permits deviations from a prescribed form that do not affect the form's substance or mislead the reader.[2] In addition, the evidence does not seem to have included the guidelines from the Superintendent of Real Estate, which at the relevant time suggested the use of *indefinite* rental periods to developers in appropriate circumstances.

When dealing with a Rental Disclosure Statement (Form J), differences between the *Strata Property Act* and the *Condominium Act* may also be important. Unlike the *Condominium Act*, the *Strata Property Act* does not set out what ingredients a Rental Disclosure Statement (Form J) must contain.[3] Instead, the *Strata Property Act* merely requires the use of a prescribed form, the contents of which are established in the regulations.[4]

Since each case depends significantly on its particular facts, including the wording of the particular Rental Disclosure Statement (Form J), an owner whose Form J describes the rental period as *indefinite* should obtain legal advice before relying on it, in view of the *Abbas* decision.

---

[1] At the time, the prescribed form was found in B.C. Reg. 74/78.
[2] *Interpretation Act*, R.S.B.C. 1996, c. 238, s. 28.
[3] *Strata Property Act*, s. 139.
[4] *Strata Property Act*, s. 139(1) and *Strata Property Regulation* (Form J).

Subsequent Purchaser?

The subsequent purchaser cannot rely on the Rental Disclosure Statement (Form J) as his or her authority to rent the strata lot, even if the rental period in the Statement has not yet expired. The right to rely on the Rental Disclosure Statement (Form J) to rent the strata lot ended when the first purchaser conveyed the strata lot to a subsequent purchaser.

However, the owner should then consider whether one of the other delaying provisions in the *Strata Property Act* or the regulations, or one of the exemptions, will postpone the application of the rental restriction bylaw as described below.

Rental Disclosure Statement Filed Before July 1, 2000

If a developer filed a Rental Disclosure Statement under the former *Condominium Act*, that Act promised that the first purchaser of the strata lot designated for rental could lease or continue to lease the strata lot for the period disclosed in the Statement.[1]

The *Condominium Act* defined a purchaser as:[2]

> **A person who purchases a strata lot from an owner developer, and any subsequent purchasers of that strata lot, but does not include an affiliate, trustee, assignee or nominee of an owner developer, or any person whose business includes the development, sale or management of real property to whom the owner developer has transferred any right, title or interest in the land included in the strata plan, unless that person personally occupies the strata lot;**

As long as an owner of the strata lot was the first purchaser, and did not fall within any of the exceptions

---

[1] *Strata Property Act*, s. 31(5), (6).
[2] *Ibid.*, s. 1.

noted in the definition, that owner would be permitted to continue to rent the strata lot until the rental period in the Rental Disclosure Statement expired.[1] Despite this definition, the ability of a subsequent purchaser to rent the strata lot under the protection of the Rental Disclosure Statement was less clear.

Regulation 74/78 of the *Condominium Act* limited the definition of purchaser for certain purposes, to a first purchaser.[2] The regulation, however, did not limit the definition of purchaser for the purpose of the section that promised that a purchaser could lease or continue to lease for the period in the Rental Disclosure Statement.

As a result, since the definition of purchaser in the *Condominium Act* includes *subsequent* purchasers, some persons argued that unless a person falls within the exceptions specifically noted in the definition, *all* purchasers, and not just first purchasers, are permitted to rent strata lots under the protection of the Rental Disclosure Statement, despite a rental restriction bylaw. Others argued that including all subsequent purchasers in the application of a Rental Disclosure Statement would prevent many rental restriction bylaws from having practical effect. While the *Condominium Act* was in force, uncertainty remained over the question whether a Rental Disclosure Statement protected only the developer and the first purchaser, or whether its protection extended also to a subsequent purchaser.

First Purchaser?

If a residential strata lot is designated for rental in a Rental Disclosure Statement filed under the former *Condominium Act*, the *Strata Property Act* and the regulations protect the first purchaser in the same way that the legislation

---

[1]*Condominium Act*, s. 31(5), (6).
[2]B.C. Reg. 74/78.

protects first purchasers where the Rental Disclosure Statement was filed on or after July 1, 2000.[1]

This means that if the owner is the first purchaser, the Rental Disclosure Statement preserves that owner's right to rent the unit for the rental period specified in the statement. If the rental period has not expired, the owner remains able to rent the strata lot, despite any rental restriction bylaw. This is so even though the rental restriction bylaw may apply to other residential strata lots.

If, however, the rental period has expired, the first purchaser will no longer be able to rent the strata lot under the protection of the Rental Disclosure Statement. In that case, the owner should determine whether one of the other delaying provisions, or one of the exemptions, in the *Strata Property Act* or the regulations will postpone the application of the rental restriction bylaw, as described below.

Where the Rental Period is Described as "Indefinite"

For the reasons explained earlier, if a developer describes the rental period in the Rental Disclosure Statement as *indefinite*, the first purchaser should obtain legal advice about the owner's ability to rely on that Statement to rent the strata lot.

In *Abbas v. The Owners, Strata Plan LMS 1921*,[2] the Rental Disclosure Statement stated that the developer reserved the right to lease all of the units in the building for an *indefinite* period. The court held, in part, that the owner could not rely on the Rental Disclosure Statement to rent her strata lot because the Rental Disclosure Statement did not comply with statutory requirements.

---

[1] *Strata Property Act*, s. 143(2) and *Strata Property Regulation*, s. 17.14.
[2] *Abbas v. The Owners, Strata Plan LMS 1921*, (13 April 2000), Vancouver No. A992516 (B.C.S.C.).

Subsequent Purchaser?

The *Strata Property Act* distinguishes between the effects of Rental Disclosure Statements on subsequent purchasers. The distinction depends on the date the developer filed the Rental Disclosure Statement. The Act does not protect the rental rights of a subsequent purchaser affected by a Rental Disclosure Statement filed on or after July 1, 2000.

The *Strata Property Act* and regulations, however, recognize that in the case of a Rental Disclosure Statement filed under the former *Condominium Act*, a subsequent purchaser may have purchased his or her residential strata lot in the belief that he or she could continue to rent the strata lot despite any rental restriction bylaw. Accordingly, the *Strata Property Act* and regulations give a subsequent purchaser of a strata lot governed by a Rental Disclosure Statement filed under the *Condominium Act* an extended period of protection.

The regulations state that if a strata lot was designated as a rental strata lot under the former *Condominium Act*, and has been sold by the first purchaser, a rental restriction bylaw does not apply until:

- the date the rental period expires as disclosed in the Rental Disclosure Statement, or

- January 1, 2006,

whichever occurs first.[1]

If the owner of the strata lot is a subsequent purchaser, and the period that the strata lot may be rented under the Rental Disclosure Statement has not expired, that owner can continue to rent the strata lot until January 1, 2006, despite any rental restriction bylaw.

---

[1] *Strata Property Regulation*, s. 17.15.

In many cases, developers filed Rental Disclosure Statements under the former *Condominium Act* that provided for rentals for an indefinite period of time. In those cases, a subsequent purchaser may only rent until January 1, 2006, unless that owner can take advantage of one of the other delaying provisions in the *Strata Property Act* or the regulations, or one of the exemptions that will postpone the application of the rental restriction bylaw, as described below.

For example, if a subsequent purchaser's tenant was renting the strata lot at the time the bylaw was passed, the application of a rental restriction bylaw is delayed until one year after that tenant vacates the strata lot. The year may extend beyond January 1, 2006.[1] Even if the tenant did not vacate until after January 1, 2006, the owner would continue to have a year after the tenant ceased to occupy the strata lot before the bylaw became effective against that strata lot.[2]

Delaying Provisions

For strata lots to which a rental restriction bylaw would apply (for example, where the right to rent is not preserved by a Rental Disclosure Statement), the general rule is that a bylaw that prohibits or limits rentals does not apply:

- if there is a tenant occupying a strata lot at the time of the bylaw's passage, until one year after the tenant ceases to occupy the unit, or

- one year after the bylaw is passed,

whichever occurs last.[3]

---

[1] *Strata Property Act*, s. 143(1).
[2] *Ibid.*
[3] *Ibid.*

This means that in every case where a rental restriction bylaw is passed, its application must be delayed for at least one year.

For a strata lot without a tenant in place when the rental restriction bylaw was passed, the bylaw will not apply for one year. This is the case even if the owner occupied the strata lot at the time the bylaw was passed. Owners should be aware that the *Residential Tenancy Act* limits the grounds upon which an owner can require a tenant to terminate a month-to-month lease.[1] Therefore, an owner wishing to rent during this period should consider entering a fixed-term tenancy agreement with his or her tenant that will expire *before* the date the rental restriction bylaw will apply to the strata lot.

In cases where a rental restriction bylaw is passed while a tenant is occupying a strata lot, the bylaw will not apply until one year *after* that tenant has moved out. This provision may benefit a subsequent purchaser who is no longer protected by a Rental Disclosure Statement. For example, an owner who purchased the strata lot from the developer may have rented the strata lot to a tenant. The first purchaser may have then sold the strata lot to a subsequent purchaser while the tenant continued to occupy the strata lot. If the tenant occupying the strata lot was the tenant in place at the time the bylaw was passed, although the subsequent purchaser cannot take advantage of the Rental Disclosure Statement, the subsequent purchaser can take advantage of the delaying provision. The subsequent purchaser will have one year after the tenant leaves before the rental restriction bylaw applies to the strata lot.

During the one year period after the tenant has moved out, and before the rental restriction bylaw applies, an owner may wish to rent the strata lot. As indicated above, owners should be very careful with respect to the

---

[1]*Residential Tenancy Act*, S.B.C. 2002, c. 78, ss. 46-49 and 51-53.

term of the tenancy agreement so they are not obligated to continue to rent to a tenant once the rental restriction bylaw takes effect.

Exemptions to Rental Restriction Bylaws

Under certain circumstances, even though a rental restriction bylaw would normally apply to a strata lot, an owner may be exempted from the application of the bylaw.

Family Members

A bylaw that prohibits or limits rentals cannot prevent an owner from renting a strata lot to a member of the owner's family.[1]

For the purposes of exemptions from rental restriction bylaws, the regulations define a family member as a:[2]

- spouse of the owner,

- parent or child of the owner, or

- parent or child of the spouse of the owner.

The term *spouse* includes an individual who has "lived and cohabited with the owner, for a period of at least 2 years at the relevant time, in a marriage-like relationship, including a marriage-like relationship between persons of the same gender."[3] Neither the Act nor the regulations define the term *child*. Presumably, the term *child* refers to the tenant's *relationship* to the owner, not the tenant's age. In the author's view, the term *child* in this definition includes an adult child.

---

[1]*Strata Property Act*, ss. 141(2) and 142(2).
[2]*Strata Property Regulation*, s. 8.1.
[3]*Ibid.*, s. 8.1(2).

Hardship

An owner may apply to the strata corporation for an exemption from a rental restriction bylaw on the grounds that it causes hardship to the owner.[1] A strata corporation cannot unreasonably refuse the owner's request.[2] In granting an exemption, the strata corporation may impose a time limit.[3]

Though the owner must apply in writing, he or she is entitled to a hearing.[4] The regulations define a hearing as an, "opportunity to be heard in person at a council meeting."[5]

If the strata corporation fails to give its written decision within two weeks of receipt of the application or, in the case of a hearing within the following week, the exemption is automatically allowed.[6]

In *Als v. The Owners, Strata Corporation NW 1067*,[7] the Supreme Court of British Columbia set out some guidelines for assessing an application for a hardship exemption under the *Strata Property Act*. The owner's work required him to live in France for an extended period. The fair market value of the owner's strata lot had declined in recent years and the owner would likely suffer a substantial loss if he sold the unit. The owner wished to rent his residential strata lot while he was overseas. The owner applied twice to the strata council for an exemption from the strata corporation's rental bylaw on the ground that the corporation's prohibition against rentals caused the owner hardship. Although the owner provided some financial information with his hardship application, he refused to give the strata council detailed financial information

---

[1] *Strata Property Act*, s. 144.
[2] *Ibid.*, s. 144(6).
[3] *Ibid.*, s. 144(5).
[4] *Ibid.*, s. 144(2), (3).
[5] *Strata Property Regulation*, s. 8.2.
[6] *Strata Property Act*, s. 144(4).
[7] *Als v. The Owners, Strata Corporation NW 1067* (2002), 97 B.C.L.R. (3d) 393, 47 R.P.R. (3d) 310, [2002] B.C.J. No. 145, 2002 B.C.S.C. 134; [2003] B.C.J. No. 628, 2003 B.C.S.C. 431 (application to vary order) (S.C.).

about his circumstances, such as a financial statement, because he thought it too intrusive. On each occasion, council dismissed the owner's application for failure to provide sufficient evidence that the rental prohibition caused the owner hardship. When the owner applied to the Supreme Court of British Columbia for a remedy, the Court upheld the strata council's decision. In *Als*, the Court found that the strata council correctly refused the owner's hardship application because the owner failed to supply sufficient information to allow council to decide whether the owner actually suffered hardship.

The *Als* case makes several things clear.

First, although the *Strata Property Act* fails to define the term *hardship*, the definition in the *Shorter Oxford English Dictionary* may serve as a guideline. That work defines *hardship* as, "hardness of fate or circumstance, severe toil or suffering, extreme privation."

Second, an owner who applies for a hardship exemption must present sufficient evidence to show that the rental restriction causes hardship *to that owner*. The Court said, in part,[1]

> **It is also the case that the bylaw must cause hardship "to the owner". . . It is not enough to show a type of hardship which might necessarily apply to all non-resident owners. In the case at bar, the only financial information available from Mr. Als is that his monthly expenses are increased because he is maintaining a home in Paris as well as in Richmond. However, a duplication of expenses flows automatically for all non-resident owners and, accordingly, this duplication will not be a factor unless it can be shown that this duplication has produced hardship for a particular owner because the duplication cannot be avoided or afforded. The duplicated expense for a very rich owner would not create hardship whereas the duplication of expense without corresponding rental income might**

---

[1] *Als v. The Owners, Strata Corporation NW 1067*, [2002] B.C.J. No. 145 at para. 23 (S.C.).

> **create hardship for an owner of modest means. The duplicated expense for someone who is not in a position to move back into the strata unit may cause a hardship which cannot be avoided as there is a good reason why an owner cannot move into the strata unit in order to avoid the duplication.**

Although the Court did not address the extent of proof required, it is likely that an owner must show hardship on a balance of probabilities. That is, the owner must show that it is more likely than not that the rental restriction in question creates hardship to that owner.

Third, although it is relevant to show that the strata unit has decreased in market value such that the owner will suffer a loss if forced to sell the unit, this factor alone is not sufficient to prove hardship *without evidence of the effect of the loss on the particular owner's financial position.*

Breaches of Rental Restriction Bylaws

The *Strata Property Act* requires that the strata corporation set out in its bylaws the maximum amount it may fine an owner.[1] The Act also permits the bylaw to specify the frequency with which the fine will be imposed for a continuing violation.[2]

The Standard Bylaws set $50 as the maximum fine for breach of a bylaw.[3] The Standard Bylaws also provide that if a contravention of a bylaw continues, without interruption, for longer than seven days, a fine may be imposed every seven days.[4]

---

[1] *Strata Property Act*, s. 132.
[2] *Ibid.*, s. 132(2).
[3] *Schedule of Standard Bylaws*, s. 23.
[4] *Ibid.*, s. 24.

A strata corporation may amend its bylaws to impose larger fines, subject to the *Strata Property Act* and regulations.[1]

Maximum Fines

Normally the maximum permissible fine for a breach of a bylaw is $200, but the regulations permit a maximum fine of $500 for a breach of a residential rental restriction bylaw.[2]

The regulations also provide that the maximum frequency for which a strata corporation may levy a fine for a continuing breach of a bylaw is once every seven days.

If a strata corporation has set the fine for breach of a rental restriction bylaw at the maximum permitted by the regulations and provided for the maximum frequency at which the fine can be imposed, an owner who rents his or her strata lot in breach of a rental restriction bylaw may face very large fines. For example, at the rate of $500 per week, the fines may amount to $2,000 per month.

Rental Restriction Breach

If an owner rents a strata lot in violation of a rental restriction bylaw, the tenant cannot be considered to be in contravention of the bylaw.[3] As a result, the strata corporation may not attempt to collect the fine from the tenant.

In addition, a tenant who discovers that the landlord is in contravention of a rental restriction bylaw may end the tenancy agreement without penalty within 90 days of discovering the landlord's breach by giving notice to the landlord.[4] If a tenant gives notice in these circumstances,

---

[1]For information about amending bylaws, see Chapter 20, *Amending Bylaws*.
[2]*Strata Property Regulation*, s. 7.1(2).
[3]*Strata Property Act*, s. 145.
[4]*Ibid.*, s. 145(1).

the landlord must pay the tenant's reasonable moving expenses to a maximum of one month's rent.[1]

---

[1] *Ibid.*, s. 145(2).

Chapter 23

AGE RESTRICTION BYLAWS

The statutory bylaws do not restrict the age of persons who may occupy a strata lot.¹ The *Strata Property Act* contemplates that some strata corporations will amend their bylaws to create age restrictions. To understand the law governing age restrictions in British Columbia, it is first necessary to understand the provincial *Human Rights Code*.²

How the *Human Rights Code* Governs Age Restrictions

The *Human Rights Code* is a statute that governs how persons treat one another in their private dealings with each other. Depending on the activity under consideration, the Code prohibits discrimination on various grounds.

If there is a conflict between the Code and any other statute, the Code prevails.³ In addition, the *Strata Property Act* specifically says that a bylaw is not enforceable to the extent that it contravenes the *Human Rights Code*.⁴

In strata matters, the *Human Rights Code* effectively distinguishes between renting a residential strata lot and selling one,⁵ creating the following result. Assuming that an age restriction bylaw meets all of the requirements for enforceability under the *Strata Property Act*, a strata corporation may always enforce an age restriction against an owner, but never against a tenant, with one exception.

---

¹For information about statutory bylaws, see Chapter 19, *Statutory Bylaws and the Effect of the Strata Property Act.*

²*Human Rights Code*, R.S.B.C. 1996, c. 210.

³*Ibid.*, s. 4.

⁴*Strata Property Act*, s. 121(1)(a).

⁵*Human Rights Code*, ss. 9 and 10.

The only time a strata corporation may enforce its age restriction bylaw against a tenant is where the restricted age is at least 55 years old.

Age and Family Status Discrimination Against Tenants

When renting a residential strata lot, section 10 of the *Human Rights Code* specifically prohibits age and family status discrimination against tenants.

The *Human Rights Code* only permits discrimination against tenants because of age or family status if the entire rental facilities are reserved for persons aged 55 years or older. The relevant provisions of section 10 provide, in part:

> 10. (1) A person must not
>
> > (a) deny to a person or class of persons the right to occupy, as a tenant, space that is represented as being available for occupancy by a tenant, or
> >
> > (b) discriminate against a person or class of persons regarding a term or condition of the tenancy of the space,
> >
> > <u>because of the . . . family status, . . . or . . . age of that person</u> or class of persons, or of any other person or class of persons.
>
> (2) <u>Subsection (1) does not apply</u> in the following circumstances: . . .
>
> > (b) as it relates to family status or age,
> >
> > > (i) <u>if the space</u> is a rental unit in residential premises in which every rental unit <u>is reserved for rental to a person who has reached 55 years of age</u> or to 2 or more persons, at least one of whom has reached 55 years of age,[1] (Emphasis added)

---

[1] *Human Rights Code*, s. 10.

If, for example, an owner of a residential strata lot refuses the tenant because the tenant is younger than the age required by an age restriction bylaw, or because the tenant has children, the owner will be in violation of the Code unless the restricted age is at least 55 years old. The owner cannot argue that the strata corporation's bylaw prevents him or her from renting to the tenant with children because the *Strata Property Act* states that a bylaw is not enforceable if it contravenes the *Human Rights Code*.[1]

Age and Family Status Discrimination Against Purchasers

Although the *Human Rights Code* prohibits discrimination on various grounds against persons who purchase dwelling units, neither age nor family status are listed among the prohibited forms of discrimination.[2] Instead, the grounds include, among other things, discrimination based on race, colour, religion, marital status, disability and sexual orientation.

Since the *Human Rights Code* does not prohibit discrimination against purchasers based on their age or family status, a strata corporation's age restriction bylaw may be applied to a purchaser of a strata lot. If the purchaser who becomes an owner is in violation of the bylaw, the strata corporation may enforce the age restriction bylaw against that owner.

Are Age Restrictions Permissible Under the *Strata Property Act*?

The *Strata Property Act* clearly contemplates that some strata corporations will amend their bylaws to restrict the

---

[1] *Strata Property Act*, s. 121.
[2] *Human Rights Code*, s. 9.

occupancy of residential strata lots on the basis of the age of the occupants. Certainly, the Act does not prohibit age restriction bylaws.

Sometimes owners who oppose an age restriction bylaw argue that the bylaw unreasonably restricts their right to sell their strata lot. The *Strata Property Act* states that a bylaw is not enforceable to the extent that it prohibits or restricts the right of an owner of a strata lot to freely sell, lease, mortgage or otherwise dispose of the strata lot or an interest in the strata lot. Note, however, that the Act specifically exempts an age restriction bylaw from the application of this provision.[1]

The leading case on point is *Marshall v. Strata Plan No. NW 2584.*[2]

The *Marshall* case weighed provisions in the former *Condominium Act* against the *Human Rights Act,*[3] which preceded our *Human Rights Code* and whose age and family status discrimination prohibitions were effectively the same as those in the current legislation.

Case Study

Mr. and Mrs. Marshall were an elderly couple in their 70s. In February 1990, they purchased their strata lot. From the time they bought their unit, the Marshalls' adult son, James, lived with them.

In 1995, the strata corporation passed a bylaw which provided, in part:

---

[1] *Strata Property Act*, s. 121.
[2] *Marshall v. Strata Plan No. NW 2584* (1996), 27 B.C.L.R. (3d) 70; 3 R.P.R. (3d) 144; [1996] B.C.J. No. 1716 (S.C.).
[3] *Human Rights Act*, S.B.C. 1984, c. 22.

1. AGE RESTRICTION . . .

b. Every strata lot is reserved for the use of individual(s) 55 years of age and older.

c. Individual(s) under the age of 55 years (with the exception of a spouse) shall not reside at (the strata development).

At the time, James was 51 years old. The Marshalls unsuccessfully sued the strata corporation to set aside the bylaw.

The Marshalls acknowledged that the *Human Rights Act* lacked any prohibition against age discrimination in the sale of strata lots and permitted age discrimination in rentals to persons 55 or older where every rental unit is reserved for that age group. However, the Marshalls argued, among other things, that the bylaw restricting age was unenforceable under section 29 of the *Condominium Act* (now section 121(1)(c) of the *Strata Property Act*) even though the *Human Rights Act* seemed to permit the bylaw restriction.

In most cases, section 29 of the *Condominium Act* made bylaws unenforceable if they prohibited or restricted an owner from transferring, leasing or otherwise dealing with his or her strata lot. The Marshalls claimed that the age restriction diminished the value of their strata lot and fettered their ability to sell or lease it.

In considering whether to permit a prohibition against age discrimination in the sale or rental of property, the Court referred to *Winnipeg School Division No. 1 v. Craton,* a Supreme Court of Canada decision which found that human rights legislation has a special nature and reflects important public policies.[1] In that regard, the Court in the *Marshall* case commented on the legislative intent of the *Human Rights Act:*[2]

---

[1]*Winnipeg School Division No. 1 v. Craton,* [1985] 2 S.C.R. 150.
[2]*Marshall v. Strata Plan No. NW 2584,* [1996] 27 B.C.L.R. (3d) 70 at para. 23 per Henderson, J.

> As far as rental accommodation is concerned, the Legislature has prohibited discrimination against tenants on the basis of age, but has made an express exception for premises in which every rental unit is designed for people 55 years of age or older. Clearly, the legislation recognizes the legitimacy of retirement communities where people of advancing years may live together with other members of their own generation. The Legislature has made a policy choice to permit this differentiation, based upon age, to exclude younger tenants. The benefits resulting from permitting older people to band together in retirement communities must be taken to outweigh the adverse consequence of placing some rental accommodation beyond the reach of younger people.

The Court held that the *Human Rights Act* should prevail over section 29 of the *Condominium Act*. The *Human Rights Act* permitted the age restriction in the strata corporation's bylaw, even though the *Condominium Act* did not. The Court held that the bylaw was valid.

In upholding the age restriction, the Court also refused to follow its earlier decision in *453048 British Columbia Ltd. v. The Owners, Strata Plan KAS 1079*, a case in which the court had previously struck down an age restriction bylaw.[1] In *Marshall v. Strata Plan No. NW 2584*, the court distinguished the earlier case on the basis, that in the previous decision, the court failed to consider the *Human Rights Act* and the principles set out by the Supreme Court of Canada in *Winnipeg School Division No. 1 v. Craton*.

Apparently in response to the decision in *Marshall v. Strata Plan No. NW 2584,* the *Strata Property Act* specifically provides, in part:

---

[1] *453048 British Columbia Ltd. v. The Owners, Strata Plan KAS 1079* (1994), 43 R.P.R. (2d) 293 (B.C.S.C.).

121 (1) A bylaw is not enforceable to the extent that it . . .

> **(c) prohibits or restricts the right of an owner of a strata lot to freely sell, lease, mortgage or otherwise dispose of the strata lot or an interest in the strata lot.**

> **(2) <u>Subsection (1)(c) does not apply</u> to . . .**

>> **(c) <u>a bylaw restricting the age of persons who may reside in a strata lot.</u>**[1] (Emphasis added)

Note that if the events giving rise to the claim in the *Marshall* case occurred today, it would not be necessary for the Marshalls to sue the strata corporation to set aside the age restriction so their son could continue living with them. The *Strata Property Act* states that a bylaw that restricts the age of persons who may reside in a strata lot does not apply to a person who resides in the strata lot at the time the bylaw is passed.[2]

Applying Age Restriction Bylaws

Against Owners

Any age restriction bylaw can be applied against an owner, assuming that the bylaw otherwise meets the requirements for enforceability. Whether the bylaw prohibits children under 19 years of age, or anyone under the age of 45, the bylaw may be applied to an owner of a strata lot. This is so even if the same bylaw cannot be applied against a tenant.

---

[1] *Strata Property Act*, s. 121.
[2] *Ibid.*, s. 123(2).

Against Tenants

In a development with residential rentals, an age restriction is not enforceable against tenants if the restriction sets the minimum age at less than 55 years.

For example, a strata corporation's age restriction bylaw that restricts occupancy to persons who have reached 45 years of age cannot be enforced against tenants who are younger than 45 because that amounts to discrimination against tenants on account of age. Similarly, even if the tenants are older than 45 but their children are not, the bylaw cannot be applied to the children. That would amount to discrimination against the tenants on the grounds of their family status.

On the other hand, an age restriction that reserves every strata lot for persons who have reached age 55 is enforceable against tenants. This is because the age restriction falls within the *Human Rights Code* exception permitting discrimination against tenants where every rental unit is reserved for persons who have reached age 55.

Adult-Only Developments

Since age restriction bylaws with age limits under 55 years cannot be applied to tenants, it might seem that a strata corporation could indirectly enforce its age restriction by simply prohibiting all rentals in the complex. In other words, no rentals, no tenants, and, therefore, no age restriction problems. That approach, however, does not work. Under the *Strata Property Act*, a strata corporation with a rental prohibition bylaw may never completely rule out residential rentals for the following reasons.

First, a rental restriction bylaw does not apply to family members under the *Strata Property Act*.[1] The regulations define *family* or *family member* to mean a spouse of the owner, a parent or child of the owner, or a parent or child of the spouse of the owner.[2] The term *spouse* includes an individual who has, "lived and cohabited with the owner, for a period of at least 2 years at the relevant time, in a marriage-like relationship, including a marriage-like relationship between persons of the same gender."[3] Neither the Act nor the regulations define the term *child*. Presumably, the term *child* refers to the tenant's *relationship* to the owner, not the tenant's age. In the author's view, the term *child* in this definition includes an adult child. As a result, even if a rental restriction bylaw prohibits all rentals, any strata lot owner will always be able to rent to a family member. As a tenant, the family member will be protected from discrimination based on age or family status under the *Human Rights Code*.

Second, a strata corporation that prohibits residential rentals may also permit an exemption from the bylaw on the grounds of hardship.[4]

A strata corporation must be aware that an age restriction bylaw that uses an age less than 55 years can never be effective against all strata lots.

Grandfathering

The *Strata Property Act* also grandfathers new bylaws imposing age restrictions. A bylaw restricting the age of persons who may reside in a strata lot does not apply to someone residing there when the bylaw is passed.[5]

---

[1] *Strata Property Act*, s. 142.
[2] *Strata Property Regulation*, s. 8.1(1).
[3] *Ibid.*, s. 8.1(2).
[4] *Strata Property Act*, s. 144.
[5] *Ibid.*, s. 123(2).

Chapter 24

ENFORCING BYLAWS AND RULES

The strata council is responsible for enforcing the bylaws and rules, subject to the *Strata Property Act*, the regulations and the bylaws, by following a series of mandatory steps.[1]

Enforcement Procedures

1. The strata council must first receive a complaint that a person has contravened a bylaw or rule.[2] Before proceeding with the complaint, the strata council may give the person a warning or an opportunity to comply with the bylaw or rule.[3]

2. If the strata council wishes to proceed with the complaint, it must give particulars of the complaint to the relevant owner or tenant, in writing. If a tenant is the subject of the complaint, the strata corporation must also notify that person's landlord about the allegation.[4]

   The *Strata Property Act* sets out how the strata council must deliver its written particulars to the owner or tenant who is the subject of the complaint.[5] For more information about delivering a notice, see Chapter 12, *Meetings*.

3. The strata council must then give the person accused of wrongdoing a reasonable opportunity to answer the complaint. If that person wishes a hearing, the strata

---

[1]*Strata Property Act*, s. 26.
[2]*Ibid.*, s. 135(1).
[3]*Ibid.*, s. 129(2).
[4]*Ibid.*, s. 135.
[5]*Ibid.*, s. 61.

council must hold one.[1] According to the regulations, a hearing means, "an opportunity to be heard in person at a council meeting."[2]

If a strata council member is the subject of the complaint, he or she must not participate in any decision about the allegation.[3] If all of the owners are on council, however, the member is permitted to participate in the decision.[4]

4. After considering any response, the strata council must promptly provide its written decision in the matter to the person affected.[5] The same requirements that govern delivery of the written particulars apply to delivering the written decision.[6]

5. Once the strata council has complied with these requirements, it can enforce the bylaw or rule.

Enforcement Methods

The *Strata Property Act* permits a strata corporation to enforce a bylaw in several ways. The strata corporation may impose a fine, remedy a contravention or deny access to a recreational facility.

Fines

The strata corporation can impose fines against owners and tenants to the extent permitted by the bylaws.[7] Every strata corporation must set out in its bylaws the maximum amount it may fine an owner or tenant for each violation of a bylaw or rule.[8]

---

[1] *Strata Property Act*, s. 135.
[2] *Strata Property Regulation*, s. 7.2.
[3] *Strata Property Act*, s. 136(1).
[4] *Ibid.*, s. 136(2).
[5] *Ibid.*, s. 135(2).
[6] *Ibid.*, s. 61(1).
[7] *Ibid.*, s. 130.
[8] *Ibid.*, s. 132(1).

If the strata corporation uses the Standard Bylaws, the maximum fines are as follows:[1]

- $50 for each contravention of a bylaw, and

- $10 for each contravention of a rule.

If the contravening activity or default continues without interruption for more than seven days, the Standard Bylaws permit the strata corporation to impose a fine every seven days.[2]

A strata corporation may amend its bylaws to set different maximum fines for the breach of different bylaws and rules. The corporation may also amend its bylaws to establish the frequency at which different fines may be imposed for a continuing contravention of a bylaw or rule.[3] The amounts and frequency of any fines, however, must not exceed the maximums established in the regulations.[4] The regulations set the following maximum fines:

- $200 for each contravention of a bylaw, other than a rental restriction bylaw,

- $500 for each contravention of a rental restriction bylaw, and

- $50 for each contravention of a rule.[5]

According to the regulations, the maximum frequency with which a strata corporation may impose a fine for a continuing contravention of a bylaw or rule is every seven days.[6]

---

[1] *Strata Property Act, Schedule of Standard Bylaws*, s. 23.
[2] *Ibid.*, s. 24.
[3] *Strata Property Act*, s. 132.
[4] *Ibid.*
[5] *Strata Property Regulation*, s. 7.1.
[6] *Ibid.*

Remedial Work

If an owner or tenant fails to carry out work to remedy a bylaw or rule violation, the strata corporation can do the work and charge the person responsible for the reasonable costs of the work.[1] The strata corporation may carry out remedial work on a member's strata lot, common property or common assets.

Denial of Recreational Facilities

When a bylaw or rule violation relates to the use of a recreational facility, the *Strata Property Act* permits a strata corporation to deny an owner, tenant, occupant or visitor the use of that facility if it is part of the common property or a common asset.[2] The strata corporation may only deny access for a reasonable length of time.

Vicarious Liability

Owners who lease their strata lots are vicariously liable for the fines or remedial costs incurred by their tenants.[3] This means that although the strata corporation has fined a tenant, or required a tenant to pay the costs of remedying a breach of the bylaws or rules, the owner may be required to pay the amount owing. An owner cannot avoid vicarious liability, even where his or her powers and duties have been assigned to a tenant, either intentionally or automatically, to long-term tenants or family members.[4]

If an owner, as landlord, pays a fine or costs levied against his or her tenant, the tenant is liable to reimburse the landlord for the amount paid.[5]

---

[1] *Strata Property Act*, s. 133.
[2] *Ibid.*, s. 134.
[3] *Ibid.*, s. 131(1).
[4] *Ibid.*, ss. 147 and 148.
[5] *Ibid.*, s. 131(2).

No Liens for Unpaid Fines

Under the former *Condominium Act*, many strata corporations collected unpaid fines by registering liens against the strata lot titles of owners who failed to pay their fines, even though this practice was illegal.[1] The *Strata Property Act* expressly prohibits the registration of a lien for an unpaid fine.[2]

Some strata corporations use the following technique to circumvent the restriction against liens for unpaid fines. Bearing in mind that a strata corporation may file a lien for unpaid strata fees, some strata corporations amend their bylaws to state that whenever an owner pays his or her strata fees, the payment is first applied to outstanding fines, then to strata fees.

Suppose, for example, that the monthly strata fees for an owner's strata lot are $225 and the owner has an unpaid $100 fine. When the owner makes his or her next monthly payment of $225, the strata corporation allocates the first $100 of that payment towards the unpaid fine, and the remaining $150 towards strata fees. Of course, this leaves an unpaid balance of $100 in the payment of the owner's monthly strata fees. Subject to certain procedural requirements for filing a lien, the strata corporation can now file a lien against the title to the owner's strata lot for $100, representing arrears for strata fees.

---

[1]The *Condominium Act*, s. 37(2) permitted a strata corporation to file a lien if an owner defaulted in the payment of his or her share of the common expenses. A lien for an unpaid fine is not a common expense of the strata corporation.
[2]*Strata Property Act*, s. 116(3).

Collecting Fines and Costs for Remedial Work

Sue in Court

The strata corporation may sue an owner or tenant for a fine in the Provincial Court of British Columbia: Small Claims Division, if the amount claimed is $10,000 or less, excluding interest and costs.[1] For larger claims, the strata corporation must sue in the Supreme Court of British Columbia. If the strata corporation succeeds in court, the corporation may register its judgment against the title to the owner's strata lot. Depending on the circumstances, the strata corporation may also pursue other collection remedies to enforce its judgment, such as garnishment. For information about legal proceedings, see Part VI, *Court Actions and Arbitration.*

Before suing to collect money from an owner or tenant, the *Strata Property Act* sets out some mandatory prerequisites.

1. The strata corporation must give the owner or tenant at least two weeks' advance written notice demanding payment.[2]

2. The notice must indicate to the owner or tenant that the strata corporation may sue him or her if the strata corporation does not receive payment within two weeks.[3]

3. If a mortgage lender has filed a Mortgagee's Request for Notification (Form C) with the strata corporation, the corporation must give a copy of the notice to the lender.[4]

---

[1] *Small Claims Act*, R.S.B.C. 1996, c. 430, s. 3.
[2] *Strata Property Act*, ss. 112 and 113.
[3] *Ibid.*, s. 112.
[4] *Ibid.*, ss. 60, 112 and 113(b) and *Strata Property Regulation*, s. 4.5.

4. The strata corporation must deliver the notice in accordance with the Act. The requirements for delivering the notice to an owner or tenant are described in Chapter 12, *Meetings*.[1] If a mortgage lender has filed a Mortgagee's Request for Notification (Form C), the corporation must also deliver a copy of the notice to the mortgage lender by leaving it with the individual named, if any, in the Mortgagee's Request for Notification (Form C) or by mailing it to the lender at the address given in the Request.[2]

If there is a dispute over whether an owner or tenant owes money to the strata corporation for a fine, and court proceedings have been started, the owner or tenant may pay the disputed amount into court, if the rules of court allow payment into court. Alternatively, the owner or tenant may pay the disputed amount to the strata corporation in trust, in which case the corporation must hold the money and any accrued interest in trust pending resolution of the dispute.[3] After the dispute is resolved, the strata corporation must pay the money out of trust to the party entitled to it and to the extent required by the court or an arbitrator.[4]

Arbitrate

Before arbitrating against an owner or tenant, the strata corporation must first comply with the same advance notice requirements required before suing, including, where required, giving a copy of the notice to a mortgage lender, all of which are described immediately above.[5] In addition, the provisions permitting an owner or tenant to

---

[1]*Strata Property Act*, s. 61.
[2]*Ibid.*, ss. 60, 61(1) and *Strata Property Regulation*, s. 4.5 and Mortgagee's Request for Notification (Form C).
[3]*Strata Property Act*, s. 114.
[4]*Ibid.* For information about a Certificate of Payment (Form F), see Chapter 13, *Record Keeping*.
[5]*Strata Property Act*, s. 112.

pay a disputed amount into court or trust apply equally to arbitrations.[1]

The *Strata Property Act* contains a procedure for arbitrations. For information about the specific steps in arbitration, see Chapter 28, *Arbitration.*

Refusal to Provide a Certificate of Payment (Form F)

The strata corporation may withhold a Certificate of Payment (Form F) until the owner pays his or her fine, or otherwise makes satisfactory arrangements.[2]

If an owner wishes to sell his or her strata lot, or to register a lease or an assignment of lease for the strata lot, the owner must, among other things, file a Certificate of Payment (Form F) at the Land Title Office.[3] The owner must obtain the Certificate of Payment (Form F) from the strata corporation or its strata manager, if it has one. The Certificate of Payment (Form F) states whether the owner owes money to the strata corporation and, if so, whether the money claimed by the strata corporation has been paid into court or trust, or whether the owner has otherwise made satisfactory arrangements to pay the money to the strata corporation.[4] The certificate may include the strata corporation's claim for unpaid fines.[5]

The strata corporation does not have to deliver its Certificate of Payment (Form F) until the owner has paid all money owing to the strata corporation, or has paid any disputed amounts into court or trust, or the owner has otherwise made satisfactory arrangements with the strata corporation to pay the debt. If, for example, the owner needs

---

[1] *Strata Property Act*, s. 114.

[2] For information about a Certificate of Payment (Form F), see Chapter 13, *Record Keeping.*

[3] *Strata Property Act*, s. 256.

[4] *Ibid.*, s. 115.

[5] *Ibid.*, s. 115(5).

a Certificate of Payment (Form F) to complete the sale of his or her strata lot to a buyer, the strata corporation may refuse to issue the certificate until the owner pays all sums owing to the strata corporation, including unpaid fines. In most cases, this is a compelling incentive for the owner to pay his or her fines.

Supreme Court's Authority to Relieve Fines

The *Law and Equity Act* permits a justice of the Supreme Court of British Columbia to relieve an owner or tenant from paying some or all of a fine.[1]

Section 24 of the *Law and Equity Act* says,

> **24. The court may relieve against all penalties and forfeitures, and in granting the relief impose any terms as to costs, expenses, damages, compensations and all other matters that the court thinks fit.**

In general, the court is more likely to reduce or cancel a fine under this section where the strata corporation could have taken steps sooner to enforce its bylaw or rule rather than allowing the size of the fine to grow unreasonably large in the circumstances.

Lau v. Strata Corporation No. LMS 463,[2] is a good example.

Case Study

Lau and her associates offered to buy a commercial strata unit in a shopping mall. One of the unit's walls was an exterior wall. Persons entering the unit gained

---

[1]*Law and Equity Act*, R.S.B.C. 1996, c. 253.
[2]*Lau v. Strata Corporation No. LMS 463*, [1996] B.C.J. No. 1728 (S.C.).

access only through the mall, whose business hours ended at 9 pm.

After the purchase, Lau and her associates planned to lease the unit to a holding company to operate a video arcade.

Since the holding company wished to operate the arcade beyond normal mall hours, the seller, on behalf of the buyers, asked the strata corporation for permission to install a door in the exterior wall. The strata corporation agreed to permit the exterior door on the condition, among other things, that the new owners install washrooms in the unit for the use of the arcade's clientele. The strata corporation required washrooms in the unit because the mall's washrooms would not be available to the arcade's customers after 9 pm.

In June 1994, the new owners installed the exterior door shortly after purchasing the unit. However, they did not install washrooms inside their unit.

When the strata corporation found out, it decided to impose fines. In September 1994, the strata corporation wrote a letter to the holding company setting out the fines. Under the strata corporation's bylaws, the corporation could impose an initial fine of $50 followed by a maximum fine of $150 for each further occurrence of the bylaw violation.

Upon receipt of the September letter, the holding company immediately blocked off the door and stopped using it. In March 1995, approximately six months later, the holding company removed the door and restored *the exterior wall. By that time, the accumulated fines amounted to $28,754, made up largely of fines at the rate of $150 per day for the continuing infraction.*

Lau and her associates sued the strata corporation for an order cancelling the fines, among other things.

The court held that the strata corporation was entitled in this case to impose fines for breach of the strata corporation's bylaws. However, the court found the total amount of the fines unreasonable. After receipt of the strata corporation's September letter, the holding company blocked the door. Rather than allow extensive fines to accumulate, the strata corporation had the authority to remove the door and restore the exterior wall. The strata corporation could have charged back the restoration expense against the new owners and registered a Certificate of Default under the former *Condominium Act* against their title. Instead, the strata corporation allowed excessive fines to accumulate. In these circumstances, the court applied the provisions of the *Law and Equity Act* to reduce the total amount of the fines to $2,500.

Part V

REPAIRS

When considering a repair or maintenance problem, it is important to keep in mind two separate questions. First, who is responsible to carry out the repair or maintenance work? Second, who is ultimately responsible to pay for that work?

The *Strata Property Act* consistently uses the phrase, *repair and maintain*, which suggests that repairs differ from maintenance. Neither term is defined in the legislation. Despite any technical difference in their meaning, the legislation clearly treats both repairs and maintenance the same. Accordingly, every reference below to repairs includes maintenance, unless the context requires otherwise.

Chapter 25

CARRYING OUT REPAIR OR MAINTENANCE WORK

To answer the question, "Who is responsible to carry out certain repair work?" a strata corporation must look to the *Strata Property Act* and the corporation's bylaws. In this chapter, we assume that a strata corporation has the Standard Bylaws under the Act. To the extent that a strata corporation amends its bylaws to deal differently with repairs, the answers will differ. Before applying the analysis in this chapter, verify whether the repair bylaws under consideration are those found in the Standard Bylaws. If a strata corporation's repair bylaws differ from the Standard Bylaws, the corporation's particular bylaws will govern the answer.

When do the Standard Bylaws Under the *Strata Property Act* Govern Repairs?

The *Strata Property Act* deals more clearly with the subject of repairs than the former *Condominium Act*. Unfortunately, the most significant repair provisions are found in the Standard Bylaws, rather than in the body of the Act. Although most strata corporations will eventually use the Standard Bylaws in the *Strata Property Act*, some strata corporations will not.

To identify a strata corporation's statutory repair bylaws and the extent to which those bylaws are altered by any amended bylaw, see Chapter 19, *Statutory Bylaws and the Effect of the Strata Property Act*. It is essential to identify a strata corporation's repair bylaws *before* approaching any repair problem.

Common Property and Common Assets

1. Strata Corporation's Responsibility

The *Strata Property Act* requires a strata corporation to repair common property and common assets.[1] In particular, if property is designated as common property and has not been designated as limited common property (LCP), the strata corporation must repair it. This is a statutory duty and the strata corporation cannot escape its responsibility. *Tadeson v. Strata Plan NW 2644*[2] is a good example.

Case Study

A residential strata complex contained 35 units. The building envelope suffered water penetration. An engineering report recommended extensive repairs to the building envelope, which was common property.

The strata council presented special resolutions (now called "3/4 vote" resolutions) at two separate general meetings to carry out the repairs. In each case, the resolutions failed because too many owners objected to the cost of the work.

In frustration, three owners applied to the Supreme Court of British Columbia for an order requiring the strata corporation to carry out the repairs.

The court ordered the repairs and authorized a special assessment (now called a special levy) to all of the owners for $312,645 to pay for the work.

---

[1] *Strata Property Act*, s. 72. See also *Schedule of Standard Bylaws*, s. 8(a), (b).
[2] *Tadeson v. Strata Plan NW 2644* (1999), 30 R.P.R. (3d) 253 (B.C.S.C.).

The court held that the strata corporation must fulfill its statutory duty to repair. The eligible voters, by defeating the special resolutions, could not, in effect, agree to excuse the strata corporation from its statutory obligation to repair the common property.

A strata corporation's obligation to repair common property, or a common asset, must be judged with a test of reasonableness. The principle is summarized in *Wright v. Strata Plan No. 205*,[1] a case decided under the former *Condominium Act*, as follows,

> **As appears from the record of its proceedings the Council was at all times alive to its repair and maintenance responsibilities; and throughout the period of the plaintiff's ownership of her strata lot took steps to remedy the defects which she drew to its attention . . .**
>
> **The defendants (the court used the term "defendants" to refer to the strata corporation) are not insurers. Their business, through the Strata Council, is to do all that can reasonably be done in the way of carrying out their statutory duty; and therein lies the test to be applied to their actions. Should it turn out that those they hire to carry out work fail to do so effectively, the defendants cannot be held responsible for such as long as they acted reasonably in the circumstances: and in this instance I have to say that the defendants did just that. They cannot be found to have been negligent.**

In other words, a strata corporation must act reasonably when carrying out its duty to repair and maintain.

In *John Campbell Law Corporation v. The Owners, Strata Plan 1350*,[2] an owner sued a strata corporation for damages on several grounds, including breach of statutory duty, and negligence. The damages occurred when sewage backed up into the owner's unit from a sewer pipe that was common property. The owner claimed the strata

---

[1] *Wright v. Strata Plan No. 205* (1996), 20 B.C.L.R. (3d) 343 at. paras. 29-30; [1996] B.C.J. No. 381 (S.C.); aff'd (1998), 43 B.C.L.R. (3d) 1, 103 B.C.A.C. 249 (C.A.).

[2] *John Campbell Law Corporation v. The Owners, Strata Plan 1350* (2001), 46 R.P.R. (3rd) 96, 8 C.C.L.T. (3rd) 226 (B.C.S.C.).

corporation was strictly liable as a result of a breach of its statutory duty to repair and maintain in section 72 of the *Strata Property Act*. The central question was whether, under the *Strata Property Act,* a strata corporation is strictly liable for a breach of its statutory duty to maintain and repair, or liable only where the corporation fails to act reasonably. The court reaffirmed that a standard of reasonableness prevails, saying in part,[1]

> **I conclude that if a strata corporation such as the defendant (strata corporation) has taken all reasonable steps to inspect and maintain its common facilities, consistent with the practice of other such associations generally, they should not be held liable for damages arising as a result of any strict statutory liability nor should they be put in the position of acting as an insurer by default.**

By analogy to the standard of care of a reasonable person in the law of negligence, the *John Campbell* case effectively confirms a standard of care of the reasonable strata corporation in a claim for breach of statutory duty. An owner wishing to sue a strata corporation for damages for breach of the statutory duty to repair must show that the corporation failed to take all reasonable steps to inspect and maintain the relevant property, consistent with the practice of other strata associations generally. As in a negligence suit, the claimant in a suit against a strata corporation for breach of the statutory duty to repair must present evidence to establish the relevant inspection, repair and maintenance practices among other strata corporations generally. That is, one has to first establish a benchmark before one can prove that someone has failed to achieve the benchmark. By establishing, in evidence, the norm among other strata corporations, the court may

---

[1]*John Campbell Law Corporation v. The Owners, Strata Plan 1350* (2001), 46 R.P.R. (3rd) 96, 8 C.C.L.T. (3rd) 226 (B.C.S.C.).

then measure whether the strata corporation in question acted reasonably in the circumstances. A claimant who fails to produce such evidence risks the dismissal of his or her lawsuit for failure to establish the relevant benchmark.

In the *John Campbell* case, the sewage back-up occurred when roots from a tree on a neighbouring property blocked the strata corporation's sewage pipe. Since the strata corporation had never before experienced problems with the pipe, the corporation had not previously inspected it for potential blockages. Nor did the corporation have any policy for regularly inspecting the sewage pipe. There was no evidence, however, to suggest that other strata corporations made regular inspections of their sewer pipes, whether or not a problem had occurred. In addition, the evidence revealed that most strata corporations do not usually flush sewer pipes unless a problem has first presented itself. The court dismissed the owner's claims for breach of statutory duty and negligence. The court found that unless there was some obvious reason to regularly inspect the sewer pipe, the lack of an inspection policy could not be held against the strata corporation. Bearing in mind the evidence concerning the inspection and maintenance practices of other strata corporations, the strata corporation in question acted reasonably. Even though the strata corporation never inspected or maintained the sewer pipe before the incident, there was no reason to be concerned about a sewage blockage, especially where no other strata corporations inspected their sewer pipes in similar circumstances.

Similarly, a strata corporation acts *unreasonably* if it attempts without justification to shift its responsibility to repair common property to an owner.[1] For example, in

---

[1] As at the date of writing this edition, it appears that a strata corporation may only compel an owner to repair common property on the basis of a prior agreement between the corporation and the owner. For example, this might occur where an owner asks the strata corporation for permission to alter common property and the corporation, as a condition of its approval, requires the owner to agree to maintain that common property. See Chapter 25, *Carrying Out Repair or Maintenance Work*.

Taychuk v. The Owners, Strata Plan LMS 744,[1] certain pipes inside a strata lot were common property. The pipes supplied badly discolored water to the unit and the strata corporation was responsible to repair the water problem. Except for one period of roughly 18 months, the strata corporation took consistent steps over seven years to solve the problem, including consulting experts, flushing the system, and replacing certain valves. Progress stalled for approximately 18 months when the strata corporation proposed installing a particular filtration system in the owners' unit and insisted that the owners would have to bear the cost of replacing the filters and maintaining the system. The owners objected. The owners commenced legal proceedings and, for a time, the strata corporation took no further steps to solve the problem. The court found that the strata corporation breached its duty to act reasonably by making the filtration option dependant on the owners paying to maintain it. Since it was the strata corporation's duty to repair and maintain the common property, it was not reasonable for the strata corporation to require the owners to assume that obligation.[2]

The court declared that the strata corporation breached its duty to repair during the relevant period. The court gave the successful owners liberty to apply again to the court if the discoloration problems returned. The court also awarded costs in favour of the owners who brought the application.

An owner cannot be relieved from paying his or her proportionate share of a special levy to repair common property merely because the strata corporation has, in the past, breached its duty to the owner to act reasonably regarding the repair of that common property.[3] In the *Taychuk* case, the successful owners asked the court for a

---

[1] *Taychuk v. The Owners, Strata Plan LMS 744* (2002), 7 R.P.R. (4th) 302, [2002] B.C.J. No. 2653, 2002 B.C.S.C. 1638 (S.C.).

[2] *Ibid.*, at para. 42.

[3] *Ibid.*

remedy in the nature of an order to exempt them from paying any share of a special levy to raise funds to repair the common property hot water system. The court held that the *Strata Property Act* does not permit such a remedy.

The court, however, exempted the successful owners under section 167(2) of the *Strata Property Act* from paying any of the strata corporation's legal expenses in the proceeding.[1]

In addition, if injury is caused by a strata corporation's failure to repair common property, or a common asset, the corporation may incur liability. *Cater (Guardian Ad Litem) v.* Ghag Enterprises Ltd. *(No. 1 and 2),*[2] is a good illustration.

Case Study

The owner leased the strata unit to a young family. At the time, the owner's representative told the tenants that the lease, in effect, entitled them to use the driveway in front of the unit.

The driveway was common property. The driveway contained a hole described as a depression about three to four feet wide and five inches deep. The depression was in plain view and remained there for some months.

The tenants' eight-year-old daughter rode her bike through the depression and fell. She suffered a broken leg. On behalf of their daughter, the tenants successfully sued the owner of the unit and the strata corporation for damages under the Occupiers Liability Act.

---

[1] For information about an owner's obligation to contribute to the cost of a lawsuit in which the owner sues the strata corporation, see Chapter 27, *Lawsuits.*

[2] *Cater (Guardian Ad Litem) v. Ghag Enterprises Ltd. (No. 1)* (1991), 17 R.P.R. (2nd) 98, [1991] B.C.J. No. 656 (S.C.) and *Cater (Guardian Ad Litem) v. Ghag Enterprises Ltd. (No. 2),* [1991] B.C.J. No. 2451 (S.C.).

The *Occupiers Liability Act* defines the term *occupier* as a person who is in physical possession of premises or has responsibility for, and control over, the condition of the premises, the activities conducted on those premises and the persons allowed to enter those premises.[1] Under the *Occupiers Liability Act,* every occupier has a duty to take care that persons are reasonably safe in using the premises.[2]

The court found that the strata corporation and the owner were both occupiers within the meaning of the *Occupiers Liability Act.* Since the driveway was common property, the strata corporation was an occupier because it had a statutory duty under the condominium legislation to repair and properly maintain the driveway. The owner was also an occupier because it had legal control, as a landlord, over the premises including the associated right to use the driveway.

The court found the child partly at fault and allocated 25 per cent of responsibility for the accident to the child. The court assigned 75 per cent of the liability equally between the owner and the strata corporation, who were each 37.5 per cent responsible.

2. Owner's Responsibility

Section 72(2)(b) of the *Strata Property Act* permits a strata corporation, by bylaw, to make an owner responsible for repairs to common property, "only if identified in the regulations and subject to prescribed restrictions."[3] When the province brought the Act into force on July 1, 2000, the government specifically refrained from proclaiming section 72(2)(b) into force.

---

[1] *Occupiers Liability Act*, R.S.B.C. 1979, c. 303, s. 1. The definition remains the same in the *Occupiers Liability Act*, R.S.B.C. 1996, c. 337, being the current version of the statute.

[2] *Ibid.*, s. 3. The duty remains the same in the *Occupiers Liability Act*, R.S.B.C. 1996, c. 337, s. 3, being the current version of the statute.

[3] *Strata Property Act*, s. 72(2)(b).

Effective October 12, 2001, the province brought section 72(2)(b) of the *Strata Property Act* into force.[1] Unfortunately, however, the regulation that brought section 72(2)(b) into force does not identify any specific common property to which it applies or prescribe any restrictions. Since section 72(2)(b) only permits a strata corporation, by bylaw, to make an owner responsible for repairs to common property that is, "identified in the regulations," it appears that this section cannot be used until the government creates a regulation to identify the applicable common property. However, it appears that in at least two situations a strata corporation may *by agreement*, rather than a bylaw, compel an owner to repair common property.

First, under the Standard Bylaws, an owner may ask the strata corporation for permission to alter common property, including limited common property, or a common asset. The Standard Bylaws permit the strata corporation to require, as a condition of its approval, that the owner take responsibility for any expenses relating to the alteration.[2] Presumably, the owner will be responsible for expenses relating not only to the initial alteration but to any further expenses that arise as a result of the alteration, including repairs or additional insurance. Note, also, that section 59(3) of the *Strata Property Act* requires each Information Certificate (Form B) to disclose any agreements under which the owner takes responsibility for expenses relating to alterations to the common property or common assets, among other things.

If a strata corporation approves an owner's request to alter common property in exchange for the owner's promise to pay for any expenses relating to the alteration, the strata corporation should always record the agreement in writing. The written document will serve as an accurate record of the agreement for future strata councils and

---

[1]B.C. Reg. 241/2001.
[2]*Strata Property Act, Schedule of Standard Bylaws*, s. 6.

property managers. Experience also suggests that recording the agreement in writing tends to avoid disputes later.

Note that an owner's agreement, in exchange for permission to alter common property, is not likely binding on subsequent owners of the same strata lot. Normally, an agreement is binding only on the parties to it. If a strata corporation wishes to make an owner's agreement to pay for repairs to alterations to common property binding on subsequent owners, the corporation should seek legal advice.

At present, our land title registration system does not appear to offer any type of charge that a strata corporation might register against title to the owner's strata lot to bind subsequent owners to the agreement. From the strata corporation's perspective, the corporation may wish, as a term of the owner's agreement to repair common property, to insist that if the owner sells his or her strata lot, he or she must require the purchaser to assume the owner's obligations to the corporation under the agreement.

In theory, if an owner enters an agreement with the corporation to repair common property, that owner's liability may continue indefinitely, depending on the wording of the agreement. For instance, in the absence of wording that terminates the owner's liability upon a sale of the strata lot, an owner who sells his or her strata lot may nevertheless remain liable to the corporation for the cost of repairs, even though he or she is no longer a member of the corporation. Where repair costs are potentially significant, an owner may wish to obtain legal advice before finalizing any agreement with the strata corporation.

Second, the *Strata Property Act* permits a strata corporation to enter into a short-term, exclusive-use agreement with an owner or tenant to give that individual the right to exclusively use common assets or common property that is not designated as limited common property.[1] When a strata corporation gives an owner or tenant exclusive permission to use common property under these provisions, the corporation may make the arrangement subject to conditions.[2] It appears possible for a strata corporation to require, as part of the agreement, that the owner or tenant carry out certain repair work on the common property allocated for that person's exclusive use. To avoid disputes, the corporation should record any short-term, exclusive-use agreement in writing.

Limited Common Property (LCP)

The Standard Bylaws divide responsibility to carry out repair work on LCP between the strata corporation and each owner.

1. Strata Corporation's Responsibility

The Standard Bylaws specifically require a strata corporation to carry out repair work on LCP in certain circumstances.

The Standard Bylaws require the strata corporation to carry out all repair work on LCP that, in the ordinary course of events, occurs less often than once a year.[3] In addition, if any of the following is designated as LCP, the Standard Bylaws make the strata corporation responsible to carry out the repair work, no matter how often the repairs ordinarily occur:[4]

- the structure of the building,
- the exterior of the building,
- chimneys, stairs, balconies and other things attached to the exterior of the building,

[1]*Strata Property Act*, s. 76. For information about short-term, exclusive-use agreements, see Chapter 17, *Common Property*.
[2]*Ibid.*, s. 76(2).
[3]*Strata Property Act, Schedule of Standard Bylaws*, s. 8(c).
[4]*Ibid.*

- doors, windows and skylights on the exterior of a building or that front on the common property, or

- fences, railings and similar structures that enclose patios, balconies and yards.

The Standard Bylaws differ significantly from the approach taken under the former *Condominium Act*. Under the former Act, an owner typically carried out all routine repairs on LCP for the exclusive benefit of his or her strata lot.[1]

2. Owner's Responsibility

If the common property has been designated as LCP, the strata corporation may, by bylaw, make an owner who has a right to use the LCP responsible for its repair.[2]

The Standard Bylaws require every owner with the use of LCP to repair it, except to the extent that the strata corporation has that responsibility under the bylaws.[3]

Under the Standard Bylaws, for example, if a parking stall is designated as LCP, the owner is responsible to carry out most repair work on the parking stall. Any repair, however, that occurs less often than once a year, such as repainting lines, or resurfacing, is the responsibility of the strata corporation to carry out.

Strata Lot

The Standard Bylaws divide responsibility to carry out repair work on a strata lot between the strata corporation and each owner.

---

[1] See, for example, the statutory bylaws in the *Condominium Act*, ss. 115(c) and 128(3).

[2] *Strata Property Act*, s. 72(2). For information about designating common property as limited common property, see Chapter 17, *Using Common Property*.

[3] *Strata Property Act, Schedule of Standard Bylaws*, s. 2(2).

1. Strata Corporation's Responsibility

The Standard Bylaws require a strata corporation to repair the following parts of strata lots:[1]

- the structure of the building,

- the exterior of the building,

- chimneys, stairs, balconies and other things attached to the exterior of a building,

- doors, windows and skylights on the exterior of a building or that front on the common property, and

- fences, railings and similar structures that enclose patios, balconies and yards.

The *Strata Property Act* also permits the strata corporation, by bylaw, to take responsibility for the repair and maintenance of specified portions of a strata lot.[2] For example, a strata corporation may amend this provision in the Standard Bylaws to expand or reduce the corporation's duty to carry out repair work on particular portions of a strata lot.

2. Owner's Responsibility

The Standard Bylaws require each owner to repair and maintain his or her strata lot, except to the extent that the strata corporation has that responsibility under the bylaws.[3]

Typical Disputes

Deciding who is responsible to carry out repair work is likely the most common area of dispute among strata corporations and owners. Despite the prevalence of these

---

[1] *Strata Property Act, Schedule of Standard Bylaws*, s. 8(d).
[2] *Strata Property Act*, s. 72(3).
[3] *Strata Property Act, Schedule of Standard Bylaws*, s. 2(1).

disputes, strata managers receive little guidance in this area. The courts have not produced much case law concerning repairs because most disputes are settled informally or through arbitration.

As a general rule, the legislation, and in particular the statutory bylaws, have always assigned responsibility according to whether the subject of the repair is common property, a common asset, LCP or a strata lot.

In reality, many repair problems include features shared between a strata lot and a neighbouring unit, LCP or common property. In many cases, the former *Condominium Act* overlooked the practical difficulties in assigning responsibility where strata lots are physically linked in various respects to other strata lots or to LCP or common property.

One of the few sources of information in this area is *Understanding and Improving the Condominium Concept*,[1] by Gerry Fanaken in which the author relates his extensive experience in solving these disputes over many years under the former *Condominium Act*. With the author's permission, the following guidelines are adapted from that text, taking into account changes introduced by the *Strata Property Act* and some of the most common disputes. Among other things, the *Strata Property Act* expands the definition of common property.[2] The changes in the definition of common property will also change the approach to some repair problems.

For the most part, the disputes described below under the *Condominium Act* did not distinguish between the responsibility to carry out the repair work and the ultimate responsibility to pay for the repair. Readers should keep in mind that, under the *Strata Property Act*, the two obligations will not necessarily be the responsibility of the same party.

---

[1] Gerry Fanaken, *Understanding and Improving the Condominium Concept*, (Vancouver, Vancouver Condominium Services Ltd., 1994) p. 45 to 55.

[2] *Condominium Act*, s. 1(1) (definition of "common property") and *Strata Property Act*, s. 1(1) (definition of "common property").

Hot Water Heating Systems

Many strata complexes have a gas-heated boiler to heat water, which is then circulated through pipes to the individual strata lots. This type of system is often used to heat the complex or, alternatively, to supply hot water to the strata units. If the complex uses hot water to heat the facilities, each strata lot typically has a thermostat to regulate the temperature of the suite. The thermostat usually controls some form of zone valve, which regulates the flow of hot water to and from the unit. Some zone valves are located inside strata lots, others are located in a common property area.

Condominium Act

In the past, if the thermostat failed, the strata corporation held the owner responsible because it was located inside the strata lot.

If the zone valve failed, and it was located within the common property, the strata corporation accepted responsibility. If the failed zone valve was inside a strata lot, most strata corporations still accepted responsibility. These strata corporations considered the zone valve to be an integral part of the building's heating system. On the other hand, some strata corporations imposed liability on the owner because the valve was inside the strata lot.

Strata Property Act

The *Strata Property Act* expands the definition of common property to include,

1. (1) **"common property" means ...**

   (b) **pipes ... and other facilities for the passage**
       or provision of water . . . heating and
       cooling systems, ... if they are located ...

       ii) **wholly or partially within a strata lot, if**
           they are capable of being and intended
           to be used in connection with the
           enjoyment of another strata lot or the
           common property. (Emphasis added)

Under this definition, clearly the zone valve and, arguably, the thermostat, are common property.

If so, under the Standard Bylaws, the strata corporation must carry out repair work on the zone valve and, in appropriate cases, the thermostat.

Windows and Doors

With the exception of bare land strata plans, virtually every strata development has windows and doors.

Condominium Act

The statutory bylaws under the *Condominium Act* required the strata corporation to maintain and repair the exterior of buildings excluding, among other things, windows and doors included in a strata lot.[1] A plain reading of this provision suggested that if a strata lot's exterior window broke, it was the owner's responsibility to carry out the repair work.

To complicate matters, the property insurance policies carried by most strata corporations included exterior windows, subject to a deductible. If an exterior window broke, most strata corporations assumed responsibility in view of their insurance coverage. However, many strata

---

[1] *Condominium Act*, s. 116(f).

corporations charged back the deductible to the owner because the statutory bylaws excluded windows from the strata corporation's responsibility.

Strata Property Act

The *Strata Property Act* and its Standard Bylaws clarify the respective responsibilities of a strata corporation and an owner to repair property that is common property, or designated as LCP or which is part of a strata lot.

Common Property

If a window or door is common property or a common asset, the strata corporation must carry out the repair work on it.[1]

Limited Common Property

Section 8(c) of the Standard Bylaws deals, in part, with a strata corporation's responsibility to carry out repair work on LCP as follows:

> **8. The strata corporation must repair and maintain . . .**
>
> > **(c) limited common property, but the duty to repair and maintain it is restricted to**
> >
> > > **(i) repair and maintenance that in the ordinary course of events occurs less often than once a year, and**
> > >
> > > **(ii) the following, no matter how often the repair or maintenance ordinarily occurs:**
> > >
> > > > **(A) the structure of a building;**
> > > >
> > > > **(B) the exterior of a building;**
> > > >
> > > > **(C) chimneys, stairs, balconies and other things attached to the exterior of a building;**

---

[1]*Strata Property Act*, s. 72(1) and *Schedule of Standard Bylaws*, s. 8(a), (b).

> **(D)** <u>doors, windows and skylights on the exterior</u> **of a building or that front on the common property;**
>
> **(E)** **fences, railings and similar structures that enclose patios, balconies and yards;**
> (Emphasis added)

Accordingly, under the Standard Bylaws, if an exterior window or door is LCP, the strata corporation must carry out the repair work.

Strata Lot

Section 8(d) of the Standard Bylaws also deals, in part, with a strata corporation's responsibility to carry out repair work on a strata lot as follows:

> **8. The strata corporation must repair and maintain . . .**
>
> **(d)** **a strata lot in a strata plan that is not a bare land strata plan, but the duty to repair and maintain it is restricted to:**
>
>   **(i)** **the structure of a building,**
>
>   **(ii)** **the exterior of a building,**
>
>   **(iii)** **chimneys, stairs, balconies and other things attached to the exterior of a building,**
>
>   **(iv)** <u>**doors, windows and skylights on the exterior**</u> **of a building or that front on the common property, and**
>
>   **(v)** **fences, railings and similar structures that enclose patios, balconies and yards.**
>   (Emphasis added)

Accordingly, if an exterior window or door is part of a strata lot, the Standard Bylaws require the strata corporation to carry out the repair work on that window or door, as the case may be.

Electricity

Most strata lots have their own fuse boxes, including a master electrical on/off switch for the unit, and a meter. In most residential complexes, the meter is usually kept with all the other meters in a meter room. Typically, the meter room is part of the common property.

Condominium Act

If a strata lot experienced a power loss and the source of the problem could be isolated and fixed within the strata unit, including its fuse box, most strata corporations considered the owner responsible. For example, a power failure might be caused by an overloaded circuit or a defectively wired appliance in the strata unit.

On the other hand, if the difficulty was in the meter room, and the meter room was part of the common property, the strata corporation usually took responsibility to fix it. For example, a defect in the main trip switch in the meter room might cause a power failure in the strata unit. Since the defect arose in the meter room, which was common property, the strata corporation was responsible.

Strata Property Act

Strata corporations dealing with electrical problems under the *Strata Property Act* will likely follow their past practice under the former *Condominium Act*. Note that the definition of common property in the *Strata Property Act* says, in part:[1]

---

[1] *Strata Property Act*, s. 1(1) (definition of "common property").

1. (1) "common property" means . . .

    (b) . . . <u>wires</u> . . . and other facilities <u>for the passage or provision of</u> . . . <u>electricity</u> . . . <u>if they are located</u>

        (i) <u>within a floor, wall or ceiling that forms a boundary</u>

            (A) <u>between a strata lot and another strata lot,</u>

            (B) <u>between a strata lot and the common property</u>, or

            (C) between a strata lot or common property and another parcel of land, or

        (ii) <u>wholly or partially within a strata lot, if they are capable of being and intended to be used in connection with the enjoyment of another strata lot or the common property</u>. (Emphasis added)

This definition will help solve disputes where the source of the electrical problem can be located. If the problem occurs within a strata lot, including the fuse box, the owner will have to carry out the repair work under the Standard Bylaws.

On the other hand, if the source of an electrical problem is located in the wiring within a floor, wall or ceiling that forms a boundary with another unit or common property, the strata corporation must carry out the repair work under the Standard Bylaws. Similarly, if the problem occurs within wiring that is inside a strata lot, but the wiring is intended to be used for the enjoyment of another strata lot or the common property, the strata corporation must carry out the repair work.

Fireplaces

Some strata lots include fireplaces. In most cases, the fireplaces do not appear on the strata plan, so it is hard to say what portion, if any, extends beyond the strata lot to the common property.

Wood-burning Fireplaces

In the case of a wood-burning fireplace, the chimney may occupy both the strata lot and the common property.

Condominium Act

The *Condominium Act* did not address responsibility for chimneys. If some, but not all, strata lots had fireplaces, many strata corporations required the owners to clean and maintain the chimneys. Other strata corporations carried out annual chimney maintenance to ensure overall safety but charged back the cost to the owners with fireplaces. If all the strata lots had chimneys, the strata corporation typically carried out annual chimney maintenance.

Strata Property Act

The Standard Bylaws make the strata corporation responsible for maintaining the chimneys.[1]

Gas Fireplaces

Gas fireplaces do not require chimney maintenance but may require repairs. Neither the *Condominium Act* nor the *Strata Property Act* specifically refer to gas fireplaces.

In the past, most strata corporations considered owners responsible for repairs to gas fireplaces within their strata lots. Nothing in the *Strata Property Act* or Standard Bylaws suggests that past practices should change.

---

[1]*Schedule of Standard Bylaws*, s. 8(d).

Toilets and Bathtubs

Neither the former *Condominium Act* nor the *Strata Property Act* refer specifically to toilets or bathtubs.

Condominium Act

In the past, the location of the problem determined responsibility.

Toilets

For example, if a toilet was plugged inside the toilet itself, a strata corporation looked to the owner to fix it.

If, however, the cause of the plugged toilet was beyond the toilet somewhere in the plumbing below floor level, the strata corporation accepted responsibility because the problem occurred within the common property. This position was also consistent with the statutory bylaws under the *Condominium Act*, which provided in part:[1]

> **116. The strata corporation shall . . .**
>
> > **(d) maintain and repair, including renewal where reasonably necessary, pipes . . . existing in the parcel and capable of being used in connection with the enjoyment of more than one strata lot or common property.**

Bathtubs

Strata corporations applied the same approach to leaky bathtubs. If a leak arose, for example, in the perimeter caulking between the tub and the wall or floor, the owner was responsible. Similarly, if the bathtub developed pinhole leaks in its surface, the owner had to fix it.

---

[1] *Condominium Act*, s. 116(d).

On the other hand, if a leak arose in the bathtub drain, which was situated between the strata lot and the common property drain, the strata corporation accepted responsibility for the repair work.

Strata Property Act

Toilets

The wording of the *Strata Property Act* suggests that if the source of the problem is within the toilet, the owner remains responsible. If, however, the problem arises within the pipes, whether inside the strata lot or beyond it, the strata corporation must carry out the repair work.[1]

Bathtubs

In the case of bathtubs, under the *Strata Property Act* strata corporations will likely follow the same approach they took under the *Condominium Act*.

---

[1] *Strata Property Act*, s. 1(1) (definition of "common property").

Chapter 26

PAYING FOR REPAIRS

The *Strata Property Act* and, especially, the regulations determine who is ultimately responsible to pay for repairs.

Although a strata corporation may amend its bylaws concerning repair work, the *Strata Property Act* and the regulations govern the allocation of costs for that work. Note that many of the provisions that specifically require a strata corporation to allocate repair costs among only *some* of the owners, rather than all of them, are found in the regulations.

A strata corporation that wishes to amend its bylaws governing repairs should keep in mind the ways in which the Act and regulations allocate the cost of repair work. Although a strata corporation may amend its statutory bylaws, a corporation is still subject to the Act and regulations. If an amended bylaw purports to allocate the cost of repairs, that bylaw will be of no force or effect to the extent that it conflicts with the provisions of the Act or regulations.[1]

Assuming that a strata corporation is responsible to carry out certain repair work, the corporation must decide who ultimately pays for that work. In other words, the strata corporation must decide whether all, some, or even just one owner must pay the corporation for the cost of that work.

---

[1]*Strata Property Act*, s. 121(1).

Use This Analysis For Expenses Other Than Repairs

Repairs are just one of the many different kinds of expenses that a strata corporation may incur. The requirements for allocating expenses for repairs apply equally to every other kind of strata corporation expenditure.

We have used the subject of repairs to illustrate how the *Strata Property Act* and the regulations allocate expenses because repairs are a common source of disputes in strata communities. Readers, however, may use the analysis below to allocate *any* expenditure by a strata corporation among the owners, including expenses for repairs.

The General Rule

Under the *Strata Property Act*, the general rule is that *all of the owners* must contribute to the operating fund, the contingency reserve fund (CRF), or to a special levy, as the case may be, according to the schedule of unit entitlement.[1] The Act describes the general rule with this formula for calculating a strata lot's contribution:[2]

$$\frac{unit\ entitlement\ of\ strata\ lot}{total\ unit\ entitlement\ of\ all\ strata\ lots} \quad \text{x} \quad total\ contribution$$

When considering an expenditure for repairs, a strata corporation must first decide whether the corporation is responsible to carry out the repair work. If so, the corporation must decide whether to use the operating fund, the CRF, or a special levy, to pay for the work. Although the general rule requires *all of the owners* to contribute to the relevant fund, or to a special levy, the corporation must also decide whether the circumstances fall within one of the

---

[1] *Strata Property Act*, ss. 99 and 108(2). For information about the operating fund, the CRF, a special levy, or using a schedule of unit entitlement, see Chapter 15, *Finances*.
[2] *Ibid.*

exceptions in the *Strata Property Act* or the regulations that require the corporation to allocate the cost only among some, rather than all of the owners.[1]

In other words, if the strata corporation must carry out the repair work, then *all* of the owners must contribute to the cost of that work, unless one of the following exceptions applies.

Section 100 Exception

This exception may apply whether the expenditure for the repair comes from the operating fund, the CRF or a special levy.

Recall that the *Strata Property Act*, as a general rule, requires *all of the owners* to contribute to the operating fund, the CRF or a special levy, according to the schedule of unit entitlement.[2]

Section 100 of the *Strata Property Act*, however, permits the owners to override the general rule by passing a unanimous resolution to change the formula for calculating each strata lot's share of a contribution to the operating fund, the CRF or a special levy, as the case may be.[3] A unanimous resolution requires the affirmative vote of every strata lot.[4] A resolution that changes the general rule for contributing according to the schedule of unit entitlement is not enforceable until the resolution is filed with a Certificate (Form E) in the Land Title Office.[5] The Certificate (Form E) is found in the regulations.

Though it is a rare case where the owners unanimously agree to alter the general rule for contributing to the operating fund, the CRF or a special levy, as the case may be, the *Strata Property Act* permits the eligible voters, in effect, to agree unanimously to require some strata lots, or

---

[1]*Strata Property Act*, s. 99(2).
[2]*Ibid.*, ss. 99 and 108(2).
[3]*Ibid.*, ss. 100 and 108(2).
[4]For information about a unanimous vote, see Chapter 14, *Voting*.
[5]*Strata Property Act*, ss. 100(3).

even just one strata lot, to contribute the whole cost of particular repair work carried out by the strata corporation. This exception is equally available for contributions to the operating fund, the CRF or a special levy.

Operating Fund: Exceptions

The operating fund is for common expenses that occur at least once a year.[1]

If a strata corporation wishes to pay for repairs out of the operating fund, the *Strata Property Act* and regulations require the corporation to allocate the expenditure among some of the owners, rather than all of them, if the corporation falls within one of the following exceptions.

Repairing Common Property

Section 72(2)(b) of the *Strata Property Act* permits a strata corporation, by bylaw, to make an owner responsible for repairs to common property, "only if identified in the regulations and subject to prescribed restrictions."[2] Until the government creates a regulation to identify the applicable common property and any prescribed restrictions, it appears that this section cannot be used to pass a bylaw making an owner responsible to repair common property.[3]

It appears, however, that in at least two situations a strata corporation may *by agreement*, rather than a bylaw, compel an owner to pay the cost to repair common property.

1. Under the Standard Bylaws, an owner may ask the strata corporation for permission to alter common property, including limited common property (LCP), or a common asset. The Standard Bylaws permit the corporation to

---

[1] *Strata Property Act*, s. 92(a).
[2] *Ibid.*, s. 72(2)(b).
[3] For more information about section 72(2)(b) of the *Strata Property Act*, see Chapter 25, *Carrying Out Repair or Maintenance Work*.

require, as a condition of its approval, that the owner take responsibility for any expenses relating to the alteration.[1] It appears that an owner may be responsible for expenses relating not only to the initial alteration but also any further expenses that arise as a result of the alteration, including repairs or additional insurance.

2. The *Strata Property Act* permits a strata corporation to give an owner or tenant permission to exclusively use, or a special privilege in relation to, common assets or common property that is not designated as LCP.[2] When a strata corporation gives an owner or tenant permission to exclusively use, or to exercise an exclusive privilege over common property, the corporation may make the arrangement subject to conditions.[3] It appears possible for a strata corporation to require, as part of the agreement, that the owner or tenant carry out certain repair work on the common property allocated for that person's exclusive use.

Repairing Limited Common Property

According to section 6.4(1) of the regulations, if a contribution to the operating fund relates to and benefits only LCP, the contribution is shared only by owners of strata lots entitled to use the LCP.[4]

If these criteria are met, the regulations require the strata corporation to calculate each strata lot's share of the contribution to the operating fund according to this formula:[5]

---

[1] *Strata Property Act, Schedule of Standard Bylaws*, s. 6.
[2] *Strata Property Act*, s. 76.
[3] *Ibid.*, s. 76(2).
[4] *Strata Property Regulation*, s. 6.4(1).
[5] *Ibid.*

$$\frac{\textit{unit entitlement of strata lot}}{\substack{\textit{total unit entitlement of all strata} \\ \textit{lots whose owners are entitled} \\ \textit{to use the LCP to which the} \\ \textit{contribution relates.}}} \quad \times \quad \textit{contribution to the operating fund}$$

For instance, under the Standard Bylaws a strata corporation must carry out all repair work on LCP balconies and railings attached to the exterior of the building. Any expenses that occur once a year, or more often than once a year, to repair the balconies or railings must, under the regulations, be allocated to the strata lot owners with those balconies and railings.

Repairing a Strata Lot

If a contribution to the operating fund relates only to the repair of some, but not all, strata lots, the *Strata Property Act* and the regulations require a strata corporation to allocate the cost of the repairs solely among those strata lots if the corporation meets certain criteria.[1]

Type of Strata Lot

According to section 6.4(2) of the regulations, if a contribution to the operating fund relates to and benefits only one *type* of strata lot, and that type is identified as a type of strata lot in the bylaws, the contribution is shared only among owners of the strata lots to which the contribution relates.[2]

If these criteria are met, section 6.4(2) of the regulations requires a strata corporation to calculate each strata lot's share of the contribution to the operating fund according to this formula:

---

[1] *Strata Property Regulation*, ss. 6.4(2) and 6.5(1).
[2] *Ibid.*, s. 6.4(2).

$$\frac{\textit{unit entitlement of strata lot}}{\begin{array}{c}\textit{total unit entitlement of all}\\\textit{strata lots of the type to which}\\\textit{the contribution relates}\end{array}} \quad \text{x} \quad \textit{contribution to the operating fund}$$

The statutory bylaws do not specify different types of strata lots. A strata corporation, however, may amend its bylaws to identify a type of strata lot for the purposes of allocating expenses.[1]

There are at least several ways that a bylaw might identify different types of strata lots, including:

- A bylaw that expressly creates different types of strata lot, or

- A bylaw that creates sections to represent the interests of owners of different types of residential strata lots.

Express Bylaw

A strata corporation may enact a bylaw that identifies different types of strata lots for the purpose of allocating expenses under section 6.4(2) of the regulations. Subject to a transition exception noted below, a strata corporation must follow the usual procedure to amend its bylaws.[2]

The *Strata Property Act* does not define what may be considered a type for the purpose of allocating expenses. Accordingly, it appears that each strata corporation may use its own criteria, by means of a bylaw, for defining a type of strata lot. For instance, one type of strata lot may be those with gas fireplaces. If a strata corporation pays for the gas every month, it is an operating expense of the strata corporation. If a strata corporation has identified strata lots with gas fireplaces as a type of strata lot in a bylaw, the regulations require that the cost of the gas used in the fireplaces be allocated only among strata lots of that type.

---

[1] *Strata Property Regulation*, ss. 6.4(2) and 17.13.
[2] For information about amending bylaws, see Chapter 20, *Amending Bylaws*.

Transition

The statutory bylaws in the former *Condominium Act* permitted a strata corporation to attribute expenses to a type of strata lot *without specifically identifying each type of strata lot in its bylaws.*[1] Section 128(2) of the *Condominium Act* said,

> 128. (2) **Where a strata plan consists of more than one type of strata lot, the common expenses shall be apportioned in the following manner:**
>
> > (a) **common expenses attributable to one or more type of strata lot shall be allocated to that type of strata lot and shall be borne by the owners of that type of strata lot in the proportion that the unit entitlement of that strata lot bears to the aggregate unit entitlement of all types of strata lots concerned;**
> >
> > (b) **common expenses not attributable to a particular type or types of strata lot shall be allocated to all strata lots and shall be borne by the owners in proportion to the unit entitlement of their strata lots.**

The *Condominium Act* did not define the term *type* in section 128(2). The courts, however, held that the word *type* in that section refers to "character or form of structure" or to "a class of things having common characteristics."[2]

In the past, many strata corporations relied on section 128(2) of the *Condominium Act* to allocate different expenses in their budgets to different types of strata lots. Since the statutory bylaws in the *Condominium Act* no longer have effect as of January 1, 2002, a strata corporation must now create such a bylaw if the corporation wishes to allocate

---

[1] *Condominium Act*, s. 128(2).
[2] See, for example, *Lim v. Strata Plan VR 2654* (2001), 44 R.P.R. (3d) 243, [2001] B.C.J. No. 2040, 2001 B.C.S.C. 1386 (S.C.).

certain expenses to strata lot owners according to types of strata lots under the *Strata Property Act*.

If on July 1, 2000, when the *Strata Property Act* came into force, a strata corporation relied on a statutory bylaw under the former *Condominium Act*, or any similar bylaw, to allocate expenses according to different types of strata lots in the budget prevailing on that date, then the transition provisions in the regulations permitted the corporation to continue allocating expenses on that basis until December 31, 2001, subject to the corporation's bylaws.[1]

In addition, during the grace period for bylaws, until December 31, 2001, a strata corporation could amend its bylaws to create types of strata lots by a majority vote at a general meeting. On or after January 1, 2002, the usual voting thresholds applied.[2]

Residential Sections

The *Strata Property Act* permits a strata corporation to pass a bylaw to create separate sections to represent the different interests of, "owners of different types of residential strata lots."[3] The regulations permit different sections for the following types of residential strata lots: [4]

- apartment-style,

- townhouse-style, or

- detached house-style sections.

---

[1]*Strata Property Regulation*, s. 17.13. See also *Strata Corporation LMS 509 v. Andresen*, [2001] B.C.J. No. 225, 2001 B.C.S.C. 201 and *The Owners, Strata Plan LMS 608 v. The Apartment Owners of Strata Plan LMS 608 et al.*, [2001] B.C.J. No. 2116 (S.C.).

[2]*Ibid.*

[3]*Strata Property Act*, s. 191(1), (c).

[4]*Strata Property Regulation*, s. 11.1.

If a strata corporation passes a bylaw to create separate sections for residential strata lots of these types, the bylaw will necessarily identify different types of strata lot. In that case, section 6.4(2) of the regulations will apply to permit the corporation to allocate expenses to the different types of residential strata lot.[1]

Specified Portions Bylaw

According to section 6.5(1) of the regulations, if a strata corporation has passed a bylaw under section 72(3) of the *Strata Property Act* that makes the corporation responsible to repair specified portions of *some, but not all of the strata lots*, a contribution to the operating fund for the repair of those portions is shared only among owners of the strata lots to which the contribution relates.[2]

If these criteria are met, section 6.5(1) of the regulations requires a strata corporation to calculate each strata lot's share of the contribution to the operating fund according to this formula:

$$\frac{\textit{unit entitlement of strata lot}}{\textit{total unit entitlement of all strata lots to which the contribution relates}} \ \times \ \textit{contribution to the operating fund}$$

Section 8(d) of the Standard Bylaws

There may be a question whether section 8(d) of the Standard Bylaws constitutes a ". . . bylaw *passed* under section 72(3) of the Act," within the meaning of section 6.5(1) of the regulations.[3] If section 8(d) of the Standard Bylaws is not such a bylaw, then this exception is not available to a strata corporation whose statutory bylaws are the Standard Bylaws.

---

[1] See also *Strata Property Regulation*, s. 11.3 and *Strata Corporation LMS 509 v. Andresen*, [2001] B.C.J. No. 225, 2001 B.C.S.C. 201.

[2] *Strata Property Regulation*, s. 6.5(1).

[3] *Ibid.*

The relevant provisions of section 6.5(1) of the regulations say,

> . . . if a strata corporation has, <u>by a bylaw passed under section 72(3) of the Act</u>, taken responsibility for the repair and maintenance of specified portions of some but not all of the strata lots, a contribution to the operating fund . . . in respect of the repair or maintenance of those portions is shared only by the owners of the strata lots to which the contribution . . . relates . . . (according to unit entitlement). (Emphasis added)

Section 72(3) of the *Strata Property Act* provides,

> **72. (3) The strata corporation may, by bylaw, take responsibility for the repair and maintenance of specified portions of a strata lot.**

Section 8(d) of the Standard Bylaws provides:

> **8. The strata corporation must repair and maintain . . .**
>
> **(d) a strata lot in a strata plan that is not a bare land strata plan, but the duty to repair and maintain it is restricted to:**
>
> > **(i) the structure of a building,**
> >
> > **(ii) the exterior of a building,**
> >
> > **(iii) chimneys, stairs, balconies and other things attached to the exterior of a building,**
> >
> > **(iv) doors, windows and skylights on the exterior of a building or that front on the common property, and**
> >
> > **(v) fences, railings and similar structures that enclose patios, balconies and yards.**

If section 8(d) of the Standard Bylaws is not a bylaw "passed under section 72(3) of the Act," then this exception is not available to any strata corporation whose statutory bylaws are the Standard Bylaws.[1]

One of the prerequisites for applying section 6.5(1) of the regulations is that the relevant bylaw is *passed under section 72(3) of the Act*. The Act does not define the term *passed*, but the word certainly suggests a step taken to enact an amended bylaw by the passage of the necessary resolution at a general meeting. For example, the Act uses the term *pass* or *passage* in that context in the following provisions:

- section 8 (before the first conveyance of a strata lot, a developer may *pass* a resolution to amend the strata corporation's bylaws without holding a general meeting),

- section 11 (after the first conveyance, but before the first annual general meeting (AGM), the strata corporation may only *pass* a resolution requiring a 3/4 vote if the resolution is passed by a unanimous vote, with some exceptions),

- section 52 (where a unanimous resolution fails, if certain requirements are met, the court may intervene where the *passage* of the resolution is in the best interests of the strata corporation),

- section 122 (a strata corporation may *pass* a bylaw governing activities relating to the sale of a strata lot),

- section 197 (the eligible voters in a section may hold meetings and *pass* resolutions), and

- section 213 (if the buildings in a leasehold strata plan are destroyed or significantly damaged, the eligible voters may elect not to rebuild by a resolution *passed* by a 3/4 vote).

---

[1]For information about statutory bylaws, see Chapter 19, *Statutory Bylaws and the Effect of the Strata Property Act.*

In most cases, a strata corporation will acquire section 8(d) as a Standard Bylaw by operation of law and not because the corporation *passed* the bylaw by approving the necessary resolution. If so, in the author's view, the corporation cannot rely on section 6.5(1) of the regulations to allocate the cost of repairs among only some, rather than all of the strata lots.

By contrast, where a strata corporation has expressly adopted section 8(d) of the Standard Bylaws by the passage of the necessary resolution at a general meeting, that corporation has arguably *passed* a bylaw under section 72(3) of the Act. This might occur, for example, where a strata corporation that was already in existence on July 1, 2000, when the *Strata Property Act* came into force, subsequently passed a resolution to adopt the Standard Bylaws during the grace period, without waiting for the Standard Bylaws to come into force for that corporation by operation of law on January 1, 2002.[1]

This problem likely reflects a legislative oversight that could be cured by amending the relevant wording in section 6.5(1) of the regulations.

Contingency Reserve Fund: Exceptions

As a general rule, Contingency Reserve Fund (CRF) expenses are allocated among *all of the owners* on the basis of their unit entitlement.[2]

There appear to be only two exceptions to the general rule.

First, there is the section 100 exception, previously described.

---

[1]For information about the effect of the *Strata Property Act* on the bylaws of a strata corporation that already existed when the Act came into force, see Chapter 19, *Statutory Bylaws and the Effect of the Strata Property Act.*

[2]*Strata Property Act*, s. 99. See also *Strata Property Regulation*, ss. 6.4(3) and 6.5(2).

Second, there is an exception for an amended bylaw that apportions contributions to the CRF, if the bylaw meets certain criteria.[1] The strata corporation must have filed the amended bylaw at the Land Title Office before July 1, 2000, when the *Strata Property Act* came into force. Next, the bylaw must apportion CRF contributions according to *type* of strata lot. Last, the specific type of strata lot must be identified as a type of strata lot in the bylaws of the strata corporation or a section, as noted above. If these requirements are met, it appears that a strata corporation may apportion a contribution to the CRF to a particular type of strata lot for the purpose of repairs.

Special Levy: Exceptions

Section 108(2)(b) Exception

Section 108(2) of the *Strata Property Act* contemplates several ways that a strata corporation may allocate a special levy among the owners. First, under section 99 of the Act, which creates the general rule based on the schedule of unit entitlement, previously described. Second, under section 100, which permits the corporation to override the general rule by passing a unanimous resolution to use a different formula for allocating the unit entitlement than the formula in the general rule. Last, section 108(2)(b) says,

> 108 (2) A strata corporation must calculate each strata lot's share of a special levy
>
> (a) in accordance with section 99 (or) 100 . . . ,
>
> OR
>
> (b) <u>in another way that establishes a fair division of expenses</u> for that particular levy, in which case the levy must be approved by a resolution <u>passed by a unanimous vote</u> at an annual or special general meeting. (Emphasis added)

---

[1] *Strata Property Regulation*, s. 17.11(6).

At first glance, this provision seems redundant with the section 100 exception. Presumably, however, the section 108(2)(b) exception refers to a situation where the eligible voters wish to allocate a special levy on grounds that do not directly involve unit entitlement. For instance, suppose a strata development consists of 20 townhouses situated near a busy street with a lot of traffic noise. Suppose, too, that the five townhouses nearest the street are separated from the roadway by a wide strip of grass that is part of the strata corporation's common property. Assume that the strata corporation requires a special levy to raise $25,000 to install a landscaped sound barrier along the grassy strip. Since the five townhouses nearest the street will most directly benefit from this repair, the owners might agree by unanimous resolution under section 108(2)(b) of the Act to allocate the whole expense solely to the owners of the five townhouses, shared equally among them.

Typical Disputes: Who Pays—All or Some?

Since the advent of the *Strata Property Act* on July 1, 2000, most strata repair cases decided by the courts involve disputes whether all of the owners, or only some of them, must pay for costly repairs.

Warning: Which Statute Governs a Dispute Over Repair Costs?

This chapter explains how the *Strata Property Act* allocates expenses, and in particular repairs, among owners.

Effective July 1, 2000, the *Strata Property Act* repealed the former *Condominium Act*.[1] As a result, some persons assume that the *Strata Property Act* governs every dispute

---

[1] *Strata Property Act*, s. 294.

over repair costs on or after July 1, 2000. As at the date of this publication, it is not safe to make this assumption.

Since the *Strata Property Act* came into force, the courts appear divided on the question which statute governs a repair dispute. In each case, the answer mainly depends on whether the provincial *Interpretation Act* applies.[1] The *Interpretation Act* applies to every enactment, "unless a contrary intention appears."[2] Where the *Interpretation Act* applies, section 35 of that Act protects rights that accrued, or that continue to accrue, under the former *Condominium Act*, as follows,

> **35 (1) If all or part of an enactment is repealed, the repeal does not . . .**
>
> **(c) affect a right or obligation acquired, accrued, accruing or incurred under the enactment so repealed, ...**

In *The Owners, Strata Plan LMS 608 v. The Apartment Owners of Strata Plan LMS 608 et al.*, the court found that section 35 of the *Interpretation Act* preserved certain rights of the applicants that accrued to them under the former *Condominium Act*.[3] Even though the *Strata Property Act* repealed the *Condominium Act*, the *Interpretation Act* allowed the court to apply the relevant provisions of the *Condominium Act* to the dispute in question.

By contrast, and more recently, in *Strata Plan LMS 1537 v. Alvarez*, the court found that the *Interpretation Act* does not apply so as to preserve rights accrued under

---

[1] *Interpretation Act*, R.S.B.C. 1996, c. 238.

[2] *Interpretation Act*, s. 2.

[3] *The Owners, Strata Plan LMS 608 v. The Apartment Owners of Strata Plan LMS 608 et al.*, [2001] B.C.J. No. 2116 (S.C.). See also *Lim v. Strata Plan VR 2654* (2001), 44 R.P.R. (3d) 243, [2001] B.C.J. No. 2040, 2001 B.C.S.C. 1386 (S.C.); *The Owners, Strata Plan No. VR 1767 v. Seven Estate Ltd. et al.* (2002), 49 R.P.R. (3rd) 156, [2002] B.C.J. No. 755, 2002 B.C.S.C. 381 (S.C.); Cf. *Coupal v. Strata Plan LMS 2503* (2002), 6 B.C.L.R. (4th) 372, [2002] B.C.J. No. 2313, 2002 B.C.S.C. 1444 (S.C.) (where the parties agreed by consent that the *Condominium Act* applied).

the former *Condominium Act.*[1] Instead, the court held that the detailed provisions of the *Strata Property Act* reveal the legislature's "contrary intention" to exclude the application of the *Interpretation Act.* Consequently, the *Alvarez* case held that the *Strata Property Act* governs repair disputes.

A strata corporation that is experiencing a significant dispute over the allocation of an expense should obtain legal advice, particularly in respect of which statute governs the disagreement.

Examples: Townhouses Versus Apartments

Depending which statute governs a dispute, the legal result may be very different.

Briefly, section 128(2) of the *Condominium Act*, quoted above, enabled a strata corporation to allocate a common expense between owners of different types of strata lots with relative ease.

By contrast, the *Strata Property Act* creates a much more formal scheme, as previously described. Under the *Strata Property Act*, all the owners must contribute to a common expense, unless an exception applies. A unanimous vote or a bylaw amendment is usually required to create an exception. Apart from the section 100 exception, the existence of an exception also depends on which source of funds will be used to pay the expenditure: the operating fund, the CRF, or a special levy.

In the case of major repairs, the spending restrictions in the *Strata Property Act* also limit the availability of certain exceptions. The Act defines the *operating fund* as a fund for common expenses that occur one or more times a year.[2] A strata corporation may only use the operating fund to pay for

---

[1] *Strata Plan LMS 1537 v. Alvarez* (2003), 17 B.C.L.R. (4th) 63, [2003] B.C.J. No. 1610, 2003 B.C.S.C. 1085 (S.C.). See also *Strata Corp. LMS 509 v. Andresen*, [2001] B.C.J. No. 225, 2001 B.C.S.C. 201 (S.C.).
[2] *Strata Property Act*, s. 92(a).

repairs if the expenditure is consistent with this definition. The Act defines the contingency reserve fund (CRF) as a fund for common expenses that usually occur less often than once per year, if at all.[1] A strata corporation may only use the CRF fund to pay for repairs if the expenditure is consistent with the fund's definition.

This means that in a typical leaky condo repair, the only permissible sources of funds are the CRF or a special levy.[2] If so, the operating fund cannot be used and the exception for certain types of strata lot created by section 6.4(2) of the regulations has no application. With the notable exception of the decision in *Strata Plan LMS 1537 v. Alvarez*, some judicial repair decisions are confusing because they overlook this important factor.[3] When reading repair cases, it is important to keep this factor in mind.

Condominium Act

In *The Owners, Strata Plan LMS 608 v. The Apartment Owners of Strata Plan LMS 608 et al.*, a strata corporation asked the court to resolve a funding dispute between apartment and townhouse owners.[4] The court found that the former *Condominium Act* governed the dispute:

---

[1] *Strata Property Act*, s. 92(b).

[2] *Strata Plan LMS 1537 v. Alvarez*, [2003] B.C.J. No. 1610 at para. 55 (S.C.); *Wilfert v. Ward*, [2004] B.C.J. No. 423, 2004 B.C.S.C. 289; Cf. *Strata Corp. LMS 509 v. Andresen*, [2001] B.C.J. No. 225, 2001 B.C.S.C. 201 (S.C.). (The court found that certain repair expenses could no longer be considered unusual, but rather had become normal, foreseeable and inevitable expenses permitting the use of the operating fund. Section 6.4(2) of the regulations did not apply, however, because the bylaws did not identify different types of strata lot.)

[3] *Strata Plan LMS 1537 v. Alvarez*, [2003] B.C.J. No. 1610 at paras. 88-89 (S.C.) where Bauman, J. refers to error on this point in *The Owners, Strata Plan No. VR 1767 v. Seven Estate Ltd. et al.* (2002), 49 R.P.R. (3rd) 156, [2002] B.C.J. No. 755, 2002 B.C.S.C. 381 (S.C.).

[4] *The Owners, Strata Plan LMS 608 v. The Apartment Owners of Strata Plan LMS 608 et al.*, [2001] B.C.J. No. 2116 (S.C.).

Case Study

. *The strata complex consisted of an apartment building and townhouses.*

In 1998, the owners unanimously passed a bylaw identifying which common expenses would be borne by all of the owners, and which would be borne by owners of the apartment or townhouse units respectively (the 1998 bylaw).

A while later, leaks developed in the exterior envelope of the apartment building. An engineering report revealed that it would cost approximately $700,000 to repair the envelope in the apartment building.

In the meantime, various townhouses were sold. In every case, the townhouse purchasers relied on the 1998 bylaw when they decided to buy their units. But for the 1998 bylaw, those purchasers would not have bought townhouses in the development.

On March 31, 2001, the strata corporation, by majority vote, passed a bylaw specifying, for the purpose of the <u>Strata Property Act</u>, *that the apartment units and townhouse units constituted two types of strata lot (the 2001 bylaw).*

When the strata corporation allocated the cost of repairing the apartment building solely among the apartment owners, they argued that all of the owners, including the townhouse owners, must contribute to the repairs. The strata corporation applied to the court to resolve the dispute.

For the purpose of the proceedings, the parties conceded that the apartment and townhouse units were different types of strata lot.

The court held that the cost of repairing the apartment building must be borne solely by the apartment owners.

The court first had to decide whether the former *Condominium Act* or the *Strata Property Act* governed the situation. The court found that the *Condominium Act* applied because of the provisions in the *Interpretation Act*, previously discussed. The *Interpretation Act* provides that the repeal of an enactment (for example, the *Condominium Act*) does not affect a right or obligation acquired, or accruing, under the enactment that was repealed.[1]

Since the former *Condominium Act* governed the situation, section 128(2) of that Act provided that common expenses attributable to one or more strata lots of a particular type must be allocated to that type and borne by the owners of strata lots of that type. Under section 128(2) of the former Act, the strata corporation could continue to rely on the 1998 bylaw to allocate different expenses to the apartment and townhouse units respectively as different types of strata lot.

Even if that conclusion was wrong, the strata corporation's bylaws consisted, in part, of the statutory bylaws under the former *Condominium Act*, including section 128 of that Act. The court found, in any event, that section 128(2) of the *Condominium Act* continued to apply until the end of December 2001, under the transition provisions in the regulations.[2]

The court also held that the same result occurs if the *Strata Property Act* applies because the 2001 bylaw created two types of strata lot within the meaning of section 6.4(2) of the regulations. In the court's view, section 6.4(2) of the regulations would permit the strata corporation to allocate the repair costs solely to the apartment owners because they owned the type of strata lot to which the expense related. Section 6.4(2), however, only creates an exception

---

[1] *Interpretation Act*, s. 35.
[2] *Strata Property Regulation*, s. 17.13.

from the general rule if, among other things, the *operating fund* is the source of the relevant expenditure. The operating fund may only be used for common expenses that usually occur every year. The court in the *LMS 608* case apparently overlooked this statutory spending restriction, described previously. This is an example of the confusion created when a court overlooks the effect of the statutory spending restrictions, as mentioned earlier.

Whether applying the former *Condominium Act,* or seemingly incorrectly applying section 6.4(2) of the regulations under the *Strata Property Act*, the result was the same. The apartment owners had to pay for the repairs to their building without contribution from the townhouse owners.

Strata Property Act

In *Strata Plan LMS 1537 v. Alvarez*,[1] the court reviewed its previous decisions to date, including the *LMS 608* case, and carefully analyzed the scheme for allocating repair costs in the *Strata Property Act*. The court concluded that the detailed provisions in the *Strata Property Act* reveal the legislature's intention to resolve repair disputes with the new statute. In *Alvarez*, the court distinguished the *LMS 608* case and rejected the view that the *Interpretation Act* preserves rights under the former *Condominium Act*. The court held that the *Strata Property Act* regulated the situation.

Case Study

The strata development blended a heritage home built in 1904 with an apartment building built in 1994. The heritage home held two strata lots. The apartment portion consisted of six apartments.

---

[1]*Strata Plan LMS 1537 v. Alvarez* (2003), 17 B.C.L.R. (4th) 63, [2003] B.C.J. No. 1610, 2003 B.C.S.C. 1085 (S.C.).

The building envelope in the apartment portion, built with all the benefits of modern technology, leaked. The strata corporation estimated that it would cost approximately $160,000 to repair the building envelope for the apartment units.

At all relevant times, section 128(2) of the <u>Condominium Act</u>, quoted above, was a bylaw of the strata corporation.

On October 15, 2001 the owners unanimously passed a resolution allocating among all the owners the cost to repair the building envelope in the apartment portion of the complex.

The applicants owned a strata lot in the heritage portion of the development.

Despite previously consenting to the resolution, the applicants claimed that it was invalid. The applicants argued that the <u>Condominium Act</u> governed the repairs, and that section 128(2) of the bylaws required the strata corporation to allocate the cost to repair the apartments' building envelope solely to the owners of the apartment units.

The court found that the general rule applied; all the owners must contribute according to unit entitlement unless an exception exists. Since the expenditure to repair the building envelope was an exceptional expense, the funds must come from the CRF or a special levy. In the circumstances of this case, there was no evidence to justify any of the exceptions that the Act permits where a CRF or a special levy is used to fund repairs. Since the

Strata Property Act required everyone to pay, the resolution was consistent with what the law required. The resolution in *Alvarez* was valid and the applicants must contribute their share of the cost of the repairs.

Sections

The *Strata Property Act* permits a strata corporation to create separate sections to represent the interests of different strata owners, if certain criteria are met.[1] A section is a form of mini-government with autonomy over matters that relate solely to the section, including finances.[2] Among other things, a section may establish its own operating fund and CRF for common expenses of the section.[3] A section may also budget and require owners of strata lots within the section to pay strata fees and special levies for expenditures authorized by the section.[4]

A strata corporation, or alternatively, a section, may spend money for the benefit of all, or some, of the strata lots in the section.

Strata Corporation Expenditure

The *Strata Property Act* and the regulations expressly address the situation where the strata corporation spends money for the benefit of some, or all, of the strata lots in a section.

The requirements that govern how a strata corporation allocates expenses among the owners, as described earlier in this chapter, apply in a similar fashion when a strata corporation spends money for the benefit of strata lots in a section.[5]

---

[1]*Strata Property Act*, s. 191. For information about sections, see Chapter 10, *Sections*.
[2]*Ibid.*, s. 194.
[3]*Ibid.*, s. 194(2)(a).
[4]*Ibid.*, s. 194(2)(b).
[5]*Ibid.*, s. 194(1) and *Strata Property Regulation*, ss. 11.2, 11.3 and 17.13.

The General Rule

Where an expense of the strata corporation relates solely to the strata lots in a section, the general rule is that *all of the owners in the section* must contribute to the expense according to the schedule of unit entitlement.[1] The general rule applies whether the strata corporation acquires the money from its operating fund, the CRF, or the proceeds of a special levy.[2] Section 195 of the *Strata Property Act* describes this general rule with the following formula:[3]

$$\frac{unit\ entitlement\ of\ strata\ lot}{total\ unit\ entitlement\ of\ all\ strata\ lots\ in\ section} \quad x \quad total\ contribution$$

For example, if a strata corporation carries out repair work on strata lots in a section, then *all of the owners in the section* must contribute to the cost of that work according to unit entitlement, unless an exception applies.

The *Strata Property Act* and the regulations create exceptions to the general rule in the same manner that the legislation creates exceptions for the corporation in cases where a section is not involved, as noted earlier. For instance, if a strata corporation wishes to allocate an expense for repairs among only some of the owners in the section, rather than all of the owners in that section, the circumstances must fall within one of the following exceptions:

Section 100 Exception

In the same fashion as described above, a strata corporation may override the general rule by passing a unanimous resolution to change the formula for calculating each strata

---

[1] *Strata Property Act*, s. 195.
[2] *Ibid.*, ss. 99, 100, 108(2) and 195.
[3] *Ibid.*, s. 195.

lot's share of a contribution to the operating fund, the CRF, or a special levy.[1]

Operating Fund: Exceptions

If a strata corporation wishes to spend money from its operating fund, the following exceptions require the section to allocate the expenditure among only some, rather than all, of the strata lots in the section.

Limited Common Property (LCP)

According to section 11.2(1) of the regulations, if a contribution to a strata corporation's operating fund relates to and benefits only LCP for the exclusive use of strata lots in a section, the contribution is shared only by owners of the strata lots entitled to use the LCP. If these criteria are met, the regulations require the strata corporation to calculate each strata lot's share of the contribution according to this formula:

$$\frac{\textit{unit entitlement of strata lot in section}}{\textit{total unit entitlement of all strata lots in section whose owners are entitled to use the LCP to which the contribution relates}} \times \textit{contribution to the operating fund}$$

Strata Lot

If a contribution to the strata corporation's operating fund relates only to the repair of some, but not all strata lots in a section, the *Strata Property Act* and the regulations require the corporation to allocate the cost of the repairs solely among those strata lots, if the corporation meets the criteria for either of the following exceptions:

---

[1] *Strata Property Act.*, ss. 100 and 108(2) and *Strata Property Regulation*, ss. 11.2(3) and 11.3(2).

Type of Strata Lot

According to section 11.2(2) of the regulations, if a contribution to the strata corporation's operating fund relates to and benefits only one *type* of strata lot in a section, and that type is identified as a type of strata lot in the bylaws of the section, the contribution is shared only by owners of strata lots of that type.

If these criteria for a type of strata lot are met, the regulations require the strata corporation to calculate each strata lot's share of the contribution according to this formula:

$$\frac{\textit{unit entitlement of strata lot in section}}{\begin{array}{c}\textit{total unit entitlement of all strata lots}\\ \textit{in section of the type to which the}\\ \textit{contribution relates}\end{array}} \quad \text{x} \quad \begin{array}{c}\textit{contribution}\\ \textit{to the operating fund}\end{array}$$

The transition provisions that apply to types of strata lot, as described earlier in this chapter, also apply to a type of strata lot in a section.[1] If on July 1, 2000, when the *Strata Property Act* came into force, a strata corporation relied on a statutory bylaw under the former *Condominium Act*, or any similar bylaw, to allocate expenses according to different types of strata lot in a section in the corporation's budget prevailing on that date, then the transition provisions in the regulations permit the corporation to continue allocating expenses on that basis until December 31, 2001, subject to the bylaws. In addition, during the grace period for bylaws, until December 31, 2001, a corporation, or presumably a section, may amend its bylaws to create different types of strata lot in the section by majority vote. On or after January 1, 2002, the usual voting thresholds will apply.

---

[1]*Strata Property Regulation*, ss. 11.2(2) and 17.13.

Specified Portions Bylaw

According to section 11.3(1) of the regulations, if a section has, by a bylaw passed under section 72(3) of the Act, taken responsibility for the repair of specified portions of some but not all of the strata lots in the section, a contribution to the strata corporation's operating fund in respect of the repair of those portions is shared only by the owners of the strata lots to which the contribution relates.

If these criteria are met, the regulations require the strata corporation to calculate each strata lot's share of the contribution according to this formula:

$$\frac{\textit{unit entitlement of strata lot in section}}{\begin{array}{c}\textit{total unit entitlement of all strata lots in}\\ \textit{section to which the contribution relates}\end{array}} \quad \text{x} \quad \begin{array}{c}\textit{contribution}\\ \textit{to the operating fund}\end{array}$$

Special Levy: Exceptions

Section 108(2)(b) Exception

Section 108(2)(b) of the *Strata Property Act* permits a strata corporation to override the general rule by passing a unanimous resolution to allocate a special levy on some other fair basis that does not directly involve unit entitlement, as previously described. The regulations clearly contemplate that where a strata corporation raises money by special levy for an expenditure that benefits strata lots in a section, the eligible voters may use section 108(2)(b) to allocate the levy among the owners on a basis other than unit entitlement.[1]

---

[1] *Strata Property Regulation*, ss. 11.2(3) and 11.3(1).

Specified Portions Bylaw

According to section 6.5(1) of the regulations, if a strata corporation has passed a bylaw under section 72(3) of the Act that makes the corporation responsible to repair specified portions of *some, but not all of the strata lots*, contributions to a special levy to repair those portions are shared only among owners of the strata lots to which the contribution relates.[1]

If these criteria are met, the regulations require a strata corporation to calculate each strata lot's share of the special levy according to this formula:

$$\frac{\textit{unit entitlement of strata lot}}{\textit{total unit entitlement of all strata lots to which the special levy relates}} \quad \text{x} \quad \textit{contribution to the special levy}$$

Contingency Reserve Fund (CRF): Exceptions

If a strata corporation wishes to use the CRF to pay for repairs to strata lots in a section, there appears to be only two exceptions to the general rule that requires all of the owners in the section to contribute according to unit entitlement.[2]

First, the section 100 exception, noted above.

Second, it appears there is an exception for an amended bylaw that apportions contributions to the CRF, if the bylaw meets certain requirements.[3] The strata corporation must have filed the amended bylaw in the Land Title Office before July 1, 2000, when the *Strata Property Act* came into force. Next, the bylaw must apportion CRF contributions according to a *type* of strata lot in a section. Last, the specific type of strata lot must be identified as a type of strata lot in the bylaws of the strata corporation or

---

[1] *Strata Property Regulation*, s. 6.5(1).
[2] *Strata Property Act*, s. 195 and *Strata Property Regulation*, ss. 11.2(3) and 11.3(2).
[3] *Strata Property Regulation*, s. 17.11(6).

a section, as noted above. If these criteria are met, it seems that a strata corporation may, for the purpose of repairs, collect a contribution to the CRF from one type of strata lot in a section.

Section Expenditure

The *Strata Property Act* and the regulations do not specifically deal with the case where a section itself, rather than the strata corporation, spends money for the benefit of some, or all of the strata lots in the section.

Section 194(2) of the *Strata Property Act* says, in part,

> **194 (2)** **With respect to a matter that relates solely to the section, the section is a corporation and has the same powers and duties as the strata corporation. . . .**

Presumably, the same provisions that govern how a strata corporation may allocate expenses that benefit some or all of the strata lots in a section, as described above, apply equally to the section itself, subject to any necessary modifications.

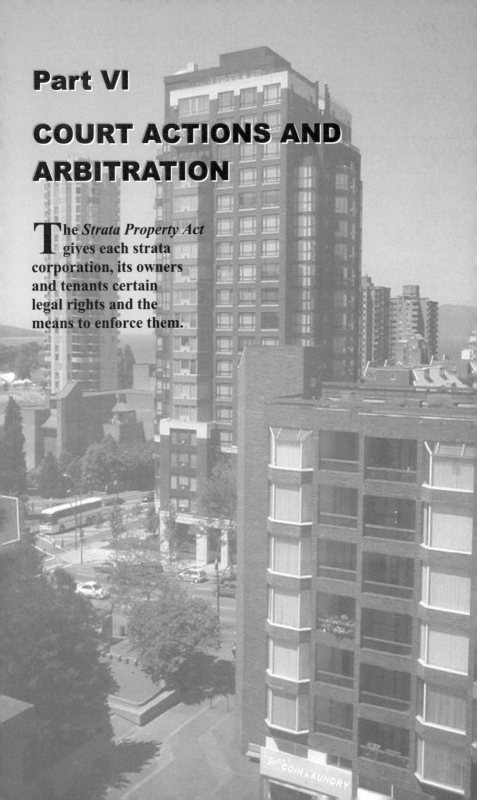

Part VI

COURT ACTIONS AND ARBITRATION

The *Strata Property Act* gives each strata corporation, its owners and tenants certain legal rights and the means to enforce them.

By the Strata Corporation

A strata corporation may sue persons against whom the corporation has a legal claim, including individual owners.

Upon application by a strata corporation to the Supreme Court of British Columbia, the *Strata Property Act* permits the court to order an owner, tenant or other person to do any of the following:[1]

- perform a duty he or she is required to perform under the Act, regulations, bylaws or rules; or

- stop contravening the Act, regulations, bylaws or rules.

On Behalf of All Owners

The *Strata Property Act* specifically permits a strata corporation to sue an owner with respect to any matter affecting the corporation, including:[2]

- the interpretation or application of the Act, regulations, bylaws or rules,

- the common property or common assets,

- the use or enjoyment of a strata lot, or

- money, including fines.

---

[1]*Strata Property Act*, s. 173.
[2]*Ibid.*, s. 171(1).

In these cases, the strata corporation sues as a representative of all the owners, except any who are being sued (a "representative lawsuit" or "representative proceedings"). Before starting a representative lawsuit against an owner, the suit must be authorized by a resolution passed by a 3/4 vote at a general meeting.[1] In these circumstances, the owner who is being sued is not an eligible voter.[2]

However, a prior resolution is not required if the strata corporation intends to proceed under the *Small Claims Act*[3] and there is a bylaw dispensing with the need for prior authorization.[4] The *Small Claims Act* gives the Provincial Court of British Columbia jurisdiction over claims for:[5]

- debt or damages,

- recovery of personal property,

- specific performance of an agreement relating to personal property or services, or

- relief from opposing claims to personal property,

if the amount claimed or the value of the personal property or services is $10,000 or less, excluding interest and costs.

Similarly, a prior 3/4 resolution of the eligible voters is not required where a strata corporation wishes to apply to the court to appoint an administrator. A majority of strata council may authorize the application for an administrator.[6] The provision of the *Strata Property Act* that normally requires the corporation to first obtain a 3/4 vote before commencing representative proceedings does not apply to an application for an administrator.

---

[1]*Strata Property Act*, s. 171(2).
[2]*Ibid.*, s. 171(3).
[3]*Small Claims Act*, R.S.B.C. 1996, c. 430.
[4]*Strata Property Act*, s. 171(4).
[5]*Small Claims Act*, R.S.B.C. 1996, c. 430, s. 3.
[6]*The Owners, Strata Plan LMS 2643 v. Kwan* (2003), 7 R.P.R. (4th) 42, [2003] B.C.J. No. 409, 2003 B.C.S.C. 293 (S.C.).

Except for any owner who is being sued, all of the owners must contribute to the expense of the lawsuit. The owners must share the expense of the representative lawsuit according to their unit entitlement.[1] However, the unit entitlement of a strata lot owned by an owner who is being sued is not used in the calculations.[2]

On Behalf of Some Owners

A strata corporation may also sue on behalf of one or more owners in respect of matters affecting only their strata lots.[3] There are two prerequisites to a suit on behalf of such owners:[4]

1. The strata corporation must obtain the written consent of those owners, and

2. The eligible voters must authorize the suit by a resolution passed by a 3/4 vote at a general meeting.

Only those owners on whose behalf the suit is brought must contribute to its expense.[5] Each of those owners must contribute his or her proportionate share of the expense of bringing the lawsuit.[6] The owners share the legal expense on the same basis used to allocate strata fees.

Failure to First Authorize Legal Proceedings

The requirements for authorizing legal proceedings under the *Strata Property Act* differ significantly in at least one respect from the former *Condominium Act*. Like the *Strata Property Act*, the *Condominium Act* also required a 3/4

---

[1] For information about the schedule of unit entitlement, see Chapter 15, *Finances*.
[2] *Strata Property Act*, s. 171(5), (6).
[3] *Ibid.*, s. 172.
[4] *Ibid.*, s. 172(1).
[5] *Ibid.*, s. 172(2).
[6] *Ibid.*, s. 172(3).

vote to authorize a strata corporation to take representative proceedings, and in addition, in the case of a suit on behalf of owners in respect of their strata lots, to obtain the written consents of those owners.[1] In the case of lawsuits commenced while the *Condominium Act* was in force, the courts allowed a strata corporation to first commence a representative proceeding, or to sue on behalf of owners in respect of their strata lots, and to later ratify the suit by passing the necessary special resolution (now called a 3/4 vote) and obtaining, where required, the owners' consents.[2]

The *Strata Property Act* is different because it expressly requires a strata corporation to *first* obtain the 3/4 vote, and any written consents, *before* commencing the lawsuit, as described above. If a strata corporation commences a representative proceeding, or a suit on behalf of owners concerning their strata lots, on or after July 1, 2000, when the *Strata Property Act* came into force, without first obtaining 3/4 vote approval and any necessary consents, the lawsuit will be a nullity.[3]

Where a strata corporation commences a representative proceeding, or a suit on behalf of owners respecting their strata lots, another party to the lawsuit may demand that the corporation produce evidence to prove compliance with the relevant statutory requirement for approval by 3/4 vote and, where necessary, written consents. Information about these matters is not privileged and, upon demand, another party to the lawsuit is entitled to it.[4]

---

[1] Authority for a strata corporation to bring representative proceedings: *Condominium Act*, ss. 15(1)(a); *Strata Property Act*, s. 171 and authority for a strata corporation to sue on behalf of owners about matters affecting individual strata lots: *Condominium Act*, s. 15(7)(b) and *Strata Property Act*, s. 172.

[2] See, for example, *The Owners, Strata Plan No. NW 651 v. Beck's Mechanical Ltd.* (1980), 20 B.C.L.R. 12 (S.C.); *Strata Corporation VR 2673 v. Comissiona*, (2000) 80 B.C.L.R. (3d) 350, [2000] B.C.J. No. 1681 (S.C.).

[3] *The Owners, Strata Plan LMS 888 v. The City of Coquitlam et al.* (2003), 15 B.C.L.R. (4th) 154, 11 R.P.R. (4th) 95, [2003] B.C.J. No. 1422 (S.C.).

[4] *Strata Plan VR 1280 v. Oberti Architecture et al.* (2003), 13 B.C.L.R. (4th) 191, [2003] B.C.J. No. 129, 2003 B.C.S.C. 112 (S.C.) leave to appeal to B.C.C.A. dismissed, [2003] B.C.J. No. 762, 2003 B.C.C.A. 213 (C.A.).

The requirement to first authorize legal proceedings with a 3/4 vote does not, however, exist when a strata corporation sues to enforce its lien,[1] or where the corporation applies to court to appoint an administrator.[2]

Against the Strata Corporation

Owners, tenants and others can sue a strata corporation. A person may sue a strata corporation with respect to any matter relating to the common property, common assets, bylaws or rules, or any act or omission by the corporation.[3]

If sued, the strata corporation may join, as a party, any owner whose act or omission gave rise to the claim against the corporation.[4]

The strata corporation must promptly inform the owners about the lawsuit.[5] The expense of defending the suit is shared by all of the owners in the same proportions by which strata fees are allocated. However, an owner who is suing the strata corporation is not required to contribute to the corporation's defence.[6]

If a person's lawsuit succeeds, a judgment against the strata corporation is a judgment against all the owners, except the owner who sued the strata corporation.[7] The owners of the remaining strata lots are liable to pay the judgment according to the same proportions used to allocate strata fees among all the owners.[8]

---

[1] *The Owners, Strata Plan VR 1008 v. Oldaker et al.*, [2004] B.C.J. No. 74, 2004, B.C.S.C. 63.

[2] *The Owners, Strata Plan LMS 2643 v. Kwan* (2003), 7 R.P.R. (4th) 42, [2003] B.C.J. No. 409, 2003 B.C.S.C. 293 (S.C.).

[3] *Strata Property Act*, s. 163.

[4] *Ibid.*, s. 168.

[5] *Ibid.*, s. 167(1).

[6] See, for example, *Taychuk v. The Owners, Strata Plan LMS 744* (2002), 7 R.P.R. (4th) 302, [2002] B.C.J. No. 2653, 2002 B.C.S.C. 1638. (S.C.).

[7] *Strata Property Act*, ss. 166(1) and 169(2).

[8] *Ibid.*, s. 166(2).

To Compel the Strata Corporation to Perform a Duty

The *Strata Property Act* permits a broad class of persons to sue a strata corporation if it fails to perform its duties, or otherwise contravenes the Act, regulations, bylaws or rules. The Act permits the following to apply to the Supreme Court of British Columbia for an order requiring the strata corporation to perform its duty under the Act:[1]

- an owner,

- a tenant,

- the mortgagee of a strata lot, or

- an interested person.

The Act does not define the term interested person.

For an example of this type of legal proceeding, see *Tadeson v. Strata Plan NW 2644* described in Chapter 25, *Carrying Out Repair or Maintenance Work.*[2]

Significantly Unfair Act or Exercise of Voting Rights

An owner, or his or her tenant, may also apply to the Supreme Court of British Columbia to prevent or remedy a *significantly unfair* action by the strata corporation.[3] Alternatively, an owner or tenant can apply to the court to prevent or remedy a *significantly unfair* exercise of voting rights by a person who holds 50 per cent or more of the votes, including proxies, at a general meeting.[4]

---

[1] *Strata Property Act*, s. 165.
[2] *Tadeson v. Strata Plan NW 2644* (1999), 30 R.P.R. (3d) 253 (B.C.S.C.).
[3] *Strata Property Act*, s. 164(1)(a).
[4] *Ibid.*, s. 164(1)(b).

Section 164 of the *Strata Property Act* provides,

164. (1) On application of an owner or tenant, the Supreme Court may make any interim or final order it considers necessary to prevent or remedy a significantly unfair

   (a) action or threatened action by, or decision of, the strata corporation, including the council, in relation to the owner or tenant, or

   (b) exercise of voting rights by a person who holds 50% or more of the votes, including proxies, at an annual or special general meeting.

(2) For the purposes of subsection (1), the court may

   (a) direct or prohibit an act of the strata corporation, the council, or the person who holds 50% or more of the votes,

   (b) vary a transaction or resolution, and

   (c) regulate the conduct of the strata corporation's future affairs.

In these circumstances, the court has broad powers to direct or prohibit any act by the strata corporation, the strata council, or by a person holding 50 per cent or more of the votes. In addition, the court can vary a transaction or resolution and regulate the strata corporation's future affairs.[1]

In *Reid v. The Owners, Strata Plan No. LMS 2503*,[2] the superior courts considered for the first time the meaning of the term *significantly unfair* in section 164 of

---

[1] *Strata Property Act*, s. 164(2).
[2] *Reid v. The Owners, Strata Plan No. LMS 2503*, [2001] B.C.J. No. 2377; 2001 B.C.S.C. 1578 (S.C.), aff'd (2003), 179 B.C.A.C. 82, 12 B.C.L.R. (4th) 67, [2003] B.C.J. No. 417, 2003 B.C.C.A. 126 (C.A.), leave to appeal to S.C.C. dismissed without reasons 22 April 2004, [2003] S.C.C.A. No. 500.

the *Strata Property Act*. The term *significantly unfair* is a feature that is new to condominium legislation in British Columbia. Previously, the *Condominium Act* permitted an owner to seek relief in arbitration, or in the Supreme Court of British Columbia, if the affairs of a strata corporation, or a strata council, were exercised in a manner that was oppressive, or unfairly prejudicial, to the owner.[1]

In *Reid*, the superior courts looked to previous authority that defined the terms *oppressive conduct* and *unfairly prejudicial* under the *Condominium Act*. *Oppressive conduct* meant conduct that is burdensome, harsh, wrongful, lacking in probity or fair dealing, or that has been done in bad faith.[2] An act was *unfairly prejudicial* if it was unjust and inequitable. In the *Reid* case, the trial court found that the term *significantly unfair* in section 164 of the *Strata Property Act* would, at the very least, include conduct that was oppressive or unfairly prejudicial within the meaning of the former *Condominium Act*. The Court of Appeal apparently endorsed the trial court's position on the point, or at least, declined to disagree with it.

To decide if significant unfairness occurred, the Court of Appeal also used the definition of the word *unfair* in *The Canadian Oxford Dictionary*. In part, that dictionary defines the term *unfair* as, "not just, reasonable or objective." The court recognized that this definition of *unfair* connotes conduct that is not as severe as the conduct envisaged by the definitions of oppressive or unfairly prejudicial.

---

[1] *Condominium Act*, s. 42.
[2] See *Blue-Red Holdings Ltd. v. Strata Plan VR 857* (1994), 42 R.P.R. (3rd) 421; [1994] B.C.J. No. 2293 (S.C.) and *Esteem Investments Ltd. v. Strata Plan No. VR 1513* (1987), 21 B.C.L.R. (2d) 352; 46 D.L.R. (4th) 577 (S.C.), rev'd on other grounds (1988) 32 B.C.L.R. (2d) 324; 53 D.L.R. (4th) 377 (C.A.).

In the *Reid* case, the Court of Appeal also recognized that a strata corporation must often make decisions that balance the best interests of all of the owners against the interests of a particular owner, or group of owners. The Court of Appeal interpreted the phrase *significantly unfair* to mean that a court should not interfere with the actions of a strata council unless those actions result in something more than mere prejudice or trifling unfairness. Consequently, in *Reid* the superior courts rejected an owner's claim that he was the victim of a significantly unfair action when a strata corporation gave several persons special privileges to place certain plants on common property.

Section 164 of the *Strata Property Act* only permits a court to remedy a significantly unfair action done to an owner or tenant. A claimant cannot use this provision to remedy an injury to a strata corporation. In *Ang v. Spectra Management Services Ltd. et al.,*[1] an owner applied under section 164 to have two leases of common property declared void. The issue was whether section 164 authorized an owner to make her own application to preserve common property despite the statutory scheme which vested in the strata corporation the duty to manage and maintain that property, and to sue to preserve it on behalf of all the owners when authorized by the requisite vote. In *Ang*, the court found that the owner lacked standing to make the application. Any wrong committed in respect of the common property was an injury suffered directly by the strata corporation, not the individual owner. Section 164 is a vehicle by which an owner or tenant may redress the actions of a strata corporation that are significantly unfair to that owner or tenant.

---

[1] *Ang v. Spectra Management Services Ltd. et al.,* [2002] B.C.J. No. 2506, 2002 B.C.S.C. 1544.

Significant unfairness seems a difficult threshold to establish. An informal review of cases to the date of publication suggests that most applications for an order to remedy a significantly unfair action fail. When such applications are successful, however, the courts have used section 164 of the *Strata Property Act* very creatively.[1]

---

[1]See, for example, *The Owners, Strata Plan No. VR 1767 v. Seven Estate Ltd. et al.* (2002), 49 R.P.R. (3rd) 156, [2002] B.C.J. No. 755, 2002 B.C.S.C. 381 (S.C.) (Order to alter schedule of unit entitlement).

Chapter 28

ARBITRATION

Provided that certain conditions exist, the *Strata Property Act* permits arbitration among a strata corporation, owners and tenants if a dispute concerns any of the following:[1]

- the interpretation of the Act, regulations, bylaws or rules;

- the common property or common assets;

- the use or enjoyment of a strata lot;

- money owing under the Act, regulations, bylaws or rules, including fines;

- an action or threatened action by the strata corporation;

- the exercise of voting rights by a person who holds 50% or more of the votes, including proxies at a general meeting.

The availability of arbitration depends on two conditions.[2] First, the individuals in the dispute must be owners or tenants at the time the disagreement arises. Second, the dispute must be one to which neither the *Residential Tenancy Act*[3] nor the *Commercial Arbitration Act*[4] apply.

After court proceedings commence, the dispute cannot be referred to arbitration.[5]

---

[1]*Strata Property Act*, s. 177(3).
[2]*Ibid.*, s. 175(2).
[3]*Residential Tenancy Act*, S.B.C. 2002, c. 406, as amended.
[4]*Commercial Arbitration Act*, R.S.B.C. 1996, c. 55, as amended.
[5]*Strata Property Act*, s. 178(1).

However, if the arbitration proceedings start first, and someone then initiates court proceedings over the same matter, any party to the arbitration may apply to the court for an order to suspend the court proceedings while the arbitration continues.[1]

Transition

If an arbitration commenced before July 1, 2000, when the *Strata Property Act* came into force, the arbitration provisions in the Act do not apply. According to the regulations, an arbitration *commenced* before July 1, 2000 if an arbitrator was appointed under section 44 of the former *Condominium Act* before that date. If so, the arbitration procedures in section 45 of the former *Condominium Act* govern the arbitration.[2]

Arbitrations Involving the Strata Corporation

In the same way that a strata corporation can sue and be sued, the strata corporation can begin an arbitration or be served with a Notice Beginning Arbitration (Form L).[3] This form, and those described below, are found among the forms in the regulations.

Begun by the Strata Corporation

Before beginning an arbitration, the strata corporation must be authorized by a 3/4 vote at a general meeting.[4] The person against whom the arbitration will proceed is not an eligible voter for the purpose of that 3/4 vote.[5]

---

[1] *Strata Property Act*, s. 178(2).
[2] *Strata Property Regulation*, s. 17.16.
[3] *Strata Property Act*, s. 177.
[4] *Ibid.*, ss. 176 and 171.
[5] *Ibid.*, ss. 167 and 171.

All owners, except the person against whom the strata corporation is proceeding, must contribute to the expenses of the arbitration according to unit entitlement.[1] The calculation to allocate the expenses must not use the unit entitlement of the person against whom the arbitration is proceeding.

Against the Strata Corporation

If a strata corporation is served with a Notice Beginning Arbitration (Form L), it must inform the members as soon as feasible.[2]

The expenses of the arbitration are shared by all owners, except the person beginning the arbitration, according to unit entitlement.[3]

In the same way that owners are liable for court judgments against the strata corporation all owners, except the owner that began the arbitration, are liable for monetary awards made by an arbitrator.[4] Owners must pay the award in proportion to their unit entitlement.[5]

Procedure

Unlike the former *Condominium Act*, the *Strata Property Act* contains very detailed procedures for the arbitration process. Section 179 of the Act prescribes the forms and time frames that apply to begin an arbitration process.

To begin an arbitration, a Notice Beginning Arbitration (Form L) must be used. The party receiving the Form L has two weeks to reply using a Notice of Reply (Form M). If the Form M does not resolve the identity of the arbitrator, the person initiating the arbitration must respond within

---

[1]For information about the schedule of unit entitlement, see Chapter 15, *Finances*.
[2]*Strata Property Act*, ss. 167 and 176.
[3]*Ibid.*
[4]*Ibid.*, ss. 169 and 176.
[5]*Ibid.*, ss. 167 and 176.

one week using a Notice Responding to Reply (Form N). For information about the requirements for delivering a Notice, see Chapter 12, *Meetings*.

The Act also contains a detailed process for choosing an arbitrator.[1] The party beginning the arbitration must provide the name of one or more arbitrators, or a method for appointing an arbitrator in the Notice Beginning Arbitration (Form L). The party responding can agree, or provide an alternative recommendation. The party initiating the arbitration can agree or reject the alternatives proposed. If the parties are unable to agree on either one or more arbitrators, or a method for appointing an arbitrator, each party can appoint one arbitrator and the two arbitrators must either name a third person to be the sole arbitrator, or name a third person to act with them.[2]

If an arbitrator is not appointed within six weeks after the arbitration process is started (i.e., after the Form L was given to the other party), either party may apply to the Supreme Court of British Columbia for an order appointing an arbitrator.[3]

The Act also contains a procedure for the arbitration and includes a requirement for the arbitrator to give written reasons for his or her decision.[4]

An arbitrator's decision is final and binding, subject only to review under the *Judicial Review Procedure Act*[5] or an appeal to the Supreme Court of British Columbia on a question of law.[6]

Despite its detail, the *Strata Property Act* does not clearly state what process should be used if either the party receiving the Notice Beginning Arbitration does not respond, or one of the parties in the arbitration process fails to respond within the time limit provided by the Act.

---

[1] *Strata Property Act*, s. 179.
[2] *Ibid.*, s. 179(6).
[3] *Ibid.*, s. 179(7).
[4] *Ibid.*, ss. 183 and 185(2).
[5] *Judicial Review Procedure Act*, R.S.B.C. 1996, c. 241.
[6] *Strata Property Act*, s. 187.

The *Strata Property Act* states that a party receiving the Notice Beginning Arbitration (Form L) *must* give the party who began the arbitration a Notice of Reply (Form M) within two weeks. However, if the party receiving the Form L fails to respond, it would appear that if the party initiating the arbitration was the strata corporation, it could apply to the court for an order compelling the other party to respond.[1] Similarly, if the strata corporation failed to respond to the Form L, an owner could apply to the court for an order compelling the strata corporation to perform a duty it is required to perform under the Act.[2]

Alternatively, if the party receiving the Notice Beginning Arbitration (Form L) does not respond, the party beginning the arbitration may choose to wait six weeks and apply to the court for an appointment of an arbitrator.[3] Section 179 provides that an application may be made for the appointment of an arbitrator if, *for any reason*, either an arbitrator or a panel of arbitrators has not been appointed.

In either case, it appears necessary for the party beginning arbitration to make an application to the court to move the arbitration process forward if the other party does not respond to the Notice Beginning Arbitration (Form L).

If the party receiving the Notice Beginning Arbitration (Form L) responds after the two-week requirement, the party beginning the process would likely choose to ignore the delay. However, what if the party that started the proceedings fails to give the other party a Notice Responding To Reply (Form N) within the one-week period? If the party receiving the Form L is unwilling to waive the time limit, it may be necessary for the party who began the arbitration to issue a new Form L and start the process again.

---

[1]*Strata Property Act*, s. 173.
[2]*Ibid.*, s. 165.
[3]*Ibid.*, s. 179(7).

Chapter 29

OWNER VERSUS STRATA CORPORATION

If an owner is involved in a lawsuit or arbitration against the strata corporation, the *Strata Property Act* limits that owner's responsibility for costs and restricts the owner's ability to attend meetings and obtain information from the corporation about the proceedings.

If an owner:

- is sued by a strata corporation,

- is joined in a suit against a strata corporation,

- sues a strata corporation,

- begins an arbitration proceeding against a strata corporation,

- is a party to an arbitration begun by a strata corporation, or

- is joined in an arbitration which is proceeding against a strata corporation,

the following limitations apply to that owner. The Act provides that the owner:[1]

- is not liable to contribute to legal costs that a court or arbitrator requires the strata corporation to pay,

- does not have the right to information or documentation relating to the suit, including legal opinions, and

- does not have a right to attend those portions of any annual or special general meeting or council meeting at which the suit is dealt with or discussed.

---

[1]*Strata Property Act*, ss. 169 and 176.

The *Strata Property Act* also states that if a strata corporation pays an amount to an owner in full or partial satisfaction of the owner's claim against the strata corporation, that owner is not liable to share in the cost of the payment with the other owners.[1]

---

[1] *Strata Property Act*, s. 169(2).

Chapter 30

APPOINTMENT OF AN ADMINISTRATOR

Applications to the Court

The *Strata Property Act* permits certain persons to apply to the Supreme Court of British Columbia to appoint an administrator for a strata corporation. Any of the following may apply for the appointment of an administrator:[1]

- the strata corporation,

- an owner,

- a tenant,

- a mortgagee, or

- other person having an interest in a strata lot.

The court may appoint an administrator if, in the court's opinion, the appointment is in the best interests of the strata corporation.[2] In making the appointment, the court may order that the administrator exercise or perform some or all of the powers and duties of the strata corporation.

If a strata corporation wishes to apply to the court to appoint an administrator, a majority of strata council may authorize the application.[3] It is not necessary for the eligible voters to first authorize the application by passing a 3/4 vote at a general meeting. Although section 171 of the

---

[1] *Strata Property Act*, s. 174.
[2] *Ibid.*, s. 174(2).
[3] *The Owners, Strata Plan LMS 2643 v. Kwan* (2003), 7 R.P.R. (4th) 42, [2003] B.C.J. No. 409, 2003 B.C.S.C. 293 (S.C.).

Strata Property Act normally requires the corporation to first obtain a 3/4 vote before commencing a lawsuit, that section does not apply to an application for an administrator.

Since applications to appoint an administrator proceed by Petition in the Supreme Court of British Columbia, an applicant must comply with Rule 10(4) of the Rules of Court. The effect of Rule 10(4) is that, unless the Rules of Court provide otherwise, the applicant must serve a copy of the Petition and each supporting affidavit, "on all persons whose interests may be affected by the order sought."[1] Since every owner is likely a person affected by the order sought, personally serving every owner may be very costly if there is a large number of owners. In that case, the better approach is to obtain an order for substituted service under Rule 12 of the Rules of Court. Where for any reason it is impractical to serve a document in the usual way under the Rules of Court, Rule 12 permits the court to order a substituted form of service. The Rules of Court govern the service of documents in court proceedings, not the notice provisions in the *Strata Property Act*.[2]

In *Lum v. Strata Plan VR519*, a number of owners applied to the court to appoint an administrator under section 174 of the *Strata Property Act*.[3] Although the court in the *Lum* case decided that an administrator was not necessary, the court set out the following factors that should be considered when determining whether the appointment of an administrator is in the best interests of the strata corporation:

1. Is there a demonstrated inability to manage the strata corporation?

---

[1] Rules of Court, B.C. Reg. 221/90, R. 10(4).
[2] *Re Strata Property Act and Owners, Strata Plan LMS 2643*, 2002 B.C.S.C. 1811 (S.C.).
[3] *Lum v. Strata Plan VR519*, [2001] B.C.J. No. 641, 2001 B.C.S.C. 493 (S.C.).

2. Is there substantial misconduct or mismanagement, or both, in relation to the affairs of the strata corporation?

3. Is the appointment of an administrator necessary to bring order to the affairs of the strata corporation?

4. Is there a struggle within the strata corporation among competing groups that impedes or prevents proper governance of the strata corporation?

5. Will the appointment of an administrator have any reasonable prospect of bringing order to the affairs of the strata corporation?

The court also noted that, in addition to these factors, the cost of an administrator to a strata corporation must always be considered.

In the *Lum* case, the court also agreed that, "the democratic government of the strata community should not be overridden by the court except where absolutely necessary."[1]

Sometimes a strata corporation requires significant and potentially expensive repairs, but the eligible voters are so deadlocked over which particular repair to choose that the corporation cannot obtain the necessary 3/4 vote to authorize the expenditure from the contingency reserve fund (CRF), or to approve a special levy. In such cases, some owners and strata corporations consider applying to the Supreme Court of British Columbia for an administrator to oversee the repairs.[2] Before applying for an administrator to manage repairs, an owner or strata corporation should

---

[1]*Lum v. Strata Plan VR519*, [2001] B.C.J. No. 641, 2001 B.C.S.C. 493 (S.C.). See also *Andrews v. Leno*, [2001] B.C.J. No. 1350, 2001 B.C.S.C. 963; *McGowan v. Strata Plan NW1018*, [2002] B.C.J. No. 959 at para. 70, 2002 B.C.S.C. 673 at para. 70 (S.C.); *The Owners, Strata Plan LMS 2643 v. Kwan* (2003), 7 R.P.R. (4th) 42, [2003] B.C.J. No. 409, 2003 B.C.S.C. 293 (S.C.).

[2]See, for example, *The Owners, Strata Plan LMS 2643 v. Kwan* (2003), 7 R.P.R. (4th) 42, [2003] B.C.J. No. 409, 2003 B.C.S.C. 293 (S.C.).

obtain legal advice. In *Cook v. Strata Plan N-50*[1] the court held that the power to appoint an administrator under the former *Condominium Act* did not permit the court to authorize an administrator to act without a special resolution (now called a 3/4 vote) where one is required by the statute. In other words, under the *Condominium Act*, a court could not authorize an administrator to approve an expenditure from the CRF because the Act required the owners to approve it by special resolution. The question is whether the *Cook* case should still apply in view of the *Strata Property Act*?

In *The Owners, Strata Plan LMS 2643 v. Kwan*, the court ordered the appointment of an administrator under the *Strata Property Act* to carry out building envelope repairs. The eligible voters were deadlocked over repair options, including whether to raise $150,000 to pay for certain investigations and repairs, or to raise $11,000 to obtain another engineering opinion. In each case, 3/4 votes to resolve these questions failed. The court held that the building envelope needed repair and that the deadlock put the strata corporation in breach of its statutory obligation to repair it. The court granted the strata corporation's application for an administrator, "to exercise the powers and perform the duties as the Strata Corporation and the Strata Council . . . with respect to the repair of the building envelope." Although the court did not expressly specify the administrator's powers, the decision seems to imply the power in the administrator to choose between the $11,000 and the $150,000 options respectively. In *Kwan*, the court never expressly addressed whether the *Cook* case might inhibit the authority of the administrator. Although the court in *Kwan* referred to the *Cook* case, the court referred to a different decision in *Cook* on another point.

---

[1] *Cook v. Strata Plan N-50*, (1995) 16 B.C.L.R. (3rd) 131, 131 D.L.R. (4th) 393 (S.C.)

On the other hand in *Toth v. The Owners, Strata Plan No. LMS 1564*,[1] the court acknowledged *Cook* and declined for the time being to appoint an administrator to oversee repairs, including the power to impose a special levy. The court gave liberty to bring the application again in the future.

Finally, in *Strata Plan LMS 1537 v. Alvarez*,[2] the court acknowledged the issue, but declined for the time being to decide whether the *Cook* case still applied.

Paying for the Administrator

The court may set the administrator's remuneration.[3] When considering the appointment of an administrator, strata owners should keep in mind that the remuneration and expenses of the administrator are paid by the strata corporation.[4] As a common expense of the strata corporation, all owners are responsible to contribute to the administrator's costs according to unit entitlement.

---

[1] *Toth v. The Owners, Strata Plan No. LMS 1564*, (19 August 2003), Vancouver L022502 (B.C.S.C.).

[2] *Strata Plan LMS 1537 v. Alvarez* (2003), 17 B.C.L.R. (4th) 63, [2003] B.C.J. No. 1610, 2003 B.C.S.C. 1085 (S.C.).

[3] *Strata Property Act*, s. 174(3).

[4] *Ibid.*, ss. 1(1) (definition of "common expenses"), 92, 99 and 174(4).

Part VII

PHASING

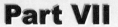

T he *Strata Property Act* permits a developer to add buildings to a development in phases. The Act also addresses some of the practical problems that occur when this happens.

Chapter 31

PHASES

Developing in Phases

A developer who wants to build multiple buildings over time can develop the strata project in phases. This is called a phased strata development.

For example, suppose a developer has a piece of land large enough for five buildings, each one containing ten strata lots. To start, the developer may only be able to afford to build one building. The developer needs the proceeds from the sale of the ten units in the first building to finance construction of the second building, and so on. In this case, the developer proceeds with a phased development. With each phase, the developer adds a new building to the development.

When the developer deposits the strata plan for the first phase of a development with the Land Title Office, the strata corporation is created. As the strata plan for each subsequent phase is deposited, the owners in that phase become members of the strata corporation that was created when the first phase was deposited.[1]

Condominium legislation in British Columbia has permitted phasing since the 1970's. For instance, the former *Condominium Act* dealt with phasing in Part 2 of that Act.[2] The transition provisions in the regulations excuse a developer from various phasing requirements under the *Strata Property Act* if the developer deposited the first phase of the strata plan in the Land Title Office before July 1, 2000.[3] In such cases, the relevant provisions of the former *Condominium Act* still apply.

---

[1] *Strata Property Act*, s. 228.

[2] For a helpful review of phasing requirements under the former *Condominium Act*, see M.J. Campbell, "Phasing of Projects" (The Canadian Institute Conference on Condominium Development, Vancouver, January 25, 1994).

[3] *Strata Property Regulation*, s. 17.17.

Legal Effect of a New Phase

The *Strata Property Act* applies to a phased strata plan, subject to the modifications in Part 13 of the Act, *Phased Strata Plans*, or the regulations.[1]

A "phased strata plan" is a strata plan that is deposited in successive phases under Part 13 of the Act.[2] Each phase must be deposited in the Land Title Office in the order set out in the Phased Strata Plan Declaration.[3] In other words, there is a single strata plan that is, in effect, modified as each phase is deposited.

The *Strata Property Act* distinguishes between the first phase of a strata plan and any phase other than the first phase. To simplify terminology, we use the term *new phase* to describe any phase other than the first phase.

The developer must immediately notify the strata corporation when each new phase is deposited at the Land Title Office.[4]

When a phase is deposited, the land in that phase is consolidated with the land shown in any earlier phase in the strata plan.[5] Although, technically speaking, the deposit of a new phase creates a new strata corporation, that strata corporation is automatically amalgamated with the strata corporation previously created when the developer filed the first phase of the strata plan.[6] Similarly, owners of strata lots in the new phase automatically become members of the strata corporation previously created when the developer filed the first phase of the strata plan.[7]

The following schematic illustration shows how a developer's parcel of land ultimately becomes a phased strata development that is subdivided into strata lots with

---

[1] *Strata Property Act*, s. 218.
[2] *Ibid.*, s. 1(1) (definition of "phased strata plan").
[3] *Ibid.*, s. 221(2).
[4] *Ibid.*, s. 229.
[5] *Ibid.*, s. 228(1)(a).
[6] *Ibid.*, s. 228(1)(b).
[7] *Ibid.*, s. 228(1)(c).

common property. Suppose a developer owns a parcel of land that she intends to develop in two phases:

Figure 1
Registered Owner of a Parcel

Developer is
the registered
owner of the
parcel of land.

The developer begins by depositing the strata plan for Phase One at the Land Title Office.

Figure 2
Phase One and the Remainder

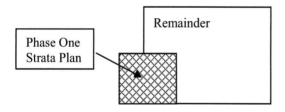

This divides the developer's parcel into two pieces; one used for Phase One of the strata development and the Remainder, being the land set aside for Phase Two. The developer owns the Remainder. By depositing the strata plan for Phase One, the developer creates a strata corporation and subdivides the land within Phase One into strata lots and common property.[1] The Registrar of Land Titles will record the developer as the registered owner of each of the newly-created strata lots in Phase One.

---

[1] *Strata Property Act*, s. 2.

Until the developer deposits a strata plan for Phase Two, the Remainder is a single parcel of land that is technically not yet part of the strata development. Until the developer deposits a strata plan for Phase Two, the developer is free to sell the Remainder to someone else.

At the appropriate time, the developer deposits the strata plan for Phase Two at the Land Title Office.

Figure 3
Phases One and Two

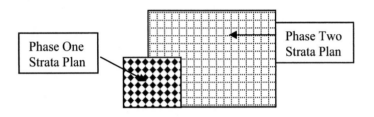

Although, technically speaking, the deposit of a new phase creates a new strata corporation, that strata corporation is automatically amalgamated with the strata corporation previously created when the developer filed the strata plan for Phase One.[1] When the strata plan for Phase Two is deposited, the land in that phase is consolidated with the land shown in Phase One.[2] Similarly, the deposit of the strata plan for Phase Two subdivides the land in that phase into strata lots and common property. The Registrar of Land Titles will record the developer as the registered owner of each of the newly-created strata lots in Phase Two. The developer, or any purchaser who buys a Phase Two strata lot from the developer, automatically becomes a member of the strata corporation that was created previously when the developer filed the strata plan for Phase One.[3]

---

[1] *Strata Property Act*, s. 228(1)(b).
[2] *Ibid.*, s. 228(1)(a).
[3] *Ibid.*, s. 228(1)(c).

In this illustration, the developer's parcel of land has now been subdivided in two successive phases into strata lots with common property.

Mandatory Meeting

Following the deposit of a new phase, section 230 of the *Strata Property Act* requires the strata corporation to hold an annual general meeting (AGM) within six weeks following:

- the date on which 50 per cent plus one of the strata lots in the new phase have been conveyed to purchasers, or

- the date that is six months after the deposit of the new phase,

whichever occurs first.[1]

At an AGM under section 230 of the *Strata Property Act,* the eligible voters must elect two additional council members from among the owners in the new phase. The two additional council members will hold office until the next AGM of the strata corporation.[2] If the bylaws contain a limit on the size of the strata corporation's council, the limit is deemed to be increased to accommodate the temporary addition of extra members under these provisions.[3]

Consequences of Calling the Section 230 Meeting an AGM

It is not clear why section 230 of the *Strata Property Act* characterizes the meeting as an AGM instead of a special

---

[1]*Strata Property Act*, s. 230. Note that the timing requirement in section 230 of the *Strata Property Act* for the AGM in a new phase differs from the one used in the first phase. Under section 16 of the Act, a developer must call the first AGM in the first phase within six weeks of the earlier of the date on which 50 per cent plus one of the strata lots have been conveyed to purchasers, or nine months after the date of the first conveyance.

[2]*Strata Property Regulation*, s. 13.5(1).

[3]*Ibid.*, s. 13.5(3).

general meeting. This characterization will cause some strata corporations to hold multiple AGM's in the same year with consequent inconvenience and confusion.

In the ordinary course of events, the Act requires every strata corporation to hold an AGM within two months of the corporation's fiscal year-end.[1] In practice, this usually works out to one AGM per calendar year.

Suppose, in the ordinary course of events, that the eligible voters in the first phase hold their AGM on January 15 of a particular year. If, however, the developer deposits Phase Two on January 30 of that year, section 230 of the Act requires the corporation to hold another AGM at the latest by July 30, being six months after the new phase was deposited at the Land Title Office. In this example the strata corporation incurs the cost of two AGM's in the same year; one on January 15 and another on July 30.

Section 103 of the *Strata Property Act* requires a strata corporation to prepare a budget, "to be passed by majority vote at each annual general meeting." The notice for every AGM must also include a budget and certain financial statements, each of which must contain prescribed information.[2] In addition, the regulations suggest, but do not expressly state, that when a mandatory AGM is held under section 230 of the Act, the eligible voters will approve a budget at the meeting.[3] In the example above, section 230 of the Act caused a strata corporation to hold two AGM's in the same year, one on January 15 and another on July 30. Section 103 of the Act suggests that the strata corporation must go through the inconvenience and expense of preparing and approving a new budget twice in the same year, six months apart.

Characterizing a meeting under section 230 of the *Strata Property Act* as an AGM may also create confusion. Several examples come to mind.

---

[1] *Strata Property Act*, s. 40.
[2] *Strata Property Act*, ss. 45(4) and 103(2) and *Strata Property Regulation*, ss. 6.6 and 6.7.
[3] *Strata Property Regulation*, ss. 13.4(3)(d) and (4)(c).

Confusion may occur with regard to the election of strata council members. First, there appears to be a conflict between the Act and the regulations. In the ordinary course of events, section 25 of the Act says that at *each* AGM the eligible voters *must* elect a council. The wording of section 25 of the Act does not recognize any exception for an AGM held under section 230 of the Act. By contrast, section 13.5(1) of the regulations says that at an AGM under section 230 of the Act, "two additional members of the council must be elected from the owners of strata lots in the new phase to hold office until the next AGM of the strata corporation." If section 25 of the Act prevails, the eligible voters must elect a whole new council at each AGM, including an AGM under section 230 of the Act. If section 13.5(1) of the regulations governs, the voters will only elect "two additional members of the council."

Second, the regulations fail to provide for the situation where there are multiple AGM's in a year under section 230 of the Act. Section 13.5(1) of the regulations says that the two additional council members elected at an AGM under section 230 of the Act will, "hold office until the next AGM of the strata corporation."

Recall how, in the example above, a strata corporation incurred the cost of two AGM's in the same year; one on January 15 and another on July 30. Suppose that on March 30 of the same year, the developer deposited Phase Three at the Land Title Office. With regard to the newest phase, section 230 of the Act requires the corporation to hold yet another AGM by September 30 at the latest, being six months after Phase Three was deposited. In this illustration, the strata corporation has three AGM's in the same year; the first on January 15 in the ordinary course of events, the second for Phase Two on July 30 and the third for Phase Three on September 30. According to section 230 of the *Strata Property Act*, the two additional council members elected on July 30 at the AGM for Phase Two will only hold office, "until the next AGM of the strata corporation." What happens to those two council members on September 30, being the next AGM of the strata corporation? Do the two council members from Phase Two lose their council seats, while two additional council members are elected from among the owners in Phase Three? Only legislative amendments, or a judicial interpretation, will resolve this confusion.

Similarly, characterizing a meeting under section 230 of the *Strata Property Act* as an AGM may create confusion about the status of certain rules. The strata council may make rules governing the use, safety or condition of common property or common assets.[1] A rule ceases to have effect at the first AGM held after it is made, unless the eligible voters at the meeting ratify the new rule by majority vote.[2] In situations where section 230 of the Act causes a strata corporation to hold multiple AGM's in the same year, as in the examples above, some corporations may overlook the need to ratify a recent rule, in which case the rule ceases to have effect.

Phased Strata Plan Declaration

A developer intending to build a development in phases must obtain the approval of an approving officer on a Phased Strata Plan Declaration (Form P) before filing the strata plan for the first phase in the Land Title Office.[3] An approving officer is an official appointed under the *Land Title Act*.[4] Typically, an approving officer is a municipal engineer, a chief planning officer, or some other person appointed by local government to approve subdivisions, among other things.[5]

---

[1]*Strata Property Act*, s. 125(1). For information about rules, see Chapter 21, *Rules*.
[2]*Ibid.*, s. 125(6).
[3]*Strata Property Act*, s. 222.
[4]*Land Title Act*, R.S.B.C. 1996, c. 250, s. 1 (definition of "approving officer").
[5]*Ibid.*, ss. 77, 77.1, and 77.2.

Form P sets out a variety of information including:

- the number of phases to be constructed,

- the number of units,

- the general type of residence or other structure to be built in each phase,

- the unit entitlement for each phase,

- the election date, being the date by which the developer will elect whether to proceed with each phase,

- the schedule setting out the estimated date for the beginning and completion of construction for each phase.

Under previous condominium legislation, a developer deposited a form similar to the Phased Strata Plan Declaration (Form P). Under the former *Condominium Act*, for example, a developer deposited a Form E, Declaration of Intention to Create a Strata Plan by Phased Development.[1] Note that if before July 1, 2000, when the *Strata Property Act* came into force, a developer obtained approval for a Form E under section 77 of the *Condominium Act*, the transition provisions in the regulations excuse the developer from certain requirements governing the Phased Strata Plan Declaration (Form P).[2]

Amending the Form P and Election Dates

A developer's Phased Strata Plan Declaration (Form P), or Form E, as the case may be, is not written in stone. There may be many reasons why a developer wishes to alter his or her plans and, consequently, to amend the phased development declaration form.

---

[1] *Condominium Act*, s. 77.
[2] *Strata Property Regulation*, s. 17.17(1).

Where a strata corporation is in dispute with a developer regarding the amendment of a Form P, or the completion of a phase, the corporation should obtain legal assistance. The issues are complex and may involve applications to the Supreme Court of British Columbia.

1. The Election Date

The election date is one of the most important features of a Phased Strata Plan Declaration (Form P) or, in the case of a declaration filed under the *Condominium Act*, a Form E. An election date is the last day by which the developer must choose whether to proceed with a phase.

The Phased Strata Plan Declaration (Form P), or Form E, as the case may be, expresses a developer's intention to construct the development in phases. It is not a promise. Until the election date for each phase, the developer may elect *not* to build that phase.

The *Strata Property Act* and the former *Condominium Act* contain similar schemes governing election dates. The operation of the schemes is set out below.

2. The Developer May Elect Not to Proceed

If a developer wishes not to proceed with a phase, section 235 of the *Strata Property Act* requires the developer to notify the strata corporation and the approving officer in writing of the developer's election not to proceed. The developer must also register a similar notice against title to the developer's remainder parcel, being the land previously set aside for the future phase.

Section 232 of the *Strata Property Act* permits a developer to amend an election date in a Phased Strata Plan Declaration (Form P). The developer must apply to the approving officer to amend the Form P. The approving officer may not allow an extension greater than one year. Nor may the approving officer grant more than one extension. For all other extensions, the developer must apply to the Supreme Court of British Columbia.

If a developer fails to give notice electing to not proceed, or to otherwise amend the election date, section 231 of the *Strata Property Act* conclusively deems the developer to have elected to proceed with that phase as set out in the Phased Strata Plan Declaration (Form P). In other words, the developer is bound to proceed if the developer fails to elect in time to quit, or to otherwise extend the election date by amending the Form P.

The Condominium *Act* contains substantially the same scheme. If the developer elects *not* to proceed with a phase, the *Condominium Act* requires the developer to inform the strata corporation in writing and file a notice to that effect on title.[1]

If a developer fails to give notice electing to not proceed, the *Condominium Act* deems that the developer has elected to continue with the project.[2]

Under the *Condominium Act*, however, a developer could apply to amend the election date, even where the Act deemed the developer to have elected to proceed because the developer failed to elect otherwise by the election date. In *Lakewood Development Ltd. v. Surrey (City)*,[3] a developer was deemed to have elected to proceed with two unbuilt phases because the developer failed, before the election date, to notify the strata corporation of any plan to not proceed. Even though the election dates for the two phases had passed approximately three years earlier, the Supreme Court permitted the developer to apply to amend the Form E to extend the election dates for both unbuilt phases.

---

[1] *Condominium Act*, s. 79(1).
[2] *Ibid.*, s. 78(7).
[3] *Lakewood Development Ltd. v. Surrey (City)*, [1999] B.C.J. No. 1788 (S.C.).

3. Where the Developer Elects Not to Proceed: A Developer's Obligations for the Cost of Common Facilities

If a developer elects not to proceed with a future phase, the *Strata Property Act* and the *Condominium Act* provide certain remedies to a strata corporation to compensate for common facilities. There are at least two principal concerns.

First, suppose the developer incorporates an expensive common facility, such as a recreation centre, into Phase One of a ten-phase development. Suppose also the developer anticipates that each phase will contain ten strata lots for a total of 100 strata lots. Purchasers in Phase One reasonably expect that the strata development will ultimately contain 100 strata lots, the owners of which will all contribute to the cost of maintaining this expensive common facility. What happens if the developer elects not to proceed after Phase One? A relatively few strata owners now carry the burden of a recreation centre designed to be maintained by many owners.

Alternatively, suppose the developer of our ten-phase development promises to build a luxurious recreation centre in Phase Ten. Purchasers in Phase One buy their strata lots in the expectation that their development will ultimately have a first class recreation centre. What happens if the developer elects not to proceed after Phase One? Purchasers may feel misled and the fair market values of their respective strata lots may reflect the loss of amenities in future phases.

What is a "Common Facility"?

In general, we can regard a common facility as common property that constitutes a major amenity in a phased strata plan.

The former *Condominium Act* and the *Strata Property Act* both use the term common facilities, but the meaning of the phrase appears more restricted in the current legislation. The *Condominium Act* defined a common facility as:[1]

> **. . . a facility that is available for the use of all the owners, and, without limiting the generality of the foregoing, may include a laundry room, playground, swimming pool, recreation centre, clubhouse or tennis court.**

The *Condominium Act* did not restrict the use of the phrase common facilities to any particular kind of strata plan. The *Strata Property Act* uses the term common facilities *only* in connection with *phased* developments. For the purpose of the phasing provisions, the Act defines common facilities as,[2]

> **. . . a major facility in a phased strata plan, including a laundry room, playground, swimming pool, recreation centre, clubhouse or tennis court, if the facility is available for the use of the owners.**

The prescribed Form E in the *Condominium Act* required a developer to specify "any common facility to be developed in conjunction with a particular phase."[3] Under the *Strata Property Act*, the Form P contains a similar requirement.[4]

---

[1] *Condominium Act*, s. 1(1) (definition of "common facility").
[2] *Strata Property Act*, s. 217.
[3] *Condominium Act*, Form E, para. 2(a).
[4] *Strata Property Regulation*, Form P, para. 2(a).

4. Remedies Under the *Strata Property Act*

If a developer elects *not* to proceed, the *Strata Property Act* allows the strata corporation to apply to the Supreme Court of British Columbia for an order requiring the developer to compensate the corporation for certain losses connected with common facilities.[1]

Where there are common facilities in *existing* phases, the *Strata Property Act* permits the Supreme Court to order the developer to contribute to the expenses of the corporation that are attributable to those facilities as if the developer had elected to proceed, unless otherwise agreed between the strata corporation and the developer. The court may also order the developer to pay security for that purpose.[2]

Where there are common facilities in *future* phases, the *Strata Property Act* is less clear. It appears that the strata corporation must first demonstrate that the developer's election not to proceed is unfair to the corporation, after which the court may order the developer to complete whatever common facilities the court considers equitable, or to pay security for the loss of those amenities.[3] Section 235(6) of the Act provides, in part, that if the court determines that the developer's election not to proceed is unfair to the strata corporation, then,

> (6) ... the court may make one or both of the following orders:
>
> (a) that the owner developer complete whatever common facilities the court considers equitable;
>
> (b) that some or all of the security provided for the common facilities be paid as provided by the court.

---

[1] *Strata Property Act*, s. 235 (compensation payable by developer where the developer elects not to proceed and the court's authority to order the developer to complete whatever common facilities the court considers equitable).

[2] *Ibid.*, s. 235(3), (4).

[3] *Ibid.*, s. 235(5), (6).

By permitting the court to order the completion of "whatever common facilities the court considers equitable," the *Strata Property Act* gives the court a broad discretion.

5. Remedies Under the *Condominium Act*

If a developer elects *not* to proceed, the *Condominium Act* also allows the strata corporation to apply to the Supreme Court of British Columbia for an order requiring the developer to compensate the corporation for certain losses connected with common facilities.

Where there are common facilities in *existing* phases, the court may order the developer to contribute to the expenses of the strata corporation that are attributable to the existing common facilities, except as otherwise agreed between the strata corporation and the developer. In that case, the developer's contribution will be based on the unit entitlement of the strata lots in the phases that the developer decided not to build.[1]

Where the developer promised common facilities in a *future* phase, the court may require the developer to pay for the loss of the common facilities that the developer promised to provide in the abandoned phase, except as otherwise agreed between the strata corporation and the developer.[2]

In addition, if a developer elected *not* to proceed, under the *Condominium Act* a strata corporation could apply to the Supreme Court,[3]

> **79. (2) . . . [F]or an order governing the provision of the common facilities to be developed in accordance with Form E and the application of the proceeds of any bond, or letter of credit or other security for the provision of those facilities.**

---

[1] *Condominium Act*, s. 79(3).
[2] *Ibid.*, s. 79(4).
[3] *Ibid.*, s. 79(2).

Two senior real estate lawyers describe the effect of this provision, in part, as follows,[1]

> **(This section) gives the court tremendous latitude to impose obligations on the owner developer. Even though the owner developer has elected not to proceed, the court may order it to construct the common facilities described in Form E.**
>
> **The court's power to order the "provision" of facilities implies that, along with ordering construction, the court may order the owner developer how to provide the facilities to the strata corporation and owners.**
>
> **For example, the court may order the owner developer to construct facilities on the remainder parcel outside the strata plan. . . .**

Where the Developer is Proceeding

Where a developer proceeds with a phase, either by choice or by virtue of a deeming provision that applies because the developer failed, for example, to elect otherwise in time, the legislation also gives the strata corporation certain rights.

If a developer fails to proceed with a phase within a reasonable time, or at a reasonable rate, the *Strata Property Act* permits the strata corporation to apply to the Supreme Court of British Columbia for an order requiring the developer to complete the phase by a set date.[2]

If the developer fails to comply with the court's order, the court may declare that the developer, "be deemed to have elected not to proceed."[3] If that occurs, the *Strata Property Act* allows the strata corporation to ask the court for an order requiring the developer to compensate the

---

[1] M. Fairweather and L. Ramsay, *Condominium Law and Practice in British Columbia*, looseleaf (Vancouver, The Continuing Legal Education Society of BC, 1996), section 9.5.

[2] *Strata Property Act*, s. 236.

[3] *Ibid.*

corporation for certain losses connected with common facilities as described above.

The *Condominium Act* contains similar provisions. Where a developer elects to proceed, the *Condominium Act* permits a strata corporation to apply to the court for an order requiring the developer to complete the next phase by a fixed date, or to elect to not proceed.[1]

Where the Developer is Proceeding: Developer's Obligations for Existing Common Facilities

Section 227(1) of the *Strata Property Act* provides, subject to certain exceptions, and in part that,[2]

> **227. (1) ... [U]ntil all phases of a phased strata plan have been deposited, the owner developer must contribute to the expenses of the strata corporation that are attributable to the common facilities.**

Subject to the regulations, section 227(2) of the *Strata Property Act* gives the following formula for calculating the developer's contribution to the common facilities in existing phases:

$$\frac{unit\ entitlement\ of\ strata\ lots\ in\ phases\ not\ deposited}{unit\ entitlement\ of\ strata\ lots\ in\ all\ phases\ whether\ deposited\ or\ not} \times \begin{array}{c} expenses\ attributable \\ to\ the\ common\ facilities \end{array}$$

Recall the recent example in which a developer built a recreation centre as a common facility in Phase One of a ten-phase development. Suppose also that the Phased Strata Plan Declaration (Form P) identifies the recreation centre common facility, and states that there will be ten phases, each consisting of ten strata lots for a total of 100

---

[1]*Condominium Act*, s. 79(6).
[2]*Strata Property Act*, s. 227(1).

strata lots, and that each strata lot will have a unit entitlement figure of one for a total of 100. In this example, the developer to date has only deposited the strata plan for Phase One, representing ten strata lots with a total unit entitlement of ten for that phase. There are nine phases remaining to deposit and they represent 90 strata lots with a total unit entitlement of 90. Finally, let's suppose the annual cost to maintain the recreation centre in Phase One is $36,000. Does the developer have to contribute to the cost of maintaining the recreation centre in Phase One? The answer is, "Yes, subject to certain exceptions in the *Strata Property Act*, the developer must contribute until all phases of the strata plan have been deposited." Using the formula from the regulations, we calculate the developer's share of the annual cost to maintain the recreation centre in Phase One, as follows:

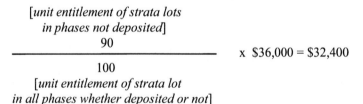

$$\frac{\substack{[\textit{unit entitlement of strata lots} \\ \textit{in phases not deposited}] \\ 90}}{\substack{100 \\ [\textit{unit entitlement of strata lot} \\ \textit{in all phases whether deposited or not}]}} \times \$36{,}000 = \$32{,}400$$

In this example, the developer must pay the strata corporation $32,400 towards the cost of maintaining the recreation centre in Phase One. As the developer deposits successive phases, the developer's contribution will decrease. This serves as an incentive to complete the project quickly.

The former *Condominium Act* contains a similar requirement. The *Condominium Act* requires a developer to contribute to the common expenses attributable to existing common facilities in proportion to the unit entitlement of the phases not yet built as set out in Form E.[1]

---

[1] *Condominium Act*, s. 80(3).

The Legal Position of the Buyer of the Remainder

Where a buyer bought a remainder parcel (land set aside for a future phase) from a developer, the *Condominium Act* did not specify the effect of a Form E on the purchaser. Historically, it appears that development lawyers considered the Form E binding on the purchaser, subject to certain considerations.[1]

By contrast, the *Strata Property Act* deals directly with the position of a purchaser who buys a remainder. Section 220 of the Act says,

> **220. If an owner developer transfers the owner developer's interest in land described in a Phased Strata Plan Declaration, the owner developer's rights and responsibilities under the declaration, this Act and the regulations transfer to the new owner developer.**

Common Facilities

For the purpose of a phased strata plan, the *Strata Property Act* defines a common facility as:[2]

> **A major facility in a phased strata plan, including a laundry room, playground, swimming pool, recreation centre, clubhouse or tennis court if the facility is available for the use of the owners.**

If a developer has promised to construct common facilities in a phase other than the first phase, the Act contains provisions intended to protect purchasers in the event the developer does not proceed with future phases. If common facilities are to be constructed in phases other

---

[1] See, for example, M.J. Campbell, "Phasing of Projects" (The Canadian Institute Conference on Condominium Development, Vancouver, January 25, 1994) at pp. 14 and 31-33.

[2] *Strata Property Act*, s. 217.

than the first, the developer must either post security in an amount that is sufficient to cover the full cost of constructing the common facility, including the cost of the land, or make other arrangements satisfactory to an approving officer to ensure completion of the common facility.[1]

Once a developer has constructed common facilities in a phase, the *Strata Property Act* requires the developer to contribute to the expenses related to that common facility on behalf of all strata lots in undeveloped phases as previously described.[2] The developer must pay to the strata corporation the proportional share of expenses attributable to the common facilities based on the unit entitlement of the strata lots in phases not yet deposited.

Obligations of the Developer

As with any newly-created strata corporation, upon deposit of the strata plan for the first phase, the developer acts as the strata council until the first AGM.[3] Part 3 of the *Strata Property Act* requires a developer to meet various requirements before handing over the development to the owners at the first AGM. How does phasing affect a developer's Part 3 obligations?

According to the regulations, a developer's duties in the first phase under Part 3 of the *Strata Property Act* do not apply in a new phase, except as set out in section 13.4 of the regulations.[4] In particular, when considering a developer's obligations in a new phase, the regulations distinguish whether, at the time the new phase is deposited, the first AGM in the first phase has been held.

---

[1] *Strata Property Act*, s. 223.
[2] *Ibid.*, s. 227.
[3] *Ibid.*, ss. 228(2) and 5.
[4] *Strata Property Regulation*, s. 13.4(1), (2).

The interaction between the Act and section 13.4 of the regulation is complex and often confusing. In some cases, only legislative changes or judicial interpretation will clarify things. In the meantime, the following table reflects the author's best efforts to simplify and explain the contrast between a developer's principal obligations in the first phase under Part 3 of the Act and the developer's duties in a new phase.

Obligations of the Developer During Phasing

Part 3 of the Act	A Developer's First Phase Obligations	A Developer's New Phase Obligations: *Before* the first AGM in the First Phase	A Developer's New Phase Obligations: *After* the first AGM in the First Phase
s. 6(1)	Creates a statutory duty of care while the developer serves as the strata council.	The same applies.[1]	No longer applies because the occurrence of the first AGM means that a strata council has been elected.
s. 6(2)	Requires the developer to make reasonable efforts to pursue any remedies under construction warranties.	The same applies.[2]	Continues to apply.[3]
s. 7	The developer must pay the actual expenses of the strata corporation until the first conveyance of a strata lot.	The same applies, until the first conveyance of a strata lot in any phase of the strata plan.[4]	No longer applies because the occurrence of the first AGM means that at least one strata lot has already been conveyed.[5]

---

[1] *Strata Property Regulation*, s. 13.4(3).
[2] *Ibid.*
[3] *Ibid.*, s. 13.4(4).
[4] *Ibid.*, s. 13.4(3)(a).
[5] *Strata Property Act*, s. 16.

Part 3 of the Act	A Developer's First Phase Obligations	A Developer's New Phase Obligations: *Before* the first AGM in the First Phase	A Developer's New Phase Obligations: *After* the first AGM in the First Phase
s. 8	Before the first convey-ance of a strata lot, the developer may pass any resolution without holding a special general meeting.	The same applies, until the first conveyance of a strata lot in any phase of the strata plan.[1]	No longer applies because the occurrence of the first AGM means that at least one strata lot has already been conveyed.[2]
s. 9	After the first conveyance of a strata lot, the developer is subject to a majority vote directing or restricting the developer in exercising the powers of a strata council.	The same applies.[3]	No longer applies because the occurrence of the first AGM means that a strata council has been elected.
s. 10	After the first conveyance of a strata lot, and before the first AGM, a unani-mous vote is necessary for the strata corporation to enter into a non-arm's length contract with the developer.	The same applies.[4]	No longer applies.
s. 11	After the first conveyance of a strata lot, and before the first AGM, most matters normally requiring a 3/4 vote need a unanimous vote.	The same applies.[5]	No longer applies.

---

[1]*Strata Property Regulation*, s. 13.4(3)(a).
[2]*Strata Property Act*, s. 16.
[3]*Strata Property Regulation*, s. 13.4(3)(a).
[4]*Ibid.*
[5]*Ibid.*

Part 3 of the Act	A Developer's First Phase Obligations	A Developer's New Phase Obligations: *Before* the first AGM in the First Phase	A Developer's New Phase Obligations: *After* the first AGM in the First Phase
S. 12	After the first conveyance of a strata lot, the developer must seed the CRF with a lump sum payment.	Following the deposit of the new phase,[1] the developer must still pay a lump sum to seed the CRF in respect of the new phase, but the developer need not establish a separate CRF. Instead, the developer must make the lump sum payment, in respect of the new phase, into the CRF of the strata corporation previously established by the deposit of the first phase of the strata plan.[2]	Following the deposit of the new phase, the developer must still pay a lump sum to seed the CRF in respect of the new phase, but the developer need not establish a separate CRF. Instead, the developer must make the lump sum payment, in respect of the new phase, into the CRF of the strata corporation previously established by the deposit of the first phase of the strata plan.[3] Note that if the eligible voters in the first phase have approved a budget at an AGM *before* the new phase was deposited, the developer must calculate the lump sum payment into the CRF as a percentage of the estimated annual operating expenses set out in the interim budget for the new phase only.[4]

---

[1]*Strata Property Regulation*, s. 13.4(3)(a)
[2]*Ibid.*, s. 13.4(3)(b).
[3]*Ibid.*, s. 13.4(4)(a).
[4]*Ibid.*, s. 13.4(4)(a) and (5)(b).

Part 3 of the Act	A Developer's First Phase Obligations	A Developer's New Phase Obligations: *Before* the first AGM in the First Phase	A Developer's New Phase Obligations: *After* the first AGM in the First Phase
s. 13	After the first conveyance of a strata lot, the developer's interim budget takes effect. The interim budget is based on a 12-month period beginning on the first day of the month following the month in which the first conveyance occurs. The interim budget will only govern until the first annual budget is approved by the eligible voters.[1]	Following the deposit of the new phase,[2] the interim budget for the new phase takes effect.[3] The budget is based on a 12-month period following the deposit of the new phase,[4] but will only govern until the first annual budget is approved by the eligible voters.[5]	Following the deposit of the new phase, the interim budget for the new phase takes effect. The budget is based on a 12-month period following the deposit of the new phase[6] but will only govern until the first annual budget is approved by the eligible voters.[7] Note that if the eligible voters in the first phase have approved a budget at an AGM *before* the new phase was deposited, the interim budget for the new phase must be based on the budget previously approved by the strata corporation.[8] Note also that in addition to supplying each prospective purchaser with a copy of the interim budget, the developer must also deliver a copy of the strata corporation's most recent budget to each prospective purchaser in the new phase before the purchaser signs an agreement of purchase and sale.[9]

---

[1] *Strata Property Act*, s. 14(1).
[2] *Strata Property Regulation*, s. 13.4(3)(a).
[3] *Ibid.*, s. 13.4(3)(c).
[4] *Ibid.*
[5] *Strata Property Act*, ss. 13 and 14(1) and *Strata Property Regulation*, s. 13.4(3)(d).
[6] *Strata Property Regulation*, s. 13.4(4)(b).
[7] *Strata Property Act*, ss. 13 and 14(1) and *Strata Property Regulation*, s. 13.4(4)(c).
[8] *Strata Property Regulation*, ss. 13.4(4)(b) and 13.4(5)(a).
[9] *Ibid.*, s. 13.4(5)(c).

Part 3 of the Act	A Developer's First Phase Obligations	A Developer's New Phase Obligations: *Before* the first AGM in the First Phase	A Developer's New Phase Obligations: *After* the first AGM in the First Phase
s. 14	After the first conveyance of a strata lot, each owner must pay strata fees based on the interim budget to the strata corporation until the first annual budget approved by the owners takes effect. To the extent the developer is an owner of unsold strata lots, the developer must also pay strata fees to the corporation.	Following the deposit of the new phase,[1] each owner of a strata lot in the new phase, including the developer as an owner of any unsold strata lots, must pay strata fees to the strata corporation based on the interim budget for that phase.[2] Every owner in the new phase must continue paying strata fees on that basis until, presumably, the eligible voters approve the first annual budget. The regulations assume this will occur at the mandatory AGM required under section 230 of the Act.[3] That section of the Act requires the corporation to hold an AGM upon the sale of 50 per cent plus one of the lots in the new phase, or six months after deposit of the new phase, whichever occurs first.[4]	Each owner of a strata lot in the new phase, including the developer as an owner of any unsold strata lots, must pay strata fees to the strata corporation, based on the interim budget for that phase. Every owner in the new phase must continue paying strata fees on that basis until the corporation holds the mandatory AGM required under section 230 of the Act. That section requires the corporation to hold an AGM upon the sale of 50 per cent plus one of the lots in the new phase, or six months after deposit of the new phase, whichever occurs first.[5] Presumably, the eligible voters will approve a new budget at the AGM under section 230 of the Act. Note that if the eligible voters in the first phase have approved a budget at an AGM *before* the new phase was deposited, the interim budget for the new phase must be based on the budget previously approved by the strata corporation.[6]

---

[1] *Strata Property Regulation*, s. 13.4(3)(a).
[2] *Ibid.*, s. 13.4(3)(d).
[3] *Strata Property Act*, s. 103 and *Strata Property Regulation*, s. 13.4(3)(d).
[4] *Strata Property Regulation*, s. 13.4(3)(d).
[5] *Ibid.*, s. 13.4(4)(c).
[6] *Ibid.*, s. 13.4(4)(c) and (5)(a).

Parking Stalls

The *Strata Property Act* permits a developer, at any time after the deposit of a strata plan, to unilaterally designate parking stalls as limited common property (LCP). Similarly, a developer who meets certain requirements may designate extra parking stalls as LCP.[1] These features of the Act are described in Chapter 17, *Common Property*. As a general rule, these provisions are not available to a developer who deposited the strata plan before July 1, 2000, when the *Strata Property Act* came into force.[2] If, however, a developer creates a phased development, these parking features in the *Strata Property Act* apply to a phase deposited after July 1, 2000, even if earlier phases were deposited before that date.[3]

Limitations on a Strata Corporation

Bylaw Amendments

Unless a strata corporation obtains the written consent of the developer, the *Strata Property Act* prevents the strata corporation from creating or amending certain types of bylaws until the AGM following the filing of the strata plan for the final phase, or until the developer has elected not to proceed with future phases.[4]

In these circumstances, a strata corporation is prevented from creating, repealing or amending bylaws relating to the:[5]

• keeping of pets

• restriction of rentals

• age of occupants, or

---

[1]*Strata Property Act*, s. 258.
[2]*Strata Property Regulation*, s. 17.19(1).
[3]*Ibid.*, s. 17.19(2).
[4]*Ibid.*, s. 13.3(2).
[5]*Ibid.*

- developer's marketing activities for the sale of strata lots in the strata plan.

Unit Entitlement Amendments

If the developer is in compliance with the dates for the beginning of construction of each phase as set out or as amended on Form P, the strata corporation is also prevented from changing the basis of calculating a strata lot's share of the contribution to the operating fund and CRF under section 100 of the *Strata Property Act.*[1]

In these circumstances, the strata corporation may not amend the basis for calculating unit entitlement until the AGM following the filing of the strata plan for the final phase, or until the developer has elected not to proceed with future phases, unless the strata corporation has the written consent of the developer.[2]

---

[1] For information about the Section 100 Exception, see Chapter 26, *Paying for Repairs.*

[2] *Strata Property Regulation*, s. 13.3(1).

APPENDICES

Appendix A

Sample Excerpts From Strata Plans

Sample Portion of a Building Strata Plan

Legend

SL   denotes strata lot

A   denotes area

PR   denotes porch (limited common property)

P   denotes patio (limited common property)

W   denotes bay window (limited common property)

C   denotes common property

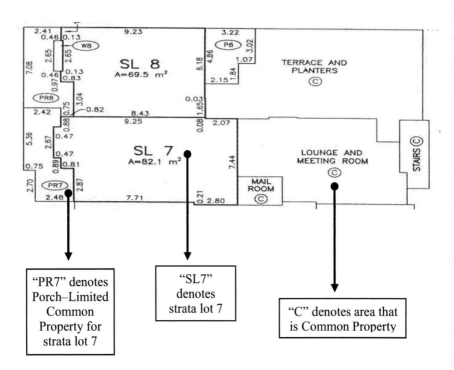

"PR7" denotes Porch–Limited Common Property for strata lot 7

"SL7" denotes strata lot 7

"C" denotes area that is Common Property

Sample Bare Land Strata Plan

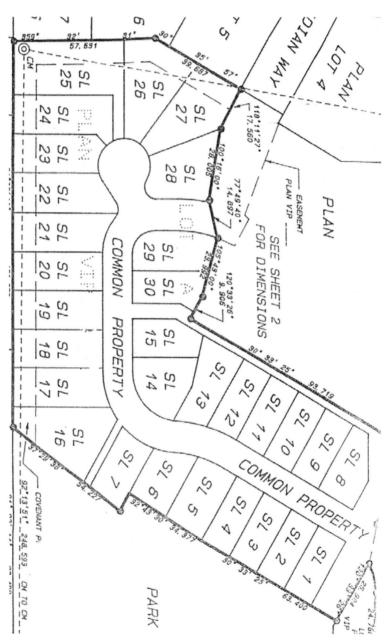

Legend: SL denotes strata lot

Appendix B

RECORDS A STRATA CORPORATION MUST KEEP

Records That a Strata Corporation Must Prepare

Section 35(1) of the *Strata Property Act* states that the strata corporation must prepare *all* of the following records:

- Minutes of annual and special general meetings and council meetings, including the results of any vote.

- A list of council members.

- A list of owners, with their strata lot addresses, mailing addresses if different, strata lot numbers as shown on the strata plan, parking stall numbers, if any, and unit entitlements.

- A list of names and addresses of mortgagees who have filed a Mortgagee's Request for Notification under section 60 of the Act.

- A list of names of tenants.

- A list of assignments of voting or other rights by landlords to tenants under sections 147 and 148 of the Act.

- Books of account showing money received and spent and the reason for the receipt or expenditure.

- Any other records required by the regulations.

In addition, section 35(3) of the *Strata Property Act* and the relevant provisions of section 4.1 of the regulation require the strata corporation to keep copies of records for the periods set out below:

The Following Records Must Be Kept Current

A list of council members and their telephone numbers or other method of contacting the council member on short notice.	s. 35(1)(b); Reg., ss. 4.1(1) and (6)
A list of owners, with their strata lot addresses, mailing addresses if different, strata lot numbers as shown on the strata plan, parking stall numbers, if any, and unit entitlements.	s. 35(1)(c); Reg., s. 4.1(6)
A list of names and addresses of mortgagees who have filed a Mortgagee's Request for Notification under section 60 of the Act.	s. 35(1)(c); Reg., s. 4.1(6)
A list of names of tenants.	s. 35(1)(c); Reg., s. 4.1(6)
A list of assignments of voting or other rights by landlords to tenants under sections 147 and 148 of the Act.	s. 35(1)(c); Reg., s. 4.1(6)
The *Strata Property Act* and the regulations.	s. 35(2)(c); Reg., s. 4.1(6)
The bylaws and rules.	s. 35(2)(c); Reg., s. 4.1(6)

The Strata Corporation Must Keep These Records for at Least Two Years

Correspondence sent or received by the strata corporation and council.	s. 35(2)(k); Reg., s. 4.1(5)

The Strata Corporation Must Keep These Records for at Least Six Years

Minutes of all general meetings and council meetings, including the results of any vote.	s. 35(1)(a); Reg., s. 4.1(3)
Books of account showing money received and spent and the reason for the receipt or expenditure.	s. 35(1)(d); Reg., s. 4.1(3)
Waivers and consents under sections 41, 44 or 46. (These sections govern the procedure for waiving notice of a general meeting, or waiving the necessity of holding a general meeting.)	s. 35(2)(f); Reg., s. 4.1(3)
Written contracts, including insurance policies.	s. 35(2)(g); Reg., s. 4.1(4)
The budget and financial statement for the current and previous years.	s. 35(2)(i); Reg., s. 4.1(3)
Income tax returns, if any.	s. 35(2)(j); Reg., s. 4.1(3)
Bank statements, cancelled cheques and certificates of deposit.	s. 35(2)(l); Reg., s. 4.1(3)
Information Certificates (Form B) issued under section 59 of the Act.	s. 35(2)(m); Reg., s. 4.1(3)
All contracts, including insurance policies, entered into by or on behalf of the strata corporation that the developer delivered to the strata corporation under section 20 of the Act.	ss. 20(2)(a)(iii) and 35(2)(n); Reg., s. 4.1(7)(b)
Copies of financial records obtained from the developer for at least six years after the transfer of control from the developer to the strata corporation referred to in section 22 of the Act.	ss. 23 and 35(2)(n); Reg., s. 4.1(7)(e)

The Strata Corporation Must Keep These Records Until the Disposal or Replacement of Certain Items

Documents obtained from the developer in the nature of: • warranties, • manuals, • schematic drawings, • operating instructions, • service guides, • manufacturer's documentation, or • other similar information respecting the construction, installation, operation, maintenance, repair and servicing of any common property or common assets, including any warranty information provided to the developer by a contractor, subcontractor or supplier to the project.	ss. 20(2)(a)(vii) and 35(2)(n); Reg., s. 4.1(7) (c), (d)

In the case of a warranty, the strata corporation must keep the document until the disposal or replacement of the relevant item, or the expiry of the warranty, whichever comes first.

The strata corporation must keep the rest of these documents until the disposal or replacement of the items to which they relate.

The Strata Corporation Must Keep These Records Permanently

The registered strata plan and any registered amendments.	ss. 20 and 35(2)(b); Reg., ss. 4.1(2) and (7)(a)
Any resolutions dealing with changes to the common property, including the designation of common property.	s. 35(2)(e); Reg., s. 4.1(2)
Decisions in court or arbitration proceedings.	s. 35(1)(h); Reg., s. 4.1(2)
Any legal opinions.	s. 35(1)(h); Reg., s. 4.1(2)
Some of the information obtained from the developer under the Act, including names and addresses of all contractors and the like who supplied labour or materials to the project, plans required to obtain building permits, any plans showing the actual location of pipes, wires and the like (sometimes called "as built" plans), and the disclosure statement and amendments, if any.	ss. 20(2)(a)(i), (ii), (iv), (v), (vi) and 35(2)(n); Reg., s. 4.1(7)(a)

Sample Strata Council Minutes
(Format may also be used for preparing minutes of general meetings.)

MINUTES NO.   XXX   / (year)

**MINUTES OF MEETING OF THE STRATA COUNCIL
STRATA PLAN XX XXX (e.g., VR 1184)
HELD ON   (date)   AT   (time)   AT   (location)**

COUNCIL IN ATTENDANCE:
(List names and position of council members and their unit numbers)

ABSENT:
(List the same information as above for those who were unable to attend)

OTHERS IN ATTENDANCE:
(List the same information as above for others who attended; e.g., a strata property manager)

1. **CALL TO ORDER**

2. **APPROVAL OF AGENDA**

3. **MINUTES OF THE PREVIOUS STRATA COUNCIL
   MEETING OF   (date)**   *(Number each set of minutes in a year consecutively; e.g., Council Minutes 2001-01, 2001-02, etc.)*

   MOTION: It was moved, seconded and carried that the minutes of the strata council meeting held   (date)   be approved as circulated.

4. **REPORTS**
   (e.g., Chairperson's, Treasurer's and Building Manager's Report)

5. **CORRESPONDENCE** *(Letters sent to the strata council)*

6. **UNFINISHED BUSINESS** *(Business from previous meeting)*

7. **NEW BUSINESS**

8. **ADJOURNMENT**

9. **NEXT MEETING** *(Date, time and location of next meeting)*

    Chairperson   **Secretary**

Appendix C

VOTING TABLES

This appendix contains Tables that summarize the principal voting thresholds under the *Strata Property Act*. The first Table organizes matters by type of vote. The second Table arranges items according to the subject matter of the relevant motion.

Table 1
Voting at General Meetings
by Type of Vote

There are three principal types of vote: majority vote, 3/4 vote, and unanimous vote.

The majority vote is the default vote. Section 50(1) of the *Strata Property Act* requires all matters at a general meeting to be decided by majority vote unless a different voting threshold is set by the Act, the regulations or the bylaws.

This Table identifies situations, by type of vote, where the *Strata Property Act*, including the *Schedule of Standard Bylaws*, and the regulations specify a particular voting threshold.

Note that a strata corporation may, in some cases, amend its bylaws to specify a different voting threshold for particular matters.

Majority Vote

A Majority Vote is Necessary . . .	Section of the Act, *Schedule of Standard Bylaws* or Regulation
To approve the first annual budget.	21(4)
To amend a proposed budget at the first AGM.	21(5)
At the second AGM to continue a strata management contract entered into before the first AGM where the contract would otherwise automatically expire under the Act.	24(2)
To direct or restrict the council in exercising its powers and performing its duties.	27(1)

A Majority Vote is Necessary . . .	Section of the Act, *Schedule of Standard Bylaws* or Regulation
To decide all matters at general meetings unless the Act, the regulations or the bylaws otherwise require a 3/4 vote or a unanimous vote.	50(1)
To approve a budget at an AGM, or failing approval at that meeting, at a subsequent special general meeting.	103(1) and 104(1)
To amend a proposed budget at the AGM.	103(4)
At an AGM, to ratify a rule made in the interim since the last AGM.	125(6)
To remove one or more council members from council (except where all the owners are on council).	*Schedule of Standard Bylaws*, s. 11(1)
To pass a resolution requiring persons who are not eligible to vote, including tenants and occupants, to leave a general meeting.	*Schedule of Standard Bylaws*, s. 26(3)

3/4 Vote

A 3/4 Vote is Necessary . . .	Section of the Act, *Schedule of Standard Bylaws* or Regulation
To ratify a contract or transaction in which a council member has a conflict of interest.	33(1)
To approve in advance payment of remuneration to a council member that is not already provided for in the budget or the bylaws.	34(c)
To approve a resolution to cancel a strata management contract.	39(1)
To amend a resolution requiring a 3/4 vote, provided that the amendment does not substantially change the resolution.	50(2)(b)
To seek judicial passage of a nearly unanimous vote.	52(2)

A 3/4 Vote is Necessary . . .	Section of the Act, *Schedule of Standard Bylaws* or Regulation
To approve a significant change in the use or appearance of common property.	71
To designate common property as limited common property without amending the strata plan.	74(1) and 75(2)
To approve a resolution for the strata corporation to acquire land.	78(1)
To approve a resolution to sell, lease, mortgage, grant an easement or a restrictive covenant over, or otherwise dispose of land that is a common asset of the strata corporation.	79
To dispose of common property in some circumstances.	80(2)
To approve a resolution for the strata corporation to acquire or dispose of personal property in some circumstances.	82(3)
To make additional contributions to the CRF after the fund reaches the maximum amount required by the Act.	93(4) Reg. s. 6.1(2)
To approve an expenditure from the CRF.	96(b)
To spend operating funds not otherwise authorized by the budget or permitted by sections 98 or 104(3) pending approval of the new budget.	97(b)
To change the dates of the strata corporation's fiscal year.	102(1)
Where a budget is not approved at an AGM, to extend beyond 30 days the time to prepare and present a budget for approval at a special general meeting.	104(1)
To deal with a surplus in the operating fund in a way that differs from the options set out in section 105(1).	105(1)
To approve a special levy.	108(2)(a)
To approve a resolution authorizing the strata corporation to borrow money.	111(1)
To amend the bylaws in a strata plan composed entirely of residential strata lots.	128(1)(a)

A 3/4 Vote is Necessary . . .	Section of the Act, *Schedule of Standard Bylaws* or Regulation
To amend the bylaws in a strata plan composed entirely of non-residential strata lots if the bylaws do not otherwise provide for a different type of vote.	128(1)(b)
To amend the bylaws in a strata plan composed of both residential and non-residential strata lots, 3/4 of the votes of the residential lots and, in the case of the non-residential lots, 3/4 of the votes unless the bylaws provide a different voting requirement for non-residential lots.	128(1)(c)
To approve a change in the number of strata lots to be rented or the rental period set out in the developer's Rental Disclosure Statement.	139(2)(b)
To decide not to use insurance proceeds to repair or replace damaged property.	159(1)
To authorize the strata corporation to sue as representative of all owners (except any who are being sued).	171(2)
To authorize the strata corporation to sue as representative of one or more owners about matters affecting only their strata lots.	172(1)(b)
To create or cancel sections representing the interests of owners of different types of strata lots or those who use their strata lots for different purposes.	193(3)
Among section members, to approve an amendment to a bylaw respecting a matter that relates solely to that section.	197(3)
To approve an application to add to, alter or repeal restrictions imposed by a leasehold landlord on strata lots in a leasehold strata plan.	207(1)
To elect not to rebuild where buildings that are part of the leasehold strata plan are damaged by more than 1/3 of their fair market value.	213(1)
To authorize the release of a bond, letter of credit or other security posted by a developer to secure the construction of common facilities in a later phase of the development.	226(1)(b)

A 3/4 Vote is Necessary . . .	Section of the Act, *Schedule of Standard Bylaws* or Regulation
To agree with a developer to relieve the developer of certain liabilities arising when the developer amends a Phased Strata Plan Declaration.	233(7)
To agree with a developer to relieve the developer of certain liabilities arising when the developer elects not to proceed with the next phase before the time set in the Phased Strata Plan Declaration for that election.	235(7)
To approve a resolution to divide a residential strata lot into two or more strata lots.	260(4)
To amend a strata plan in certain cases to make land held by the strata corporation, but not shown on the strata plan, into a new strata lot or to otherwise add that land to a strata lot.	262(3)(a)
To amend a strata plan to add land held by the strata corporation, but not shown on the strata plan, to the common property.	266(3)(a)
To approve a resolution to amalgamate with another strata corporation.	269(2)(a)
To approve an appraisal of the assessed value of a strata lot for the purposes of a conversion schedule when cancelling a strata plan and winding up the strata corporation.	273(2)(b)
To approve an appraisal of the assessed value of a strata lot for the purposes of determining an owner's share of the proceeds of distribution when cancelling a strata plan and winding up the strata corporation.	278(2)(b)
To authorize a liquidator to distribute land or property that is being disposed of when cancelling a strata plan and winding up the strata corporation.	282(1)
To approve the account and final return of the liquidator when cancelling a strata plan and winding up the strata corporation.	283

Unanimous Vote

A Unanimous Vote is Necessary . . .	Section of the Act, *Schedule of Standard Bylaws* or Regulation
In the period between the first conveyance and the first AGM, to approve a contract or transaction between the strata corporation and the developer or a person who is not arm's-length to the developer.	10
In the period between the first conveyance and the first AGM, to pass any resolution that normally requires a 3/4 vote.	11
To change the formula used to calculate a strata lot's contribution to the operating fund and the CRF.	100(1), (2)
To change the formula used to calculate a strata lot's contribution to a special levy.	108(2)(b)
In the period before the first AGM in bare land strata or entirely residential strata developments, to amend a bylaw.	127(1)
In the period before the first AGM in a mixed strata with residential and non-residential strata lots, to amend a bylaw.	127(3)
In the period before the first AGM in a mixed strata with a separate residential section, for the residential section to amend a bylaw.	127(4)(a)
To change the basis for calculating how much a leasehold landlord must pay to the leasehold tenant at the end of the strata lot lease for the leasehold tenant's interest in the strata lot.	214(3)
To amend a strata plan to designate property as limited common property or to remove a designation of limited common property.	257
To amend a strata plan, in certain cases, to divide a strata lot into two or more lots, to consolidate two or more strata lots, or to add part of a strata lot to another strata lot.	259(3)(a)

A Unanimous Vote is Necessary . . .	Section of the Act, *Schedule of Standard Bylaws* or Regulation
To amend a schedule of unit entitlement where, in strata plans, the schedule of unit entitlement is based on habitable area or square footage.	261(1)
To amend a strata plan, in certain cases, to make land held by the strata corporation into a new strata lot or to otherwise add that land to a strata lot.	262(3)(b)
To amend a strata plan, in certain cases, to add or remove land belonging to the strata corporation to or from a strata lot.	262(3)(b)
To amend a strata plan to add a strata lot, or part of a strata lot, to common property.	263(2)
To cancel a strata plan.	272
To appoint a liquidator.	277

Table 2
Voting at General Meetings
by Subject Matter

There are three types of vote: majority vote, 3/4 vote, and unanimous vote.

The majority vote is the default vote. Section 50(1) of the *Strata Property Act* requires all matters to be decided by majority vote unless a different voting threshold is set by the Act, the regulations or the bylaws.

This Table identifies situations, according to subject matter, where the *Strata Property Act*, including the *Schedule of Standard Bylaws*, and the regulations specify a particular voting threshold.

Note that a strata corporation may, in some cases, amend its bylaws to specify a different voting threshold for particular matters.

Subject	Motion	Type of Vote Required	*Strata Property Act*
Borrowing	To approve a resolution authorizing the strata corporation to borrow money.	3/4	111(1)
Budget	To approve the first annual budget.	Majority	21(4)
	To amend a proposed budget at the first annual general meeting (AGM).	Majority	21(5)
	To approve a budget at an AGM, or failing an approval at that meeting, at a subsequent special general meeting.	Majority	103(1) and (104)(1)
	To amend a proposed budget at the annual general meeting.	Majority	103(4)
	To spend operating funds not otherwise authorized by the budget or permitted by sections 98 or 104(3) pending approval of the new budget.	3/4	97(b)
	To change the dates of the strata corporation's fiscal year.	3/4	102(1)
	Where a budget is not approved at an annual general meeting, to extend beyond 30 days the time to prepare and present a budget for approval at a special general meeting.	3/4	104(1)
	To deal with a surplus in the operating fund in a way that differs from the options set out in section 105(1).	3/4	105(1)
	To change the formula used to calculate a strata lot's contribution to the operating fund and the CRF.	Unanimous	100(1), (2)
	To create a bylaw before January 1, 2002 that identifies different types of strata lots for the purpose of apportioning common expenses in a budget.	Majority	Reg., s. 17.13 (3), (4)
Bylaws	In the period before the first AGM in bare land strata or entirely residential strata developments, to amend a bylaw.	Unanimous	127(1)
	In the period before the first AGM in a mixed strata with residential and non-residential strata lots, to amend a bylaw.	Unanimous	127(3)

Subject	Motion	Type of Vote Required	*Strata Property Act*
Bylaws *(cont'd)*	In the period before the first AGM in a mixed strata with a separate residential section, for the residential section to amend a bylaw.	Unanimous	127(4)(a)
	To amend the bylaws in a strata plan composed entirely of residential strata lots.	3/4	128(1)(a)
	At any time, to amend the bylaws in a strata plan composed entirely of non-residential strata lots if the bylaws do not otherwise provide for a different type of vote.	3/4 or as otherwise set by the bylaws	127(2) and 128(1)(b)
	To amend the bylaws in a strata plan composed of both residential and non-residential strata lots, 3/4 of the votes of the residential lots and, in the case of the non-residential lots, 3/4 of the votes unless the bylaws provide a different voting requirement for non-residential lots.	Residential = 3/4 Non-residential = 3/4 or as otherwise set by the bylaws	128(1)(c)
	To create a bylaw before January 1, 2002 that identifies different types of strata lots for the purpose of apportioning common expenses in a budget.	Majority	Reg., s. 17.13 (3), (4)
Common Assets	To approve a resolution for the strata corporation to acquire land.	3/4	78(1)
	To approve a resolution to sell, lease, mortgage, grant an easement or a restrictive covenant over, or otherwise dispose of land that is a common asset of the strata corporation.	3/4	79
	To approve a resolution for the strata corporation to acquire or dispose of personal property in some circumstances.	3/4	82(3)
Common Property	To approve a significant change in the use or appearance of common property.	3/4	71
	To designate common property as limited common property without amending the strata plan.	3/4	74(1) and 75(2)

Subject	Motion	Type of Vote Required	*Strata Property Act*
Common Property *(cont'd)*	To amend a strata plan to designate property as limited common property or to remove a designation of limited common property.	Unanimous	257
	To dispose of common property in some circumstances.	3/4	80(2)
	To amend a strata plan to add land held by the strata corporation, but not shown on the strata plan, to the common property.	3/4	266(3)(a)
	To amend a strata plan to add a strata lot or part of a strata lot to common property.	Unanimous	263(2)
Contingency Reserve Fund	To make additional contributions to the CRF after the fund reaches the maximum amount required by the Act.	3/4	93(4) and Reg., s. 6.1(2)
	To approve an expenditure from the CRF.	3/4	96(b)
Developer	In the period between the first conveyance and the first AGM, to approve a contract or transaction between the strata corporation and the developer or a person who is not arm's-length to the developer.	Unanimous	10
Finances *(see also Budget, above)*	To change the dates of the strata corporation's fiscal year.	3/4	102(1)
	To deal with a surplus in the operating fund in a way that differs from the options set out in section 105(1).	3/4	105(1)
	To approve a budget at an annual general meeting, or failing an approval at that meeting, at a subsequent special general meeting.	Majority	103(1) and 104(1)
	To approve a special levy (see also *Special Levy*, below).	3/4	108(2)(a)
	To change the formula used to calculate a strata lot's contribution to the operating fund and the CRF.	Unanimous	100(1), (2)
	To change the formula used to calculate a strata lot's contribution to a special levy.	Unanimous	108(2)(b)

Subject	Motion	Type of Vote Required	*Strata Property Act*
General Meetings	In the period between the first conveyance and the first AGM, to pass any resolution that normally requires a 3/4 vote.	Unanimous	11
	To decide all matters at general meetings unless the Act, the regulations or the bylaws require a different voting threshold.	Majority	50(1)
	To pass a resolution requiring persons who are not eligible to vote, including tenants and occupants, to leave a general meeting.	Majority	*Schedule of Standard Bylaws*, s. 26(3)
	To amend a resolution requiring a 3/4 vote, provided that the amendment does not substantially change the resolution.	3/4	50(2)(b)
	To seek judicial passage of a failed unanimous vote.	3/4	52(2)
Leasehold Strata Developments	To approve an application to add to, alter or repeal restrictions imposed by a leasehold landlord on strata lots in a leasehold strata plan.	3/4	207(1)
Leasehold Strata Developments	To elect not to rebuild where buildings that are part of a leasehold strata plan are damaged by more than 1/3 of their fair market value.	3/4	213(1)
	To change the basis for calculating how much a leasehold landlord must pay to the leasehold tenant at the end of the strata lot lease for the leasehold tenant's interest in the strata lot.	Unanimous	214(3)
Legal Proceedings	To authorize the strata corporation to sue as representative of all owners (except any who are being sued).	3/4	171(2)
	To authorize the strata corporation to sue as representative of one or more owners about matters affecting only their strata lots.	3/4	172(1)(b)
Limited Common Property	To designate common property as limited common property without amending the strata plan.	3/4	74(1) and 75(2)
	To amend a strata plan to designate property as limited common property or to remove a designation of limited common property.	Unanimous	257

Subject	Motion	Type of Vote Required	*Strata Property Act*
Operating Fund	To spend money from the operating fund, if the expenditure is not previously authorized in the budget or under sections 98 or 104(3).	3/4	97
Phased Developments	To authorize the release of a bond, letter of credit or other security posted by a developer to secure the construction of common facilities in a later phase of the development.	3/4	226(1)(b)
	To agree with a developer to relieve the developer of certain liabilities arising when the developer amends a Phased Strata Plan Declaration.	3/4	233(7)
	To agree with a developer to relieve the developer of certain liabilities arising when the developer elects not to proceed with the next phase before the time set for that election in the Phased Strata Plan Declaration.	3/4	235(7)
Property Management	At the second annual general meeting to continue a strata management contract entered into before the first annual general meeting where the contract would otherwise automatically expire under the Act.	Majority	24(2)
	To approve a resolution to cancel a strata management contract.	3/4	39(1)
Rules	At an annual or special general meeting, to ratify a rule made in the interim since the last annual general meeting.	Majority	125(6)
Sections	To create or cancel sections representing the interests of owners of different types of strata lots or those who use their strata lots for different purposes.	3/4	193(3)
	Among section members, to approve an amendment to a bylaw respecting a matter that relates solely to that section.	3/4	197(3)
Short-Term, Exclusive-Use	To approve a short-term, exclusive-use arrangement that involves a significant change in the use or appearance of common property.	3/4	71 and 76
Special Levy	To approve a special levy.	3/4	108(2)(a)
	To change the formula used to calculate a strata lot's contribution to a special levy.	Unanimous	108(2)(b)

Subject	Motion	Type of Vote Required	*Strata Property Act*
Spending	To spend operating funds not otherwise authorized by the budget or permitted by sections 98 or 104(3) pending approval of the new budget.	3/4	97(b)
	To approve an expenditure from the CRF.	3/4	96(b)
Strata Corporation	To approve a resolution to amalgamate with another strata corporation.	3/4	269(2)(a)
	To approve an appraisal of the assessed value of a strata lot for the purposes of a conversion schedule when cancelling a strata plan and winding up the strata corporation.	3/4	273(2)(b)
	To approve an appraisal of the assessed value of a strata lot for the purposes of determining an owner's share of the proceeds of distribution when cancelling a strata plan and winding up the strata corporation.	3/4	278(2)(b)
	To authorize a liquidator to distribute land or property that is being disposed of when cancelling a strata plan and winding up the strata corporation.	3/4	282(1)
	To approve the account and final return of the liquidator when cancelling a strata plan and winding up the strata corporation.	3/4	283
	To appoint a liquidator.	3/4	277
Strata Council	To remove one or more council members from council (except where all the owners are on council).	Majority	*Schedule of Standard Bylaws*, s. 11(1)
	To direct or restrict the council in exercising certain powers and performing certain duties.	Majority	27(1)
	To ratify a contract or transaction in which a council member has a conflict of interest.	3/4	33(1)
	To approve in advance payment of remuneration to a council member that is not already provided for in the budget or the bylaws.	3/4	34(c)
Strata Lot	To approve a resolution to divide a residential strata lot into two or more strata lots.	3/4	260(4)

Subject	Motion	Type of Vote Required	*Strata Property Act*
Strata Lot *(cont'd)*	To amend a strata plan in certain cases to add or remove land belonging to the strata corporation to or from a strata lot.	Unanimous	262(3)(b)
	To amend a strata plan in certain cases to make land held by the strata corporation, but not shown on the strata plan, into a new strata lot or to otherwise add that land to a strata lot.	3/4	262(3)(a)
	To amend a strata plan in certain cases to divide a strata lot into two or more lots, to consolidate two or more strata lots, or to add part of a strata lot to another strata lot.	Unanimous	259(3)(a)
	To approve an appraisal of the assessed value of a strata lot for the purposes of a conversion schedule when cancelling a strata plan and winding up the strata corporation.	3/4	273(2)(b)
	To approve an appraisal of the assessed value of a strata lot for the purposes of determining an owner's share of the proceeds of distribution when cancelling a strata plan and winding up the strata corporation.	3/4	278(2)(b)
	To amend a strata plan in certain cases to make land held by the strata corporation into a new strata lot or to otherwise add that land to a strata lot.	Unanimous	262(3)(b)
Strata Plan	To amend a strata plan in certain cases to make land held by the strata corporation, but not shown on the strata plan, into a new strata lot or to otherwise add that land to a strata lot.	3/4	262(3)(a)
	To amend a strata plan to add land held by the strata corporation, but not shown on the strata plan, to the common property.	3/4	266(3)(a)
	To amend a strata plan in certain cases to divide a strata lot into two or more lots, to consolidate two or more strata lots, or to add part of a strata lot to another strata lot.	Unanimous	259(3)(a)
	To amend a schedule of unit entitlement in a strata plan where the schedule of unit entitlement is based on habitable area or square footage.	Unanimous	261(1)

Subject	Motion	Type of Vote Required	*Strata Property Act*
Strata Plan *(cont'd)*	To amend a strata plan in certain cases to make land held by the strata corporation into a new strata lot or to otherwise add that land to a strata lot.	Unanimous	262(3)(b)
	To amend a strata plan in certain cases to add or remove land belonging to the strata corporation to or from a strata lot.	Unanimous	262(3)(b)
	To amend a strata plan to add a strata lot or part of a strata lot to common property.	Unanimous	263(2)
	To cancel a strata plan.	Unanimous	272
	To approve an appraisal of the assessed value of a strata lot for the purposes of a conversion schedule when cancelling a strata plan and winding up the strata corporation.	3/4	273(2)(b)
	To approve an appraisal of the assessed value of a strata lot for the purposes of determining an owner's share of the proceeds of distribution when cancelling a strata plan and winding up the strata corporation.	3/4	278(2)(b)
	To authorize a liquidator to distribute land or property that is being disposed of when cancelling a strata plan and winding up the strata corporation.	3/4	282(1)
	To approve the account and final return of a liquidator when cancelling a strata plan and winding up the strata corporation.	3/4	283
Unit Entitlement	To change the formula used to calculate a strata lot's contribution to the operating fund and the CRF.	Unanimous	100(1), (2)
	To change the formula used to calculate a strata lot's contribution to a special levy.	Unanimous	108(2)(b)
	To amend a schedule of unit entitlement in a strata plan where the schedule of unit entitlement is based on habitable area or square footage.	Unanimous	261(1)

Appendix D

USEFUL WEBSITES

Readers may find the following websites to be useful sources of information, including links to other resources. This list is not exhaustive. A reference in this list to organizations other than the British Columbia Real Estate Association does not constitute an endorsement of any particular organization or the content of its website.

Organization	Website (www.)
British Columbia Institute of Property Inspectors	asttbc.org/bcipi
Provincial Court of British Columbia	provincialcourt.bc.ca
British Columbia Real Estate Association (BCREA)	bcrea.bc.ca
The Revised Statutes and Consolidated Regulations of British Columbia	qp.gov.bc.ca/statreg
British Columbia Superior Courts	courts.gov.bc.ca
Building Owners and Managers Association of British Columbia (BOMA)	boma.bc.ca
Canada Revenue Agency	ccra-adrc.gc.ca/menu-e.html
Canada Mortgage and Housing Corporation (CMHC)	cmhc.ca
Canadian Association of Home & Property Inspectors (BC)	cahpi.bc.ca
Canadian Condominium Institute	cci.ca
Centre for Feng Shui Research	geomancy.net
Coalition of Leaky Condo Owners	myleakycondo.com
Condominium Home Owners' Association of BC (CHOA)	choa.bc.ca
Homeowner Protection Office	hpo.bc.ca
Human Rights Code	qp.gov.bc.ca/statreg/stat/H/96210_01.htm
Independent Contractors and Businesses Association of BC	icba.bc.ca/

Organization	Website (www.)
Interior Strata Owners Association	isoa.ca
Multiple Listing Service®	mls.ca
National Home Warranty Program	nationalhomewarranty.com
Newsletter for Condominium and Homeowner Associations (U.S.)	regenesis.net
Pacific Condominium Association of British Columbia	condohelp.org
Professional Association of Managing Agents (PAMA)	pama.ca
Property Transfer Tax Regulations	qp.gov.bc.ca/statreg/reg/P/ PropertyTransfer/74_88.htm
Real Estate Council of British Columbia	recbc.ca
Resident Manager's Training Institute	rmti.ca
Residential Tenancy Office	pssg.gov.bc.ca/rto/index.htm
Residential Warranty Company of Canada	residentialwarranty.ca/home.htm
Strata Property Act Information Site	fic.gov.bc.ca/strata/index.html
Strata Property Agents of BC	spabc.org
Urban Development Institute (*Strata Property Act*: Analysis and Recommendations)	udi.bc.ca/publications/ spa_recommendations.htm
Vancouver Island Strata Owners Association	visoa.bc.ca
Vancouver Condominium Services Ltd.	vancondo.com
Web Page Condominium News	wpcn.ca

Appendix E

PERMITTED INVESTMENTS UNDER THE REGULATIONS

Apart from investing a contingency reserve fund (CRF) in an insured account at a savings institution in British Columbia, the *Strata Property Act*[1] only allows a strata corporation to invest its CRF in an investment permitted under section 6.11 of the *Strata Property Regulation* as shown below:

Section 6.11

6.11. A strata corporation may invest money from the contingency reserve fund in the following investments for the purposes of section 95(2)(a) of the Act:

(a) securities of Canada, a province, the United Kingdom, the United States of America or a municipal corporation in a province;

(b) securities the payment of the principal and interest of which is guaranteed by Canada, a province, the United Kingdom, the United States of America or a municipal corporation in a province;

(c) securities issued for school, hospital, irrigation, drainage or other similar purposes that are secured by or payable out of rates or taxes levied under the law of a province on property in that province;

(d) bonds, debentures or other evidence of indebtedness of a corporation that are secured by the assignment to a trustee of payments that Canada or a province has agreed to make, if those payments are sufficient to meet the interest on all the bonds, debentures or other evidence of indebtedness outstanding as it falls due and also to meet the principal amount of all the bonds, debentures or other evidence of indebtedness on maturity;

---

[1] *Strata Property Act*, s. 95(2).

(e) bonds, debentures or other evidence of indebtedness of a corporation incorporated under the laws of Canada or a province that are fully secured by a mortgage, charge or hypothec to a trustee on any one or combination of the following assets:

    (i) land;

    (ii) the plant or equipment of a corporation that is used in the transaction of its business;

    (iii) bonds, debentures or other evidence of indebtedness or shares of a class or classes authorized by this section;

(f) bonds, debentures or other evidence of indebtedness of a corporation incorporated under the laws of Canada or a province if the corporation has earned and paid a dividend,

    (i) in each of the 5 years immediately preceding the date of investment, at least equal to the specified annual rate on all of its preferred shares, or

    (ii) in each year of a period of 5 years ending less than one year before the date of investment, on its common shares of at least 4% of the average value at which the shares were carried in the capital stock account of the corporation during the year in which the dividend was paid;

(g) guaranteed trust or investment certificates of

    (i) a bank, or

    (ii) a corporation that is incorporated under the laws of Canada or of a province and that has a business authorization to carry on trust business or deposit business;

(h) bonds, debentures or other evidence of indebtedness of a loan corporation or similar corporation

    (i) that at the time of investment has all of the following:

          (A) power to lend money on mortgages, charges or hypothecs of real estate;

          (B) a paid up nonreturnable capital stock of not less than $500 000;

          (C) a reserve fund amounting to not less than 25% of its paid up capital, and

      (ii) the stock of which has a market value that is not less than 7% in excess of its par value;

(i) preferred shares of a corporation incorporated under the laws of Canada or of a province if the corporation has paid a dividend,

    (i) in each of the 5 years immediately preceding the date of investment, at least equal to the specified annual rate on all of its preferred shares, or

    (ii) in each year of a period of 5 years ending less than one year before the date of investment, on its common shares of at least 4% of the average value at which the shares were carried in the capital stock account of the corporation during the year in which the dividend was paid;

(j) first mortgages, charges or hypothecs on land in Canada, but only if the loan does not exceed 75% of the value of the property at the time of the loan as established by a valuator whom the trustee believes on reasonable grounds to be competent and independent;

(k) securities issued or guaranteed by the International Bank for Reconstruction and Development established by the Agreement for an International Bank for Reconstruction and Development, approved by the *Bretton Woods and Related Agreements Act* (Canada), but only if the bonds, debentures or other securities are payable in the currency of Canada, the United Kingdom, a member of the British Commonwealth or the United States of America;

(l)   fully paid common shares of a corporation incorporated under the laws of Canada or of a province that, in each year of a period of 7 years ending less than one year before the date of investment, has paid a dividend on its common shares of at least 4% of the average value at which the shares were carried in the capital stock account of the corporation during the year in which the dividend was paid;

(m)   deposits in, or non-equity or membership shares or other evidence of indebtedness of, a credit union.

Appendix F

CHARTS EXPLAINING THE APPLICATION OF A RENTAL RESTRICTION BYLAW

Relevant Legislation

The following provisions must be read together to determine how a rental restriction bylaw applies to your strata lot.[1]

Strata Property Act

143. (1) A bylaw that prohibits or limits rentals does not apply to a strata lot until the later of

     (a) one year after a tenant who is occupying the strata lot at the time the bylaw is passed ceases to occupy it as a tenant, and

     (b) one year after the bylaw is passed.

     (2) Subject to subsection (1), if a strata lot has been designated as a rental strata lot on a Rental Disclosure Statement in the prescribed form, and if all the requirements of section 139 have been met, a bylaw that prohibits or limits rentals does not apply to that strata lot until the earlier of

     (a) the date the strata lot is conveyed by the first purchaser of the strata lot, and

     (b) the date the rental period expires, as disclosed in the statement.

Strata Property Regulation

17.15 Despite section 143(2) of the Act, but subject to section 143(1) of the Act, if a strata lot is conveyed by the first purchaser of the strata lot, and the strata lot was designated as a rental strata lot on a rental disclosure statement in the prescribed form under section 31 of the *Condominium Act* and all the requirements of section 31 of the *Condominium Act* were met, a bylaw that prohibits or limits rentals does not apply to that strata lot until the earlier of

---

[1]*Strata Property Act*, s. 143; *Strata Property Regulation*, s. 17.15.

    (a) **the date the rental period expires, as disclosed in the statement;**

    (b) **January 1, 2006.**

The flowcharts below illustrate how these provisions work.

Where to Start in the Flowchart

If the strata corporation passes a bylaw restricting rentals . . .

Go to Part 1:

> if there is a Rental Disclosure Statement (Form J):
>
> - that was filed on or after July 1, 2000 under the *Strata Property Act*, and
>
> - that applies to your strata lot.
>
> (called a "Form J")

Go to Part 2:

> if there is a Rental Disclosure Statement:
>
> - that was filed *before* July 1, 2000 under the former *Condominium Act*, and
>
> - that applies to your strata lot.
>
> (called an "RDS")

Go to Part 3:

> if there is *no* Rental Disclosure Statement, or:
>
> - the Rental Disclosure Statement no longer applies to your strata lot (e.g., the rental period in the statement has expired)

PART 1

How to Apply the Rental Disclosure Statement (Form J) Filed Under the *Strata Property Act* When a Rental Restriction Bylaw is Passed

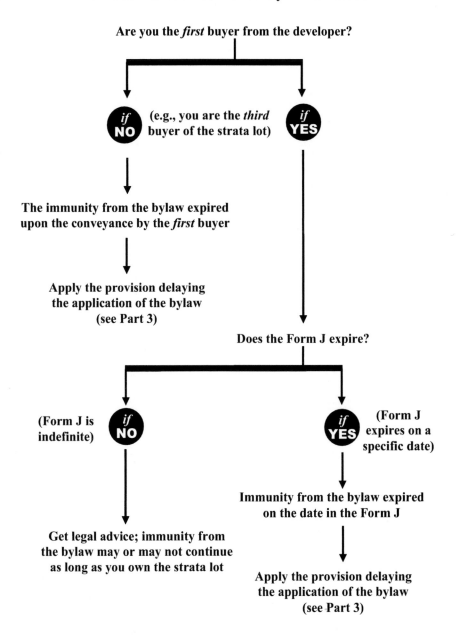

Are you the *first* buyer from the developer?

if **NO** (e.g., you are the *third* buyer of the strata lot)

if **YES**

The immunity from the bylaw expired upon the conveyance by the *first* buyer

Apply the provision delaying the application of the bylaw (see Part 3)

Does the Form J expire?

(Form J is indefinite) *if* **NO**

if **YES** (Form J expires on a specific date)

Immunity from the bylaw expired on the date in the Form J

Apply the provision delaying the application of the bylaw (see Part 3)

Get legal advice; immunity from the bylaw may or may not continue as long as you own the strata lot

PART 2

How to Apply the Rental Disclosure Statement(RDS) Filed Under the *Condominium Act* When a Rental Restriction Bylaw is Passed

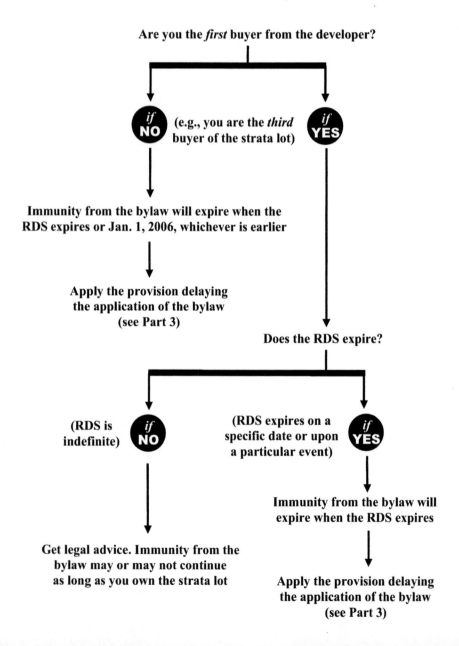

PART 3

How the Application
of Rental Restriction Bylaws are Delayed

Where the Form J or RDS does not apply, or no longer applies, to preserve the right of the strata lot owner to rent the strata lot, then:

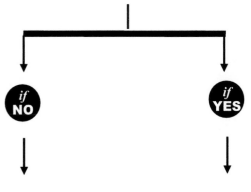

**Apply the provision delaying
the application of the bylaw**

**Is the tenant who was occupying the strata lot at the time
the bylaw was passed, still occupying the strata lot?**

if
NO

if
YES

**The bylaw applies
one year
after its passage**

**The bylaw applies
at the end of that tenant's
tenancy, plus one year**

Appendix G

Bylaw Amendments Contemplated by the *Strata Property Act*

The *Strata Property Act* contemplates that strata corporations may amend their Standard Bylaws to deal with certain matters, including the following subjects:

Subjects	The Act Contemplates Creating a Bylaw That . . .	Section
Age Restrictions	restricts the age of a person who may reside in a strata lot.	123(2)
Bylaw Amendments	in the case of non-residential strata lots, sets a voting threshold, other than a 3/4 vote, for approving a resolution to amend the bylaws.	128(1)
	relates solely to a section.	197
Fines	sets out different amounts of fines for different bylaws and rules.	132
Dispute Resolution	provides for the voluntary resolution of disputes.	124(1)
Finances	sets the amount the strata corporation may spend on expenditures that have not previously been approved.	98(2)
	establishes a schedule for the payment of strata fees and a rate of interest to be paid if an owner pays his or her strata fees late.	107(1)
	identifies different types of strata lot for the purpose of allocating costs out of the operating fund to a particular type of strata lot.	Regulation, s. 6.4(2)
	in the case of a section, identifies different types of strata lots in the section for the purpose of allocating costs out of the operating fund to a particular type of strata lot.	Regulation, s. 11.2(2)
	imposes user fees for the use of common property or common assets.	Regulation, s. 6.9(b)
General Meetings	permits attendance at a general meeting by telephone or any other method that permits everyone attending to communicate with each other during the meeting.	49(1)

Subjects	The Act Contemplates Creating a Bylaw That . . .	Section
General Meetings (*cont'd*)	except on matters requiring a unanimous vote, prohibits a vote in respect of a strata lot if the strata corporation is entitled to file a lien against that strata lot.	53(2)
Insurance	designates an insurance trustee.	156
Legal Proceedings	authorizes the strata corporation to commence certain proceedings under the *Small Claims Act* without the necessity of first obtaining approval by a 3/4 vote.	171(4)
Personal Property	sets a particular dollar amount, in excess of which the strata corporation must first obtain approval by a 3/4 vote at a general meeting, before acquiring or disposing of personal property.	82(3)
Pets	prohibits pets.	123(1)
Rentals	prohibits or limits rentals.	141
Repairs	makes owners responsible for the repair and maintenance of limited common property.	72(2)
	gives the strata corporation responsibility for the repair and maintenance of specified portions of a strata lot.	72(3)
	identifies a type of strata lot so the strata corporation can allocate certain expenses to only strata lots of that type.	Regulation, s. 6.4(2)
Sale of a Strata Lot	governs activities relating to the sale of a strata lot, including locations for posting signs and times for showing common property and holding open houses.	122
Strata Council	states that a power or a duty that would normally belong to the strata council cannot be exercised or performed by the council.	4
	permits additional classes of persons to serve on the strata council.	28(2)

Subjects	The Act Contemplates Creating a Bylaw That ...	Section
Strata Council (*cont'd*)	prohibits a person from serving on council with respect to a strata lot if the strata corporation is entitled to file a lien against that strata lot.	28(3)
	sets the number of persons on council.	29(1)
	provides for payment of strata council members for their service as council members.	34(b)

INDEX